"My main interest is making sure that all do themselves a huge favor and read *Fearless!* It chronicles the compelling life story of an individual of enormous candor, tenacity, and talent. God, Julie just opens up her heart, her secrets, her deepest thoughts in a way I found so unusual. What amazes me is how she brings together so many significant stories and key events of our generation in so few pages and makes it such an enjoyable read that runs a roller-coaster gamut from thrilling to poignant. It is hard to explain how deeply taken I was by this book." **—Pat O'Day, Radio Legend**

"Julie Blacklow is a trailblazing woman who entered the male-dominated TV news scene in Seattle in 1972 with a burning desire to witness history. Her intensely personal story shows how she succeeded; from chasing criminals, to cornering politicians and celebrities, to a raunchy encounter with a rock 'n roll legend. *Fearless* is a highly absorbing journey and at the end the reader is left grateful for having been along on the ride."
—George Lewis, NBC Correspondent, Retired

"I flat-out love what Julie has written here! Television news viewers see, but rarely get to know, the person on the screen. In *Fearless* she shares all of who she is. Julie plied her craft blessed with a big dose of sensitivity and a deep sense of justice. Those gifts were sometimes a burden, but they always showed in her work and defined her to her colleagues. I hired and coached hundreds of people with talent and integrity over many decades and though I 'inherited' her, she possessed those qualities in abundance."
—Bob Jordan, Former News Director, KING Television

"The fabric of Julie Blacklow's life is an improbable, crazy quilt that she stitches together with seamless and eloquent words. She takes us on a wild ride of dizzying highs and lows. She also survived two life-threatening illnesses and turned down an offer of money for sex from legend Chuck Berry. This seven-decades long saga is further enriched by historic vignettes that provide valuable context and substance, along with vintage photos and treasured mementoes." **—Larry Coffman, Publisher, MARKETING**

"The best reporters are those who have lived fully and embraced a wide variety of people, places, and events. They follow such experiences with honest personal reflection. That gifts us with reporters like Julie Blacklow, who possess the emotional and intellectual depth to do more than simply relate the 'facts'…but also place events in context, move us, fascinate us, and relate those experiences to our lives, all of which she's done in this stunning book. In these pages, Julie shares the best and worst of the history and human condition she has witnessed and serves as a lens…honestly examining and analyzing what she has discovered. I know of no one who wielded that lens better than Julie who challenges, educates and yes —entertains us in this remarkable memoir."
—Jeff Renner, Former KING-TV Chief Meteorologist and Science Reporter

"What a fascinating read! Julie Blacklow has lived a unique life! Packed it all in. The portrait of a strong woman—one who knows who she is and knows how to communicate clearly all the jaw-dropping highs and lows."
—Patti Payne, Columnist, *Puget Sound Business Journal*;
Founder of the Payne Group—Communicating and Connecting

Fearless

Diary of a Badass Reporter

JULIE BLACKLOW

Book Publishers Network
P.O. Box 2256
Bothell • WA • 98041
Ph • 425-483-3040
www.bookpublishersnetwork.com

10 9 8 7 6 5 4 3 2 1

Printed in the United States of America

LCCN 2019906152
ISBN 978-1-948963-30-5
ISBN 978-1-948963-31-2 (eBook)

Names: Blacklow, Julie, author.
Title: Fearless : diary of a badass reporter / Julie Blacklow.
Description: Bothell, WA : Book Publishers Network, [2019]
Identifiers: ISBN: 978-1-948963-30-5 (hard back) | 978-1-948963-31-2 (e-book)
Subjects: LCSH: Blacklow, Julie. | Women television journalists--Washington (State)--Seattle--Biography. | KING-TV (Television station : Seattle, Wash.)--History. | Women journalists--Washington (State)--Seattle--Biography. | Reporters and reporting--United States--Psychological aspects. | Horse farms--Management--Personal narratives. | Self-realization.
Classification: LCC: PN4874.B53 A3 2019 | DDC: 070.9/797772--dc23

Cover design: Scott Book
Interior design: Melissa Vail Coffman

To the people who allowed me into their lives to tell their stories in both the best and worst times and to those who watched.

Contents

PART ONE – BORN BRAVE

Part Three – In the Shadow of the Mountain – A Quieter Life

Acknowledgments

I CANNOT FIND THE PERFECT WORDS to thank Laddy Kite. For more than twenty years, we worked together at KING Television in the News Department, and he was my steadfast partner who helped me create important and memorable stories. He was one of those rare photojournalists who always had my back and never caused me to wonder if the camera was rolling. I trusted him completely. More than anyone else in my life, he never stopped encouraging, insisting, and compelling me to write a book. He is more than a professional partner. He is now my life partner, and without him at my side, helping me every step of the way, this book would not have been written. It has been a tough journey creating this book. Working with me in any capacity is a challenge. Thank you, Laddy... so very much.

Susan and Eric Manegold encouraged me to write this book and never doubted I could and should do it. Though the stories told here go back many decades, the ignition point for putting them to paper sparked at their dining room table when they said they believed in me. While I had doubts about taking a long, hard look at my life, they never did. I fell on their strong shoulders many times as I went through this process. They were always there to catch me.

I want to thank my friend Lindy, who will no longer have to listen to me talk about the book. Thank you for being my audience as I read the emerging stories to you repeatedly and for laughing and crying in all the right places. Her help was invaluable. Thank you for being my dear friend and for loving all creatures great and small.

I am forever in debt to my lifetime friend, Pepper Schwartz, who introduced a rambunctious foal to me and changed my life forever and for better.

LADDY KITE

To Jeremy, my son, thank you for the privilege of being your mother and for sharing your story with me. And I owe a debt of gratitude to his father, my former husband Richard Blacklow. Without him, I would never have found my way to Seattle and the amazing life that unfolded.

I am so grateful to my therapist, Dr. Judith Gordon, who helped me remove the obstacles in my path, move forward in my life, stop talking about the book, and write it.

Without Melissa Coffman, my publisher, editor, and literary midwife, there might not have been a book at all.

"You were the canary in the coal mine. You railed against consultants and any attention paid to ratings, and hated everyday news you considered 'road kill.' You were a rare defender of true journalism. You saw me as the guy who put a jukebox in the cathedral."

—BOB JORDAN,
Former KING Television news director

"If she was on fire she would insist on putting herself out."

—LADDY KITE,
Former KING Television news photographer

Prologue

I FAKED HAVING POLIO when I was five, a remarkably strange thing to do but an act that set in motion a life of confrontation, provocation, and making trouble when I thought it needed to be made. I attacked a racist high school librarian at sixteen, threw a bag of dog shit into the living room of the American Nazi Party headquarters, plotted to oust a family member from my home, trespassed on the property of a convicted Watergate felon to get an interview, and shoved aside two Secret Service agents to get to Richard Nixon. If I wanted something, I usually found a way to get it. I survived rape and cancer and, at the age of sixty, left a career in television news to manage a horse ranch.

After working more than forty years in the television business, I met or interviewed at least thirty thousand people, everyone from the Dalai Lama to Oprah, from John Wayne to Paul McCartney and JFK Jr. I had a very special moment with Chuck Berry, who offered me cash to give him a blowjob before a performance. Along with the rich and famous, I encountered a sordid collection of killers, rapists, and child molesters—the famous and the infamous, the whole spectrum of humanity, including an entity claiming to be thirty-five thousand years old.

I also helped a lot of people. My trigger was injustice, wherever and whenever I saw it, and the trouble I made was typically on behalf of others, those unable to stand up and fight for themselves. I had no obvious innate gifts. I could not sing, dance, or play an instrument and was not a great student. I did have other natural talents. I was born with a big mouth, a brave heart, and no tolerance for taking abuse from anybody. For most of my life, I fought for other people. But for one terrifying year when I tried to take my own life, I was forced to fight for myself and battle the television station I loved that fired me, defamed me, and took away my good name and reputation.

Along this tumultuous and thrilling journey, I learned how to write and tell a story. As a journalist, I had to remain objective, meaning I should not and could not share my personal thoughts, emotions, or experiences behind the scenes of the stories I covered. On these pages, I am no longer bound by those constraints.

Whenever I shared my adventures, people often said, "You really should write a book!"

Finally . . . I did.

LADDY KITE

PART ONE

Born Brave

"Writing is like driving at night in the fog.
You can only see as far as your headlights, but you
can make the whole trip that way."

—E. L. Doctorow

It took me more than four years to write this memoir though it was more than seven decades in the making. I went through the fog with my headlights on the entire time, driving slowly, often unsure of what lay ahead and afraid of what scary things might jump into my path, but I just kept going. E.L. Doctorow was right. You *can* make the whole trip that way.

Chapter 1

Polio in Purcellville

I MADE MY LEGS GO NUMB.

I was five years old, my chubby body crammed inside a dough-nut-shaped inner tube, splashing around in the middle of an enormous, outdoor L-shaped pool. No one was paying any attention to me, particularly my mother and father who were fawning over some of my young cousins on the pool deck. In a flash of misguided jealousy, I hatched a nefarious plan to capture their attention. I would pretend to have polio.

Purcellville, Virginia, not far from our hometown of Arlington, was a regular summer gathering place for our family. More than one hundred years before we got to the Blue Ridge Mountain retreat, Confederate and Union armies marched through the town where several of the original buildings remain. There were hot springs, good food, and comfortable cabins, as close to camping as our pampered, Jewish family ever got. For us, this was roughing it. A regular family escape, a chance to relax, hang out with relatives, and do a lot of nothing for a few days on occasional summers.

This particular summer, in 1952, should have been no different. But I made sure it was. I had learned to read a year earlier and knew from newspapers about the polio scourge raging in America. There were thousands of confirmed cases, pictures of kids in leg braces, stuck inside iron lungs, which breathed for them. It would be three years before the first vaccine was developed by Jonas Salk. I also knew polio could be transmitted through water in swimming pools.

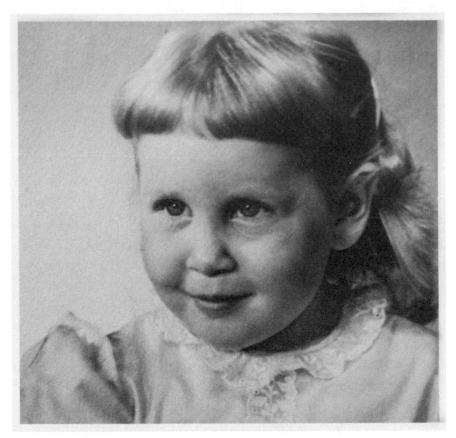

JULIE...LOOKING INNOCENT, BUT MISCHIEVOUS.

"Mommy, Daddy!" I shouted from the pool. "I can't move my legs!"

Now I had everyone's attention. My parents came running to the side of the pool, my fat, little arms paddling towards the shiny, chrome ladder, my seemingly lifeless legs dragging behind me like a limp fish. Daddy grabbed my hands and pulled me out of the water onto the cement. He cradled me, shouted for help, and rushed me to a nearby white tent where someone called a doctor. Wet and lying on a cot, I was basking in the fuss being made, all about me.

Then the doctor came in. He grabbed a paper clip, bent it into a straight line, and began scraping it along the bottoms of my feet and the sides of my legs. Somehow, I forced myself not to react to what he was doing, summoning every bit of concentration I could to stay numb. The doctor was worried. My parents were becoming frantic. And I was beginning to panic, feeling guilty at the chaos I was causing. I couldn't let this go on much longer. This was more attention than I'd bargained for. I needed to get out of this mess.

Miraculously, in a matter of minutes, I allowed the feelings in my feet and legs to return, first with a little tingle, then full sensations in both legs. A wave of relief washed over the faces of my parents, the doctor, and an assortment of aunts, uncles, and cousins in the tent. Everyone was grateful I could walk again. I felt guilty.

I never confessed the truth to my parents about what I had done, but over the years, I told the story to dozens of people who either laughed or were shocked that a child could do such an outrageous thing. I reveled in the attention I got when I was five and every time I retold the story.

I would never tell a lie quite like that again. It would be hard to top that. But I learned early on how to get the attention I desperately craved. I never lost that drive to be in the limelight but fortunately was also able to hone that skill and use it for better purposes and mostly to help other people.

YEARS LATER, I asked an expert to weigh in on what I had done.

> "I thought that was a strange thing for a five-year-old child to do. It exhibited potential sociopathic tendencies and I guess you could have turned into a dangerous person. But you had the guts to put on different faces and personae and learned at a very young age how to make things happen. That personality quirk, I think, made you more successful in your future career."

> —DR. BARBARA SCHNEIDMAN
> *Clinical Professor, University of Washington School of*
> *Medicine, Past President, American College of Psychiatrists,*
> *Chair Emeritus, American Board of Psychiatry and Neurology*

> . . . And my dear friend for more than forty years

Chapter 2

The Beginning of Me

I WAS A BIG, LOUD BABY born into a small, quiet family. I arrived on Saturday, February 22, 1947, in the midst of a raging snowstorm in Washington, DC according to my parents. The stormy weather seems now like a harbinger of the challenging life that lay ahead. My weight was not listed on the birth certificate, but in baby pictures, I was a chubby infant, another sign of future issues.

My mother, Esther, was twenty-nine, a homemaker. My father, Leonard, was thirty-three, just back from World War II and beginning to work in his father Michael's men's clothing store in Arlington, Virginia.

As all of us do, I share my birthday with millions of others, none more famous than George Washington. Born in 1732, he is renowned for his unfailing honesty, never telling a lie. After pretending to have polio, I could never make that claim. Other than our birthdays, there is little else I share with our first president, other than growing up not too far from his beloved Mt. Vernon in Virginia. He had a noble lineage, coming from English gentry. My roots came from another country and from a very different social strata . . . the Russian, Jewish, lower-middle class.

Chapter 3

From Russia with China

BOTH MY MOTHER'S AND FATHER'S FAMILIES, the Aronows and Honicks, were born and raised in Russia in the late 1800's. Life in Ukraine was comfortable with occasionally fancy clothes and even a little pony in my mother's family.

MY MOTHER'S TWIN SIBLINGS ON THEIR PONY,
YOUNG SAM HOLDING THE REINS IN RUSSIA.

MY MATERNAL GRANDPARENTS, FANNY AND ISAAC, IN RUSSIA...NEWLY MARRIED.

Her parents, Isaac and Fanny, had four children born there. My mother, Esther, was the fifth child, the only one born in America. Both families made the decision to flee their homeland in the wake of widespread, violent, and deadly attacks on Jews in the early 1900's. The anti-Semitic pogroms (a Russian word meaning havoc) were reaching a bloody climax, and my ancestors had the good sense and apparently enough money to board a crowded ship headed for America.

Part of the family lore passed down over generations was that Fanny joined the resistance, yelling and even shooting at the czar's soldiers. My mother told me I was just like Fanny, willful, brave, and indefatigable. She died when I was a baby so I only knew her from old photos and legendary stories about her. My mother said she lived on in me.

MY MATERNAL GRANDMOTHER, 'BUBBA FANNY'...IN AMERICA...
IMMACULATELY DRESSED. THE 'TOUGH, OLD BROAD' WHO MY
MOTHER SAID LIVED ON IN ME.

My grandparents, like millions of other emigrants, sailed past the Statue of Liberty on their way to Ellis Island. They were the tired, the poor, the wretched refuse Emma Lazarus wrote about on the statue. They did not know the language or the customs of their adopted country. They knew nothing about where they would live or where they would get their next meal. They had only the clothes on their backs, their children in tow, and dreams of a less chaotic life. But Fanny, being Fanny, insisted on packing up her set of Czechoslovakian china and her precious brass samovar. Those were the only material possessions she brought from her old life to her new life in America. The ornate china with its flowery design and the samovar have been with me for decades.

On special occasions, I still use her china and tell my guests where it came from. As a child, I remember my grandfather, Papa Isaac, brewing tea in the samovar, sipping the warm liquid through a sugar cube in his mouth, as was the custom back in the old country. After Fanny died, Isaac lived with us until he passed away.

Though the families did not know one another when they left Russia, they all eventually ended up in Newport News, Virginia, in the early twentieth century, a city famous for its shipbuilding industry.

Fanny was a tough, old girl. Having taken on the czar's soldiers, packing up her family, and moving halfway around the world, she was ready for anything. She started her own business at a time when women did not do those things, even if they spoke English, and Fanny only knew Russian and Yiddish. That did not stop her. She opened her confectionery store on Chestnut Avenue selling candy, cigars, and soft drinks. All five of her children and her husband, Isaac, pitched in to help run the business.

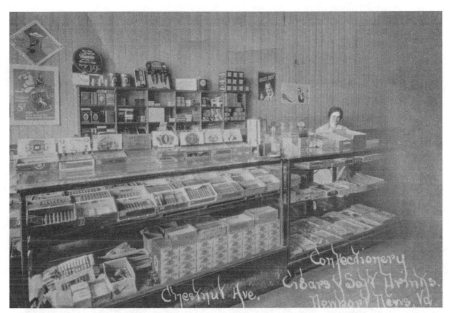

FANNY PROUDLY STANDING BEHIND THE COUNTER OF HER CONFECTIONERY STORE
ON CHESTNUT AVENUE IN NEWPORT NEWS, VIRGINIA.

My mother remembers working at the store and Fanny yelling at the kids to stop eating the profits. My mother said I was spunky like Fanny. She did not mean that as a compliment, but I took it as such.

My father's father, Michael Honick, became a tailor and later opened a men's clothing store. His wife, Mary, stayed home and raised their four children while her husband ran the business.

Both families were Orthodox Jews and continued traditions they followed in Russia. Different sets of plates during Jewish holidays, no pork, and for my father, daily prayer. Every morning at an ungodly early hour, my father, Leonard, went with his father to the synagogue and, as he would tell me many times with great disgust, hated every minute of it. He regaled me with his recurring nightmares of the stench of unwashed, old men draped in prayer shawls, bobbing up and down, reciting (davening) ancient Hebrew chants in obeisance to almighty God, a higher power my father was not entirely convinced existed.

In the small, Jewish community of immigrants, my mother and father met and eventually married. Leonard was twenty-five. Esther was twenty-one. For a while, Daddy taught English at Newport News High School. He told anyone who would listen that one of his students was

Ava Gardner, who would become a famous actress and marry Frank Sinatra. "She was so beautiful," he said, even as a teenager. He milked that story for decades.

MY FATHER, LEONARD, CORRECTING PAPERS AT NEWPORT NEWS HIGH SCHOOL, WHERE HE TAUGHT ENGLISH AND SPANISH...AND AVA GARDNER.

Chapter 4

War and Peace

T HE QUIET LIFE of a high school teacher and his young, beautiful wife was interrupted by World War II as were the lives of millions of young families. Leonard enlisted in the navy and received officer's training, earning the command of a Liberty ship delivering supplies to troops in Europe.

LEONARD IN UNIFORM...A VERY PROUD NAVY MAN.

He and his crew were lucky. More than 2,500 Liberty ships were built to help fight the war. More than a thousand were sunk by German U-boats. I am told by those who have studied World War II that duty on a Liberty ship was incredibly dangerous. The Germans did not want American supplies to get to Europe.

On May 7, 1945, my father, the man who taught English, who loved words and taught me to love them too, wrote to my mother from Belgium:

All day today the expectancy has mounted and mounted as we sat close by the radio and then, at long last, it came! We've been waiting so very long now and now peace has come to Europe. It's unreal . . . dreamlike . . . we are all kind of walking around in a daze, not knowing what to do or what to say. My "boys," now as I write this, are all standing down on the main deck below my cabin singing "God Bless America" which just about put the finishing touches on me. I sit here only yearning to be with you. But I know we are together, love.

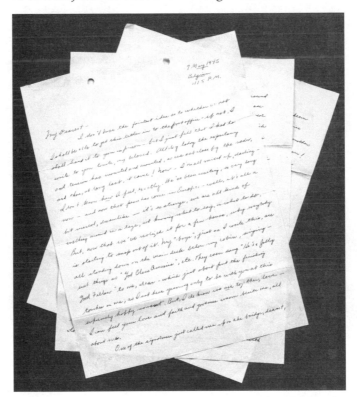

LEONARD'S LETTER TO ESTHER AT THE END OF WW II...
A STUNNING DESCRIPTION OF THE CELEBRATION AT THE WARS' END.

One of the men just called me from the bridge to watch the searchlights of the A.A. batteries [anti-aircraft guns] around the city throwing their patterns across the skies, those same searchlights which only a few short weeks ago were busy try- ing to shoot down the "buzz bombs" with which the Nazis tried so long, and so futilely, to knock out this great port. Other ships are shooting off red and green flares . . . shots being fired in the realization that it's really over. It's really starting to dawn on people.

I can't possibly jot down on this paper all the mixed-up emotions inside me. I wonder what my beloved is doing this evening to celebrate? Tomorrow at 3 p.m it all becomes official. I shall hold a general muster of all the crew and hold a silent prayer, dear, for all of the comrades who died for us.

Everybody has suddenly gone delirious with joy and well they may. If there was ever a time for celebration, this is it!

OUR LITTLE FAMILY IN OUR FILLMORE GARDENS APARTMENT.
I AM AN EARLY MEMBER OF THE BABY BOOM GENERATION.

DADDY CAME HOME. He was physically unscathed but would say many times that, as a Jewish man, he took great pride in helping to destroy the Nazi scourge.

Several months later, Esther and Leonard packed up, left Newport News, and moved to Arlington, Virginia, where my father took over his father's clothing business. The war set him on a different path, away from his beloved teaching career.

Our new home, Fillmore Gardens, was a vast complex of brick apartments, filled with young couples starting families, the beginning of the baby boom generation. My parents contributed to the boom, with me and my younger brother Alan. Mommy stayed home with us kids and did the cooking. Daddy went to work. Life was warm, safe, and secure.

Words were a very big deal in our home, and I was taught at a young age to use language correctly, with precision and intention, and to try to think before I spoke, an instruction I never quite mastered. Some of my earliest memories are sitting on my father's lap as he read the newspapers to me, from the morning's *Washington Post* and the afternoon's *Evening Star*. That is how I learned to read before I ever went to school. After dinner, my parents often played Scrabble, and though Daddy considered himself the wordsmith, my mother beat him almost every time. It drove him crazy. He sometimes accused her of cheating because she always seemed to get the best letters. Once, in a fit of rage after she had clobbered him yet again, he exploded in anger and tossed the Scrabble board up in the air, scattering tiles everywhere. It was perhaps the only time I ever saw this quiet and gentle man lose his temper.

But for his occasional eruptions over Scrabble, Leonard was as calm as Esther was stormy. She was his complete opposite—quick to criticize, quick to lose her temper, and occasionally smug and petulant when she was not getting her way. In my father's eyes, I was perfect. In my mother's, I was rambunctious and impertinent, and I often felt she did not quite know how to deal with me. She was controlling, and I was, even as a young child, uncontrollable. I could feel her frustration and confusion as to how she could have a daughter like this. I can still hear her today: "Julie . . . just behave yourself" and "Can't you be a little quieter . . . and just calm down?"

I hated her criticism then and cringe now thinking back on it.

She wanted me to act a certain way and look a certain way. She dressed me in impeccable outfits with little, matching hats and perfect socks and shoes. I looked the part of a pretty, little girl and mostly acted it, but for the occasional moments of rebellion, such as faking polio. After that memorable summer where I learned how to get attention and make things happen, I entered first grade at Patrick Henry Elementary School.

SWINGING AT FILLMORE GARDENS...PERFECTLY DRESSED
ACCORDING TO MY MOTHER'S TASTE.

Anything having to do with words was easy for me, but right from the start, I struggled with math. I remember as if it was yesterday my teacher—Virginia Sensindiver—patting me on the shoulder, leaning over and telling me, "Don't worry, honey, girls don't need to be good at math."

Even at six years old in 1953, those words shocked me. It seemed wrong to be told girls did not need to be good at something. I was getting a message early on that girls were somehow inferior, that only male proficiency mattered. I absorbed the message but never believed it.

She liked me, though, and wrote on my report card: "Julie has been an inspiration to me all year. Her behavior and her attitude in class have always been worthwhile and encouraging. She is unselfish and thoughtful of others and always displays a cheerful smile."

Just what my mother wanted and needed to hear.

Chapter 5

The Early Years

IN THE SUMMER OF 1953, our family of four moved from our small apartment to a new house across town at 2635 North Richmond Street. Our cul-de-sac was dotted with brick ramblers, about a dozen homes in total, all new but one . . . an almost-century-old, two-story, wood-framed house, built during the Civil War. I used to babysit the two young boys who lived there, but I never felt safe in that house. It felt haunted to me, as if ghosts of the past were very much present.

Reminders of the Civil War were all around us. My friends and I would sometimes find metal fragments, probably shot from muskets. We once found a rusty, old rifle in the dense and overgrown woods behind our home. We turned it over to the Smithsonian.

I walked through those woods every day on the way to my second grade at Zachary Taylor Elementary School. Almost every building and every main street and highway was connected in some way to history. We took Nellie Custis Drive to the George Washington Parkway to get to Robert E. Lee Highway. Our house was twenty minutes from the White House, fifteen minutes from the Washington Monument, the Jefferson and Lincoln Memorials, and Arlington National Cemetery. I lived in the middle of early American history, though the true horror of the absurdly named Civil War was never taught in our schools.

My good deportment continued from the first grade to Miss Harman's and Ruth McMains's second grade class at Taylor Elementary.

Miss Harman: "Julie works and plays well with her classmates and is very popular with other children. She enjoys sharing her experiences with others and speaks with poise and self-confidence before the group."

AN EARLY EFFORT AT GRABBING THE SPOTLIGHT...
PERFORMING IN SOME DANCE RECITAL DRESSED
AS SOME TYPE OF ANIMAL...AND AS A GYPSY...SORT OF.

SAME PERFORMANCE WITH A COSTUME CHANGE.
I APPARENTLY LEARNED AT AN EARLY AGE TO MAKE
EYE CONTACT WITH THE CAMERA.

Ruth McMains: "Julie has little difficulty in spelling hard words; and retains the very difficult words learned and uses them in creative stories. Her papers have been admired by many, and have raised the standards of writing and neatness for the entire class. Her creative stories have excellent ideas and seldom need any corrections. Julie is very self-confident in all areas of language arts."

POSING FOR A PHOTOGRAPH...ARRANGED BY MY PARENTS...
AND HATING EVERY MINUTE OF IT. I HAD TO WEAR A FLUFFY DRESS FOR HOURS.

I was seven years old, and my father's early emphasis on language was paying off. My teacher's comments, in a way, foretold my future.

In the white middle-class suburbs of DC, life for us in the 1950s consisted of family outings, visiting relatives, Sunday dinners at Steve's Crab House with brown butcher paper on the tables, piles of Maryland blue crabs, and greasy french fries. Summers in the steamy bog of Washington were hot, humid, and miserable until we finally got air conditioning. The highlight of the day was the arrival of the Good Humor Ice Cream man whose jingling tune could be heard blocks away. My father loved the almond-crusted vanilla bar, my mother favored the chocolate-covered, nutty drumstick, and I craved the Creamsicles with the tangy orange coating filled with vanilla ice cream.

My best friends at the time all lived nearby just around the corner from my house on Richmond Street. The Jefferson sisters were thought to be descendants of Thomas Jefferson. More precisely it was the girls' father, the six-foot, two-inch, red-headed Jeff Jefferson, who'd been told for years he was a distant relative. The documents confirming this were destroyed earlier in a fire in a Virginia courthouse, but a genealogist later told Jeff that according to subsequent research, the story appeared to be true and that he was related to someone in the Thomas Jefferson lineage. To me, the girls' father had an uncanny physical resemblance to portraits of the nation's third president so the connection always made sense to me. There were a half dozen girls in the very Catholic Mattie family, daughters of a military man who was transferred to Seattle, a place I had never heard of that seemed so very far away in the 1950's. There was Ellen who told me at the corner of Richmond Street and Twenty-Sixth Road how babies were made. She was quite insistent that our fathers put their penises into our mothers' vaginas. I did not think this could possibly be true, but she had a book with pictures, so it was hard to argue with her.

Notwithstanding our early sex education, our little gang gathered almost every Saturday in front of our black-and-white RCA television to watch *The Lone Ranger*, *Spin and Marty* from the Mickey Mouse Club, and my favorite, *Fury*. For me, it was always about the horses, not the plot. In one of my earliest baby pictures, I am astride a black pony, naked except for my diaper, my father's hand at my back holding me in the fancy saddle. I always loved horses. I hated Sunday school and going to the synagogue. In exchange for not putting up a fuss about it, I was rewarded with a trip to Bernie's Pony Ring on Sunday afternoons. We rode around and around in circles. The ponies were probably bored out of their minds, but I loved every minute of it. I nuzzled my face into the pony's warm neck, inhaling the scent of this magical creature and the aroma of the leather dampened by the horse's sweat. I never forgot how those smells made me feel—calm, peaceful, and a sense of being home.

AT BERNIE'S PONY RING...GAP-TOOTHED AND HAPPY...
MY FAVORITE PLACE AS A CHILD.

As I got older, I continued riding at stables in the Virginia suburbs, begging and pleading with my parents to buy me a horse. Instead, I got piano lessons.

My mother's two sisters lived near us, Annie in Arlington, Pauline on Connecticut Avenue in downtown Washington, DC, her brother Sam in New York, and brother Lewis, or Lolly as we called him, in southern Virginia. On holidays, they all converged at our Arlington home for big and celebratory Thanksgiving gatherings and Passover Seders. Those were wonderful times in our newly refinished basement, with its knotty-pine paneling and black-and-white checkered floors. The Ping-Pong table and other rented tables were covered in linen cloths with place settings for as many as thirty people. On Thanksgiving, there were turkeys at both ends, no shortage of yam casseroles, mashed potatoes, and the obligatory green bean glop with mushroom soup. On one particularly memorable Thanksgiving, our cat, Sneakers, jumped up on a counter where the turkey was cooling and was caught blissfully licking the big bird. We ate the other turkey.

Passovers were challenging for a couple of reasons—the annual, interminable reading of the Haggadah and the restlessness of the hungry children gathered around the table. The story of the exiled Jews and their forty-year struggles in the desert had little resonance to my bored cousins and me. Everyone around the table had to read a paragraph, and it seemed to take as long to complete the story as it took the Jews to get out of the desert. My father was the annual rabbi for the evening who repeatedly snapped at me and my cousins to be quiet. Everyone's favorite part came at the end of the story with the words, "Dinner is served."

Daddy in front of his store 'Honick's Menswear' in Clarendon.
I worked there off and on for years...helping out during the holidays.

ME, AGE 7, AT BUCKROE BEACH IN SOUTHERN VIRGINIA...
GLASSES ASKEW...GOOFING AROUND ON VACATION.

Without the invaluable help of our housekeepers Pauline and Thelma, those annual feasts would never have happened. They were our black housekeepers, probably called Negroes or colored people back then, but whatever they were called they were family to us, and I never heard my parents use those words. They helped cook and serve but always had a place at the main table, never relegated to the kitchen. Pauline Patton taught me at a very young age how to iron. While I loathe other housework, on the few occasions when something needs ironing, I pull out the board and think about her. Collars first, then sleeves and cuffs, and then the rest. Thelma eventually went to work in my father's store as a seamstress. Both were kind, gentle souls who loved our family, and we loved them.

AT AGE 8...AROUND FOURTH GRADE.
BANGS WERE POPULAR IN THE 1950'S.

Life was good, easy, and mostly fun. Until it wasn't.

On most Friday nights, my mother would ask her brother-in-law Frank to join us for dinner along with his two sons. Frank's wife, Annie, my mother's sister, died of cancer. Unstable even before her death, Frank unraveled completely after she was gone. He was a large and scary presence with a violent temper. I remember his rages and the stress I felt being in his presence, never knowing when he would erupt. At thirteen years old, I was selfish, devoid of empathy or sympathy for him or my two cousins. I resented Frank and the weekly intrusions into my family's life.

Those Friday night dinners ended in a sickening and horrifying way. Frank jumped off a building and killed himself, and my happy, comfortable family life died with him. On a bleak evening after Frank's suicide, my father arrived at our house with my two cousins, their suitcases and bags stuffed with belongings dragging behind them. My parents, with perfunctory calm, announced that the boys, now orphaned at ten and fourteen, were coming to live with us. With their pronouncement, I went from being the older sister to the only girl among three boys. I was furious, enraged that my parents would rupture the calm of our family life and do it without warning us. I felt deflated and powerless to stop this from happening, and I resented these boys from the moment they arrived. It was a ferocious and cold bitterness that took root in my psyche and never left. My cousins moved in downstairs, into the sanctuary reserved for celebratory Thanksgivings and Passovers, into my special place where I imagined future dance parties with my friends and necking with boyfriends. In an instant, on a cold, dreary, and unforgettable night, my happy place was gone.

Annie died. Frank was dead. After the arrival of the "intruders," my mother and father felt my rage and tried, in vain, to explain they felt they had no choice but to take in these children. At thirteen, I acted as if I understood, but I didn't. Outwardly, I stayed calm and tried to adapt to the new configuration of my family. But inside, I remained bitter, filled with resentment. The destruction of my family as I had known it carved a deep wound inside me that never healed. The scar tissue from that trauma remains.

I was unable to muster much compassion for my cousins perhaps because I was no longer the center of attention, just a self-absorbed, newly minted teenager. I made the best of it. Music and friends saved me. I still had my own room and my small, portable record player that held a stack of 45s. I closed the door to my room and lost myself in the sounds of Elvis Presley, the Crests, and Dion and the Belmonts. "Come Go with Me" by the Del Vikings was the first 45 I bought. When I hear it to this day, it takes me back to the safety and comfort of my bedroom.

Life in this new and awkward family was messy and chaotic. The oldest cousin thankfully left for college after a couple of years, but the younger one remained a disruptive force, psychologically damaged from the loss of his mother to cancer and his father's suicide. I recall my father telling me that the boys' father left a suicide note blaming his sons for his shocking decision to kill himself. How could his sons not be disturbed and overwhelmed? But the ability to be compassionate was lost on me. I was a selfish, teenage brat and I just wanted him out of our house.

Chapter 6

Deliverance

I WAS A JUNIOR at Washington-Lee High School in Arlington, Virginia, still rankled about my younger, troubled cousin taking up space in our rec room. Seeing a chance to escape from my unsettled home, I applied to the annual student exchange program, a weeklong trip to Hershey High School in Pennsylvania. W-L students would be matched with Hershey students, who would later come and stay with families in Arlington. I got lucky.

GIANT KISSES SERVE AS STREETLIGHTS IN HERSHEY, PENNSYLVANIA.

MILTON S. HERSHEY…THE CANDY BARON WHO FOUNDED THE
MILTON HERSHEY SCHOOL FOR ORPHAN BOYS. *BETTMAN/GETTY IMAGES*

The town founded by Milton Snavely Hershey was dotted with street-lights shaped like large, silver kisses and roads named Chocolate and Cocoa Avenue. It is often called "The sweetest place on Earth," a description that would have particular significance for me. But for the fact that Milton Hershey was forced to cancel his trip on the *Titanic* in 1912 for business reasons, there might never have been a Hershey, Pennsylvania, a candy empire, and a solution to my chaotic home life.

By 1964, the Hershey Chocolate Corporation basically owned the town that bore its name, and most of the people who lived there worked for the company. I went to classes with my exchange partner, Betsy, and one day we all boarded a bus and toured the town that candy built. We saw green fields filled with herds of grazing cows, which provided the milk, which went to the factory to make the chocolate, which went into the Hershey candy products. A perfect cycle of life. Our bus pulled up to a beautiful, large home in this verdant suburb outside the main part of town. It was one of more than a dozen mansions comprising the Milton Hershey School for Orphan Boys. In 1909, unable to have children of their own, Milton Hershey and his wife decided to use their wealth from his candy company to establish a home and school for orphan boys. In 1918, following the death of his wife, he transferred the majority of his assets, including control of the company, to a trust fund that created and supported the school in perpetuity.

I remember each home we visited had a couple living there, a mother and father to the dozen or so young boys. The children all seemed happy and well adjusted. The adults were kind and caring, no doubt selected after intense review to look after these orphaned boys. As was the custom, the boys came with almost nothing but the clothes on their backs. From the moment they arrived until they graduated from college, everything was provided for them—a stable home life and an education, all subsidized by the sale of candy and the largesse of Milton Hershey.

I found it hard to concentrate. Looking at the young boys, I could only think about the orphaned boy living in *my* house. He needed to be here in candy land, and I needed to get him here. But one troubling fact from our tour lingered in my brain. Thousands of boys applied to Milton Hershey's school. Few got in.

The next stop was the Hershey Chocolate factory, which, besides supporting the school, manufactured some of the best candy ever made. Fortunately, Milton Hershey, who started out working for a printer, was fired at the age of fourteen for accidentally dropping his hat into the machinery. His mother and aunt encouraged him to go into the candy business. He started out creating caramels, sold that company, and used the profits to perfect his milk chocolate recipe. The first Hershey bar was produced in 1900, Hershey's kisses in 1907, and the Hershey bar with almonds the next year.

We watched, mesmerized, as the candy bars came through giant machines and dropped down to an assembly line of women in clean, white aprons and hair nets who scrutinized every piece of chocolate, yanking the rejects and throwing them into a giant barrel. Any chocolate bar or Hershey's kiss deemed imperfect was tossed aside but not discarded. Tourists were encouraged to grab as much candy from the barrel as they could, devour it on the spot, or save it in a bag for later consumption. We took full advantage of the moment. But as I gorged on chocolate, my mind was elsewhere, obsessed with the question of how to get my cousin out of my home and into the Milton Hershey school.

A door opened into the chocolate factory, and the answer walked in.

Resplendent in a dark suit and tie, his hair perfectly combed, company president Samuel F. Hinkle came over to greet us. He began working at the Hershey Chocolate Corporation in the 1920s, analyzing fat, sugar, and milk content. In addition to creating Mr. Goodbar and acquiring the H. B. Reese Candy Company, once he took the helm of the company, Sam Hinkle founded a medical center. He was a brilliant businessman and community leader, and someone I needed to talk with, alone.

As the students headed back to the bus, I stayed behind to corner Mr. Hinkle. I introduced myself and told him I had a young, orphaned cousin whom I believed really needed to come to the Milton Hershey School. I wrote down my name and my cousin's name and gave it to him. He gave me the name of the person to contact to try to move this process along. In that moment, I knew the purpose of my trip had less to do with candy or meeting new friends and more with getting my family back the way I wanted it to be. I had a sense of destiny, of being in the right place at the right time. Undeterred by the stark reality of how few boys were accepted into the school, I had no doubt this was going to work.

I returned home a few days later and told my parents what they needed to do to get my cousin into the Hershey School. Our family lawyer contacted the school, and within weeks, he was on his way to "the sweetest place on Earth." He thrived there and received the care and counseling he so desperately needed. I got my family and my home back the way I needed it to be.

The wood-paneled rec room, a temporary bedroom while my cousins lived with us, was now mine again, a safe, comfortable place to listen to music, hang out with friends, watch TV, and neck, which was about as far as sex went for teenagers in the early Sixties. We kept the music loud, hoping to discourage my parents from checking on us. Three years of family turmoil were over. Mostly.

Over time, I understood why my parents felt compelled to bring my cousins into our home. None of the other relatives would take them, and my parents could not bring themselves to put them in foster care. I understood intellectually, but I never resolved the emotional pain. I never made peace with my parents' decision. Four decades later when I was in my fifties and my mother was in her eighties, I dragged her into therapy with me. I needed to say things I had never said and vent all of the resentment simmering inside me for so many years, but I needed a referee. In a small room my mother sat quietly on a couch, the therapist in a chair between us and I ranted like a petulant, spoiled teenager, thirteen years old again and furious, but I got it all out. My mother listened. She cried and asked forgiveness. I forgave her. And I forgave myself.

To THIS DAY, Hershey's is my favorite chocolate.

Chapter 7

Witness to History

I T WAS THE SUMMER OF 1963, the beginning of momentous events that shook, shattered, and rocked the world. Though almost a century had passed since the Civil War and the Emancipation Proclamation, the promise of that document was not kept. Freedom Riders were challenging segregation on buses, and from the steps of the University of Alabama, Governor George Wallace was shouting, "Segregation today, segregation tomorrow, segregation forever." In 1955, after a long day working as a seamstress, Rosa Parks refused to give up her seat on a bus to make room for white passengers. She once said the only tired she was "was tired of giving in."

Four years later, on February 2, 1959, four young, black teenagers possessed the same resolve as they calmly walked into my junior high school, Stratford. I remember National Guard troops surrounding the school as Michael, Ronald, Lance, and Gloria walked through the doors and into history. Stratford was the first public school in the state of Virginia to desegregate, and it accomplished that with little conflict.

BLACK STUDENTS ENTERING STRATFORD JUNIOR HIGH SCHOOL, MY ALMA MATER...AND THE FIRST PUBLIC SCHOOL IN VIRGINIA TO DESEGREGATE. *CENTER FOR LOCAL HISTORY, ARLINGTON PUBLIC LIBRARY.*

The county and state planned for trouble, but there was none. Almost six decades later, the Stratford school property was declared a local, historic district.

In late summer, the papers and radio were saturated with news about the upcoming March for Freedom and Jobs at the Washington Mall, a setting steeped in American history. I was compelled to go. I needed to be there, not satisfied to watch it on television but wanting to see it for myself. My friends and I drove as close as we could, but with the traffic and police blockades, we could only get as far as the Arlington side of Memorial Bridge. We parked the car and walked into a crowd of thousands, more people and picket signs than we had ever seen. We ended up near the back of this mass of humanity by the Washington Monument, sweating from the hot, humid, stifling heat so typical of a DC summer. We could not see Dr. King, Bob Dylan, or Joan Baez, but we could hear them. Especially Dr. King's powerful "I Have a Dream" speech. It felt so right to be there, black and white, young and old Americans, all gathered for the same purpose, adding our bodies and voices to the cry for justice and equal rights.

It was becoming clear to me that I had an almost pathological need to be close to important events. I was not content to read about things in a newspaper or watch them on television or have others tell me what they saw. I had to see things for myself if I was able to do that. Something happened to me that summer day in 1963, some kind of internal ignition that, once started, would never be turned off.

After the march, the speakers traveled to the White House to talk with President John F. Kennedy about proposed civil rights legislation, which would be signed by the president a year later, but not by JFK.

ON FRIDAY, NOVEMBER 22, 1963, around two in the afternoon, a crackled voice came through the loudspeaker in Shirley Fuelling's eleventh grade English class: "The president is dead. Repeating this announcement. The president of the United States is dead. All classes will now be dismissed, and students are to go to their buses and head home for the day."

We turned our heads in disbelief and just stared at each other. Was this a prank? Who would do that? But it was real.

The loudspeaker went silent. We staggered out of English class and mingled in the hallways with other students, dazed and quiet as we tried to grasp what we had heard. The president had been assassinated in Dallas. But that word, "assassination," seemed strange and antiquated, a word out of history and out of place in 1963. Unfamiliar and frightening.

President John Fitzgerald Kennedy was dead.

We went through the motions of gathering our books and whatever else we might need for the weekend. Three thousand students streamed out of Washington-Lee High School and headed home to their television sets. We were all in a state of confusion and disbelief and my mind drifted back for a moment...to a couple years earlier. I was at a slumber party at the home of a good friend, the daughter of a prominent Virginia Congressman on the same night he and his wife were hosting a fancy dinner party. We girls were confined to the upstairs balcony, but could not resist peering down between the spindles of the banister as the resplendent guests arrived in formal gowns and tuxedos. Among the glamorous crowd, President Kennedy and his beautiful Jackie walked into the foyer. His crisp, white shirt and tie were a stark contrast against his black tuxedo and her sleeveless gown was white and sparkled. For a moment, time stopped. They were elegant, perfect, young, and so beautiful they did not seem real.

As I continued walking down Twenty-Sixth Road towards Richmond Street, a large, black limousine was pulling away. No doubt it had come to retrieve our neighbor Gerald Behn, who lived at the top of our cul-de-sac.

Gerald Behn became head of the White House Secret Service soon after JFK was elected but did not make the fateful trip to Dallas on November 22. He had come up through the ranks of the Secret Service, beginning with what he called "diaper duty," watching the children of previous elected officials. Historic photos from the early 1960s show him standing close to President Kennedy on many occasions and walking behind the Kennedy family at the funeral. He is the tall, handsome man with the distinctive head of hair, always parted in the middle. He and his wife, Jean, played bridge with my parents, and one of his daughters, Barbara, was a friend of mine.

MY NEIGHBOR, GERALD BEHN, HEAD OF THE WHITE HOUSE SECRET SERVICE,
ALONGSIDE JFK JUST WEEKS BEFORE HIS ASSASSINATION.

The television set was on when I got home. My father closed his store early that Friday and would not reopen it for four days. We watched David Brinkley, Chet Huntley, and Walter Cronkite began to fill in the horrendous details about the assassination, and we saw Air Force One arrive at Andrews Air Force Base. The coffin was lowered off the plane, followed by Jackie, still wearing her blood-stained pink suit. She refused to change her clothes, saying, "I want them to see what they have done to Jack."

We stayed glued to the television set and left only to go to the bathroom or to eat. It was announced Saturday night that JFK's body would be moved to the Capitol Rotunda, allowing the public to come and pay their respects. I had to see this for myself, not content to watch this epic moment on television when it was all taking place just miles away. Most Americans recall that weekend in black and white from their TV sets. I remember it in vivid color.

I stood in a seemingly endless line of thousands of people also compelled to be there. It was sunny and cold and took hours to wind our way towards the white, marble steps and into the warmth of the US Capitol Building. People were quietly crying and hugging one another as we approached the casket, flanked by four unflinching military guards, one from each service. The casket was draped in an American flag and rested on a black catafalque, a raised box constructed to support a coffin. It was the same one that had been hastily built in 1865 for Abraham Lincoln.

As I approached the casket, I was transfixed, staring at the American flag, imagining the body of the dead president inside. We had to keep moving, pushed along by ushers waving us past the casket, allowing more than a quarter million people that day to walk past the tragic and somber scene. After four hours of waiting, I had thirty seconds to see what I had come to witness that day and was soon back out into the cold and sunshine, gazing out on a crowd of hundreds of thousands of people, dotting the landscape against a clear, blue sky. On Monday November 25, I found my way to Pennsylvania Avenue, as close as I could get to the White House to watch the funeral procession on its way to a service at St. Matthew's Cathedral in DC, and then on to Arlington National Cemetery. I saw a limousine drive by carrying Jackie and Caroline and thought I caught a glimpse of young JFK Jr. sitting on his mother's lap in his little blue suit. It was his third birthday. I would meet both of JFK's children much later in my life and theirs.

SEVERAL WEEKS after I witnessed JFK's casket, I was driving my mother's light green Corvair Monza when these words rang out from the car radio:

> *Oh yeah, I'll tell you something*
> *I think you'll understand*
> *When I say that something*
> *I wanna hold your hand*
> *I wanna hold your hand*
> *I wanna hold your hand*

The country and the world were still reeling from the death of the American president and would never be quite the same again. With the arrival of the Beatles, music would never be the same again either. I pulled off the road to hear the rest of the song and to find out who was singing it. The music was captivating, infectious, and it made me feel happy, an emotion in short supply in November of 1963.

The Beatles. I was one among millions who fell instantly in love with the music and the shaggy-haired young men making it, a perfect balm to ease the pain and misery from the death of a president. They would likely have become international superstars, no matter when they and their music exploded, but arriving on the heels of our national tragedy proved to be impeccable timing. We needed them, and they needed us.

Several of their songs were released in America towards the end of 1963, and they were coming here, scheduled to perform their first concert at the Washington Coliseum, another seismic event happening close to me. When tickets went on sale at the Coliseum box office, I cajoled my father into driving me there in the middle of the night and stand in line with me to buy tickets. We got there around five in the morning and left about six hours later with ten treasured tickets in hand . . . four dollars apiece. I knew I would have no trouble selling them to nine of my Beatles obsessed friends. The prevailing thought in my mind was *I have to be there*, as I needed to witness the Martin Luther King march and the JFK funeral. Watching snippets of this concert on television would be unacceptable.

On February 7, 1964, Pam Am Flight 101 landed in New York at John F. Kennedy Airport, renamed for the man assassinated just eleven weeks earlier. A crowd of around four thousand screaming girls and a few dozen boys stood jammed behind fences, straining for a glimpse of the Beatles. I was mesmerized watching them on TV coming down the steps from the plane, knowing I would see them in person in a few days. Two days after they landed, on Sunday, February 9, they appeared on the *Ed Sullivan Show*, and I, along with seventy-three million other Americans, was glued to my TV set. While Sullivan typically paid his guests $10,000 to appear on his show, he paid the Beatles only $3,500. Their manager, Brian Epstein, was forced to accept the deal because he believed his clients needed the exposure, no doubt a smart and ultimately lucrative decision. Dutch magician Fred Kaps had the unfortunate luck to follow the Beatles' performance on the Sullivan show. I remember nothing after the Beatles. For me, that was all the magic I needed.

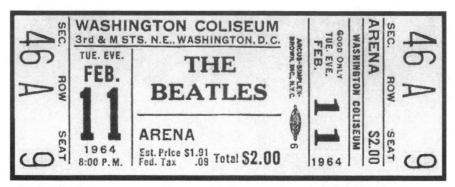

A TICKET FROM THE FIRST BEATLES CONCERT IN AMERICA, FEBRUARY 11, 1964.
THIS WAS NOT MY TICKET. WE HAD THE EXPENSIVE $4.00 SEATS.

February 11, 1964, was, without question, one of the greatest and most memorable days of my life. I was "just seventeen" and imagined myself as the girl they were singing about. Didn't we all? Other than riding horses, I had never been more excited about anything. It was a Tuesday, and as I recall, schools were closed because of a sudden and massive snowstorm that pummeled the East Coast. The weather shut down the airports in New York, forcing the Beatles to board a train to Washington for their first American concert.

Because I didn't have to go to school, I had more time to plan what I was going to wear, convinced that if I dressed just right, they would see me, return my affections, and take me back to their hotel room. Self-delusion is sometimes a wonderful thing. After much deliberation, I chose a brown, herringbone jumper, a white Villager shirt, a circle pin for my collar, and though I'd planned to wear Weejun loafers with a penny inserted on top, I was forced to wear rubber boots to trudge through the snow. This was an unfortunate but necessary fashion choice. Not a good look. Other than my wedding day, it was the only time I remembered precisely what I was wearing. The boots really ruined the whole look, and I was depressed at the thought of having to wear them. I thought it would hurt my chances of being noticed by Paul. I finished dressing, heard a car horn outside my house, and ran to join my nine friends jammed into a station wagon. In the frigid cold, we headed to the holy ground of the Washington Coliseum. Eight thousand ninety-two teenagers poured into the concrete belly of the Coliseum, typically the site of boxing matches. We were shaking with excitement as we trudged our way up to the second tier of seats. Three standing microphones were on the stage, ready for John, George, and Paul, and Ringo's iconic drum kit awaited him with the words "Ludwig" and "The Beatles" inscribed on the front. Before the show started, we walked down to the stage surrounded by dozens of policemen. We bowed towards the drums and paid homage to this sacred location in a brief moment of silence. There were three opening acts—the Righteous Brothers, Tommy Roe, and Jay and the Americans. I have absolutely no memory of those performances. None.

THE BEATLES ONSTAGE AT THE DC COLISEUM...FEBRUARY 11, 1964.
ICON/MICHAEL OCHS ARCHIVES/GETTY IMAGES

At 8:31 p.m., John, Paul, George, and Ringo swooped down from a stairway, flanked by policemen, through hordes of screaming girls and jumped onto the stage. They wore their familiar gray Beatle jackets with black trim around the collar, black Beatle boots, and the most famous haircuts in the world. They sang twelve songs in thirty-five minutes, mostly impossible to hear, the words and music drowned out by deafening screams. Because they were performing in the round, with the audience on all four sides of them, the Beatles stopped after every few songs to reposition the microphones and drums, giving everyone a chance to see their faces. Whether from the front, back, or side, they were amazing from any angle.

I think I was the only girl in the audience not screaming. I watched the people around me, and I watched the Beatles. I realized I was watching history, wanting to savor the moment, trying hard not to lose focus by yelling.

I could not believe I was there and to this day still boast about being one of only 8,092 people at the first Beatles concert in America. Twenty-seven years later, I would see Paul again in another Washington three thousand miles away. The fact that I was there when he first stepped on the stage at the Washington Coliseum would, in the future, get me a front row seat at his press conference in 1990 during his "Wings Over America" tour at Seattle's Kingdome. I did not scream then either, but I did cry.

There is an unfortunate side story to this epic moment in my life. My gym teacher's husband worked at the Shoreham Hotel where the Beatles stayed during their first visit to Washington. I asked Mrs. Causey to ask her husband to get me their autographs, which, miraculously, he did! A couple of days later, she said she had a big surprise for me and gave me a piece of Shoreham stationary signed by each of them—the souvenir of a lifetime . . . which I somehow managed to lose. It sickens me every time I think about it, but the memory of that night will never be lost.

In less than six months, the world changed. Martin Luther King, Jr. heralded a call for equality, John Fitzgerald Kennedy was gone, and the Beatles arrived. I saw all of this with my own eyes.

Chapter 8

Revulsion, Expulsion, Exclusion

THE NAZIS

L ESS THAN TWENTY YEARS after the fall of Nazi Germany, the American version of the Nazi party set up shop in Arlington, Virginia, at 928 Randolph Street, across from my high school. One of my many boy-crushes, Ricky Farber, decided to throw rocks and yell insults at the Nazis' house after a school dance. Ricky, who was Jewish, was grabbed and dragged into the house, handcuffed, and questioned at gunpoint by two thugs later arrested for assaulting Ricky. I liked Ricky even more after that.

George Lincoln Rockwell, the founder and leader of the American Nazi Party, had a fancy name, an unflagging hatred of Jews and blacks, and often sported a Hitler-like moustache. He began life as a somewhat sane person, working in advertising and publishing, and did not become a Hitler sycophant until the late 1950s and early 1960s. He once said, "When I was in the advertising game, we used to use nude women. Now I use the swastika and storm troopers. You use what brings them in."

GEORGE LINCOLN ROCKWELL STANDING SMUGLY IN FRONT OF HIS HOUSE OF NAZIS. THIS WRETCHED PLACE WAS NEAR OUR HIGH SCHOOL. © *AGE FOTOSTOCK*

The house on Randolph Street both attracted and repulsed the students at Washington-Lee High school. A large banner sometimes hung outside the shabby, Nazi headquarters and read: "White Man . . . Fight! Smash the Black Revolution Now." We never saw much of Rockwell himself, but his coterie of young, misguided punks often left anti-Semitic and racist leaflets on the windshields of cars in the student parking lot. Occasionally when the drapes were pulled back from the house, we could see a bright red flag with a black swastika in the center mounted over the fireplace. The young, Nazi aspirants sometimes called in bomb threats to several businesses owned by Jewish families, including my father's clothing store and my uncle's record store in the Clarendon shopping center. No bombs ever exploded, but the threat was scary enough. They had the audacity to picket Mario's Pizza House on Wilson Boulevard, much-beloved by W-L high school students for their pizzas and sub sandwiches, after the owners, the Levine family, refused to serve the Nazis while continuing to serve black customers. Their picket signs read: "Mario the Jew." The wannabe American Nazis were, most simply put, vermin. We students, our parents, and most of the residents of Arlington hated these people. Still, they were impossible to ignore. A cancer growing in our town.

On Halloween night in 1964, the temptation to retaliate was irresistible. Inspired by the legendary chutzpah of our classmate Ricky, several of my friends and I decided to go trick-or-treating on Randolph Street. I filled a paper bag with dog shit, courtesy of our family poodle, Tammy, hopped into a friend's car, and headed to the house of Hitler.

We pulled up in front. We were young, bold, and eager for revenge. They had threatened my father, who only twenty years earlier served in the war that defeated Hitler. I felt brave and, at seventeen years old, invincible. Lacking a gun, I carried the best weapon at my disposal, a bag of stinking excrement. I got out of the car, marched up to the door, and rang the bell. One of Rockwell's trashy Brownshirts opened the door, and without hesitation, I threw the smelly mess into the hallway. Before these idiotic, misguided storm troopers knew what had happened, I turned around, ran, jumped into the car, and we took off. I felt completely justified in what I had just done. In my mind, nothing I could do, short of killing them, would be worse than what they were doing or worse than what they stood for. It was, by comparison, a mild and completely justifiable act of retaliation.

In December of 1965, the Internal Revenue Service locked the American Nazi Party members out of their Randolph Street house for non-payment of taxes. They relocated to a couple other Virginia locations. On August 25, 1967, George Lincoln Rockwell was shot and killed leaving a laundromat in Arlington. His assailant was a recently expelled and clearly disgruntled member of Rockwell's putrid organization. Rockwell left behind an estate of $257 in cash, various writings, and a legacy of hatred.

Upon Rockwell's death, his father is quoted as saying, "I am not surprised at all. I've expected it for quite some time."

THE RACIST

Miss Ethel Leigh Joyner was the chairman of the Washington-Lee High School Library Department. She was shriveled, mean-spirited, and had very bad breath. To us students, she was known as "Zoo Breath" due to the fetid stench she exhaled when she hovered over us with stern orders to be quiet in her library. My friends and I would often curse and raise our voices in the library just to annoy her. On one memorable occasion in the cafeteria, some boys filled a condom with water and tossed it around the room to taunt Miss Joyner, who was trying in vain to maintain order while on lunch duty. She grabbed the condom and proudly strutted away, holding it high, saying with great conviction: "We don't throw balloons around the school!"

She took her job as chairman of the library very, very seriously, slinking around with pursed lips, ready to pounce on anyone who dared speak above a quiet whisper or anyone who dared speak at all. It was a hallowed place for reading, studying, and nothing else.

One afternoon in Zoo Breath's library, I was sitting at a round, wooden table, trying and failing to study and mind my own business. A couple of my friends were sitting with me, among them my dear friend Jerome Green who, but for being born black, might never have caught Miss Joyner's attention. Washington-Lee was a very big high school with about three thousand students, mostly white. The Arlington County schools had only recently been desegregated in 1960. Full integration was years away. Jerome loved everybody, and everybody loved him. I never saw him without a smile on his face, except in his senior picture. We became good friends. Jerome was co-captain of the high school football team, along with my boyfriend, Jimmy Carr.

Jerome Green: 2. J.V. Football, Graphic Arts Club; 3. Varsity Football, J.V. Track, Health Club, Graphic Arts Club, Varsity Football—Co-Captain, Health Club

JEROME GREEN, MY DEAR FRIEND.
I WAS PROUDLY EXPELLED AFTER STANDING UP FOR HIM.

On that fateful afternoon in the library, Jerome leaned over to tell me something and touched his hand to my forearm to get my attention. That simple, innocent gesture sent Miss Joyner into a frenzy. With lightning speed, she raced over to us with a menacing look on her face, much like the wicked witch from Oz flying in on her broomstick. She grabbed Jerome's hand still resting on my arm and said in a very loud "not appropriate for the library" voice, "Get your hand off of her! Black boys don't touch white girls in my school!"

First I went numb. Then I went nuts. I stood up, exploded in anger, and screamed back at her, "What the fuck are you doing, you fucking piece of shit! Don't you dare talk to him like that! Who the fuck do you think you are?"

As I kept ranting at her, she called for someone to haul me down to the principal's office. Cursing all the way, I was escorted into the sanctum where no student ever wanted to go. The place where only the bad kids went, the office of vice-principal Doris H. Matthews. Mrs. Matthews was a battle-ax of a woman . . . grim-faced, serious, and formidable. I do not recall ever seeing her smile, and she was certainly not smiling the day I faced her.

"I'm very disappointed in you, Julie. I have to take this very seriously."

I considered telling her I was very disappointed too, in Miss Joyner's contemptuous words aimed at Jerome and the bigotry and racism put on display in the library. But for once in my life, I said nothing, fully aware that Mrs. Matthews was about to impose her punishment.

She expelled me.

She told me to gather my things, whatever belonged to me, and to leave all books belonging to the school in my locker. The bell had rung and school was over for the day as dozens of my close friends gathered around me while I prepared to leave permanently. The fact that I'd been expelled . . . one of the good girls . . . was almost as shocking as Miss Joyner's actions in the library. I felt more pride than shame as I got ready to leave, somehow convinced that while my attack on Ethel Joyner was somewhat wrong, what she had said and done was worse. Just as I'd done while throwing dog shit into the Nazi headquarters, I convinced myself that my actions were completely justified.

My mother came and picked me up. She was not pleased. We drove home without speaking. Her silence was deafening and frightening.

"When your father gets home, he'll talk with you."

Indeed he did, but not in the way I expected. My father was angry, but apparently not with me. He was enraged at the school for having anyone on staff who was so obviously racist. Daddy decided to fight my expulsion.

He went to the school administration offices the next day, demanding to see whoever was in charge. I was with him. Leonard Honick was as kind and gentle a soul as you would ever meet. Other than being upset when my mother beat him at Scrabble, he never yelled or raised his voice. He never hit anyone or anything as I recall. He was a quiet man. But not that day. By the time we were escorted into some official's office, he was resolute in fighting what he believed was blatant racism in the schools and said in a clear, concise, and unquestionably serious way, "Julie will be back in school tomorrow, or I will sue you over this issue."

The facts of the previous day's events were discussed. I was appropriately admonished for my obscenity-laced outburst and forced to promise I would never do anything like that again. That was a lie. It was a false promise I was forced to make, but I would rage again. Many times.

I returned to school the next day with the support of the students and most of the faculty, but not all of them. I got an icy reception from some of the teachers, but went about my business and attended classes pretending, as best I could, that I didn't care about anyone's disapproval. "Social media" in 1965 meant actually talking to people either in person or on the phone, so the ability for mass communication, bullying, or creating memes did not exist. In time, the infamous episode with Zoo Breath in the library was forgotten by most people. But not by Jerome Green or me.

He wrote in my high school yearbook:

JEROME'S INSCRIPTION IN MY HIGH SCHOOL YEARBOOK. HE FILLED A
WHOLE PAGE THANKING ME, BUT IT WAS MY HONOR TO STAND UP FOR HIM.

Dear Julie

*Well it's finally the end of the road for high school. I am sorry
I did not have the privilege of knowing you earlier because I
have really been missing something. I do not know exactly how
to say it, but I really appreciated all that you did for me this
year. I am really going to miss you, Julie. You were more than a
friend . . . something really special to me. I hope our friendship*

does not end with the school year. They tried to separate us, but you would not let them. Well, Julie, I am running out of words so I'll say you are a girl who deserves all the best things in and out of life. Best of luck and love always. This is the end of our high school days.

Best wishes,
Jerome

STARING UP AT MIKE O'CONNELL, ONE OF MY HIGH SCHOOL CRUSHES, POSING FOR A YEARBOOK AD IN MY FATHER'S STORE.

It was, indeed, the end of high school but not the end of a longtime friendship between Jerome and me. At our high school reunions, we hugged, smiled, and relived our encounter with Zoo Breath.

REJECTION

After the unfortunate but necessary attack on Miss Joyner, my focus during the remaining months of high school was filling out college applications and deciding where I would go after graduation. I knew where I wanted to go but had little chance of getting there.

In 1965, most of the Ivy League universities were closed to women. Harvard, Yale, Columbia, Dartmouth, Brown, and my father's alma mater—The University of Virginia—all had what was known as sister schools, for women only. To me this was blatant discrimination. College officials in the 1960s considered only "the best and the brightest," according to an article from that time, a distinction that apparently did not include women. I considered filling out applications to these schools and listing my name as Jules instead of Julie and marking the gender box with an *M* for male. I regret not doing that. I really wanted to go to Columbia University, believing everyone should live in New York City at some point in their life. Decades later a part of me would get into Columbia.

I loved New York City. I often went to visit aunts, uncles, and an assortment of cousins when I was a young child and into my teenage years. Along with some of my cousins and friends, we managed to talk our way into Cafe Wha? and some of the other Greenwich Village clubs. I saw Bob Dylan and Joan Baez and dozens of other singers of the folk era, not imagining I was listening to musicians who would become some of the biggest stars in the history of American music. On one particularly sneaky weekend, I borrowed my father's new, white Oldsmobile with its red leather interior and told my parents I was going to spend the night with some girlfriends. I did drive to my friend's house, and we all piled into the car and drove to New York City's Apollo Theater to see a Motown Review. We were the only white people there. We got back to Arlington the next morning, my parents none the wiser. If my father noticed any extra mileage on the odometer, he never mentioned it.

The urge to live in New York City was not strong enough to inspire me to apply to Barnard, the women's school. I probably would not have been accepted anyway. I did not want to be in the women's school. It seemed unfair and another form of segregation. But at that time, more than fifty years ago, women just did not apply to the men's Ivy League schools. The thought of filing a discrimination lawsuit was not even an inkling of an idea in anyone's mind.

I was in the top 10 percent of my graduating class of about a thousand students, so I figured I had a pretty good shot at being accepted at the University of Pennsylvania, one of only two coed schools in the Ivy League. It was my first choice and my only chance to get into a real Ivy and go where the boys went. While my grades and test scores were good, they paled next to the SAT scores and grades of our dozen valedictorians. For them, Penn was their back-up school, their second choice. They all got accepted. I did not.

I was accepted at Northwestern, the only private, small school in the Big Ten Conference. It was coed, a good school, and as far away from home as I wanted to be. I had never been to any major city other than those on the East Coast.

The last memorable event of my senior year was the prom, a night I remember not so much for the fancy dinner or dancing but for losing my virginity. Jimmy and I double-dated with my best friend, Martha, and her boyfriend, Larry, and headed south to Jimmy's father's farm in Southern Virginia not too long after arriving at the prom. We went into separate bedrooms, and on a cold bed, I took off my prom dress and had sexual intercourse for the first time.

PROM NIGHT WITH BOYFRIEND JIMMY CARR. THE NIGHT I LOST MY VIRGINITY... THOUGH JIMMY FORGOT THAT.

Some years later at one of our high school reunions, a large group of us got together in Jimmy's hotel room and began telling stories about the first time we had "done it." Easy for me. My first sex partner was in the room with me, but when I told my story and looked over at Jimmy, he insisted no such thing ever happened. Everyone laughed as I sat slack-jawed next to Jimmy. How dare he deny it? To me there was nothing funny about it. Maybe he was drunk that night. Maybe it just didn't mean anything to him. But it happened. I know. I was there.

I spent the summer working in my father's stores, having his seamstress, Thelma, make some clothes for me for college as I prepared to get on with the next stage of my life.

The March on Washington, the JFK funeral, the first Beatles concert in America, the Nazis, getting expelled from school, and being rejected by the Ivy League were now all in my wake. I was eighteen years old, and it was time to move on. Just for the record, prior to becoming an avowed Nazi, George Lincoln Rockwell applied and was accepted at Brown University. If they wanted the best and the brightest, they clearly did not get that with him.

Chapter 9

The Winters of My Discontent

"NOW IS THE WINTER OF OUR DISCONTENT" is a phrase from Shakespeare's *Richard III*, describing a civil war in England. In the late Sixties, cities across America were erupting in political unrest largely because of the Vietnam War, and much of the chaos and discontent was on college campuses. The phrase also has come to suggest a general state of disaffection. In September 1965, on arrival in Evanston, Illinois, I was severely disaffected.

Mostly I hated college. The best gifts I got from Northwestern University were three lifelong friends, Mardee, Mary, and Dulcie who were well worth the price of admission. But I got little else. I was not mature enough, smart enough, or disciplined enough to know how to study or how to take advantage of the scholars who taught there. A thousand miles away from my high school comfort zone where everyone knew me and most people liked me, I was a stranger in a strange place, severed from my family and everything that was familiar, the streets I grew up on, my bedroom, my records, and my friends. To be a college freshman in 1965 was to arrive on the cusp of a cultural revolution, in the middle of a decade where mores, morals, and music were changing, and the Vietnam War permeated everything. A letter sent to all incoming Northwestern coeds advised us to pack an evening gown, a cocktail dress, and several cashmere sweaters, a clarion reminder of how women adorned themselves at this school. I packed none of those items. I did not own them and would not buy them.

Evanston, Illinois, is nestled along the windy shores of Lake Michigan, about twelve miles north of Chicago. More than a century before I got there, the land was uninhabited, mostly wetlands and swampy forests. By the mid-nineteenth century, before the town had electricity, a group of Methodist business leaders founded Northwestern University and named the town after John Evans. It lays claim to having invented the ice cream sundae, was the birthplace of Tinkertoys, and was the longtime headquarters of the WCTU, the Women's Christian Temperance Union. It was a dry community, which meant the sale and consumption of alcohol was illegal until 1972. It was dry *and* cold. The appalling chill of a Chicago winter was still a few months away, but part of freshman orientation was a reminder to have hats, gloves, and warm coats in our closets. They did not list those things along with the cashmere sweaters and cocktail dresses in their earlier letter. I did buy coats and gloves.

I was assigned to live in Willard Hall, named after the indomitable Frances Willard, one of the founders of the WCTU who, other than eschewing alcohol and furthering Christian principles, also pushed hard for the rights of women to vote. She was an early feminist and grew the WCTU to be the largest organization of women in the world by 1890. Unlike Frances, her eponymous building was a dull, drab red-brick edifice of a housing complex, home to several hundred coeds. Freshmen were not allowed to choose their roommates, and I was paired with a very serious, quiet, and shy girl from Dyersburg, Tennessee. She pronounced her city as a two-syllable word, "Diesberg." Southerners are often quite adept at making single syllable words polysyllabic. "Bed" morphs into "bay-ed," and "yes" sometimes becomes "yay-es." I did not know they could condense words. Betty and I were, without question, the oddest couple in Willard Hall.

Betty rarely talked and had few facial expressions. She was tough to read. I talked constantly and wore my emotions on a face that was rarely without expression. The beds were as uncomfortable as our relationship, the closets were tiny, there was no drawer space to speak of, and the worst indignity was the communal showers. I was never comfortable being naked in front of people I knew, let alone as many as a dozen teenage girls who lacked any scintilla of modesty. Adding insult to injury, I was a bather, and I would not see a bathtub until I returned home on school breaks. Meals were served at precise times, and curfews were rigid and enforced. Boys were not permitted past the lobby area, forbidden upstairs. No telephones were allowed in the rooms, those now antiquated contraptions once used to make contact with other people. A few pay phones were mounted in the hallways with strictly imposed time limits so others could have access. With the passage of more than fifty years, all the rules and customs seem absurd in the light of today. But that is how it was, and though we did not like those restrictions, we never thought to seriously challenge them.

WITH MY SORORITY CLASS...1965...STILL WITH BIG HAIR IN THE BACK ROW...
FLASHING THE PEACE SIGN...FEIGNING HAPPINESS.

One way to feel less lonely and lost was to join a sorority. Northwestern was a Greek campus with dozens of national chapters of fraternities and sororities. I decided to sign up for rush week, which can best be described as a rectal exam with no lubrication. All the girls visit the sororities and boys go to the fraternities, literally rushing in and out, shaking a few hands, and eating a few cookies as they are scrutinized and judged by those who will determine if they are good enough to warrant a return visit. The few friends I made were going to the most popular houses, Kappa Kappa Gamma, Tri Delta, and Pi Phi, so I followed them, oblivious to the fact that the welcome mat was not typically extended to Jewish girls. I learned very quickly that we had our own sororities and that I should not count on getting into the ones I wanted. If I wanted to become a pledge, a candidate for acceptance, I needed to visit the Jewish houses. It all sounded very snotty and exclusionary, which indeed it was.

Other than seeing anti-Semitic flyers stuck to windshields of cars parked at my high school and my father's store getting a bomb threat from the Nazis in Arlington, this was my first up-close and personal encounter with blatant religious discrimination. It stung, badly. Alpha Epsilon Phi was considered the cooler of the two Jewish sororities, so I went there. Feeling different, excluded, and rejected only deepened my sense of isolation. But it was there that I met Mardee and Mary, the girls who got me through four mostly discontented years.

Though I had good enough grades to get into Northwestern, I did not have a clue how to succeed there academically. At the end of my first quarter, I failed every one of my midterm exams and was put on academic probation. In the days before the internet and computers, grades were often posted in the buildings where the classes were held. I walked to the biology building where students' names and grades were posted on a large bulletin board. I worked my way through the crowd and started looking down the list from the top. By the time I got to the middle, I still did not see my name. I kept looking, lower and lower until I got to the bottom. There I was—Julie Honick, with a very large F by my name. Someone has to be last. I certainly distinguished myself by having the lowest grade of four hundred students. I never did anything half-assed.

I felt sick, embarrassed, and scared and considered for a moment drowning myself in the icy waters of Lake Michigan. Instead, I called my father from a campus pay phone. If I expected sympathy, I did not get it. My usually calm, gentle father was brutal and took no pity on me. He said I had better figure out what to do. I was on my own. He was paying for college, and that was all he could do. He could not do the work for me, could not take the exams for me, and could not help me out of this mess. It was the toughest love he ever gave me. With no real choice other than to fix this wreck in which I was now entangled, I focused on academics in lieu of boys and parties and, by the end of the quarter, had salvaged my grades enough to get off probation.

After my freshmen year in the stultifying atmosphere of Willard Hall, I shared a room in Shepard Hall with Mardee. We were the oddball duo of our sorority, never really ostracized but never really fitting in. As long as we had each other, we were okay. She was from Milwaukee, beautiful, with long, straight hair, a handsome boyfriend, and an innate talent for academic success without much studying. I envied everything about her but loved her anyway.

The most shocking and memorable event at the beginning of our sophomore year was the murder of Valerie Percy, the daughter of then-Republican US Senate candidate Charles Percy. The twenty-one-year-old had just graduated from Cornell and came home to work on her father's campaign. She was stabbed to death in her family's Kenilworth mansion, just a few miles from the Evanston campus. It was the first homicide in that wealthy community and close enough to our campus to warrant warnings and bring extra patrols around the coed dorms, including Shepard Hall. We were ordered not to walk alone anywhere on campus and to make sure our doors were locked at night. It scared us. The Percy murder remains unsolved to this day.

We were forced to declare our majors during our sophomore year. Lacking any focus or particular interest in any career and aspiring to nothing more than possibly finding a husband, I opted for a teacher's degree, a common option for women in the Sixties. It seemed a safe choice and something I thought I could always use. I never did.

I took a lot of classes in the English department—Shakespeare, American and European fiction, and writing classes. I never distinguished myself academically but never humiliated myself as badly as I did my first year. I remember often falling asleep in my classes, slumping over in what I called the "college nod," closing my eyes, and jerking my head back before I completely zoned out. I was too ignorant and woefully unaware of some of the great teachers in front of me—world-renowned scholar Richard Ellmann teaching James Joyce and Oscar Wilde, Meno Spann teaching European fiction and Goethe—and just too young to realize and appreciate the opportunities in front of me. I wish I could go back and sit in those classes again.

I remember little of my academic life at Northwestern, but I will never forget the winter weather. The winds often blew so hard off Lake Michigan that ropes were installed so students could hold on to get to classes. In 1967, a snowstorm still in the record books dumped almost two feet in a single day. Classes were canceled. The whole city shut down, and I hid under my blanket for days. My blue, Sunbeam electric blanket was my refuge over four interminable winters. I slept, studied, ate, and wrote papers huddled under that blanket, pounding away on my Smith-Corona electric typewriter. I am *not* proud to say I did not spend even one hour in the magnificent Deering Library at Northwestern, repository of some of the world's greatest books, which I could not be bothered to examine. Shameful.

Junior year was overwhelming. With twenty papers due in a three-month period, I had no chance of meeting those deadlines without help. It arrived in the body of Howard, a future venture capitalist now worth about two billion dollars. When we dated during my junior year at Northwestern, Howard was in graduate school at the University of Chicago, brilliant, funny, cocky, and immensely creative. Howard came to my rescue on a red, corduroy bedspread in my cramped room at 1900 Orrington Avenue. He sat on the bed with my typewriter between his legs as we created papers out of our heads, doing little research. Some were just fictional stories, others research papers requiring bibliographies and citations. Howard and I invented quotes and references, book titles and authors out of thin air, making it up as we went along. Beyond this confession many decades later, what is most disturbing is the fact that it really never occurred to either one of us that we would get caught. There was no internet, no Google, no Facebook, no computer-generated algorithm that might bust us. Papers were typically graded by overworked grad students and teaching assistants who had little time to verify quotes or bibliographies. To me, writing fiction seemed more reasonable than the impossible task of doing actual research. Howard saved me from certain failure.

By my senior year, I was done with campus housing. The rules and restrictions became too ridiculous to follow. Mardee, Mary, and I decided to rent an apartment and live on our own, breaking an age-old tradition of coeds living in restricted dorms. I never much liked going along with regulations or being bound by other people's rules. I even hated wearing jewelry. It made me feel restrained and tied down. I never wore rings, necklaces, or even a wristwatch. The three of us asked our parents to write letters to university administrators seeking permission to live off campus during our senior year. Reluctantly, they agreed.

The old, brick building along Sheridan Road was owned and managed by a crusty, Polish woman, Mrs. Keljik. Mary and I shared a room and Mardee got a room to herself in our two-bedroom apartment. She smoked and, though she denied it ferociously, was having regular sex and needed more privacy. Funny, the things you remember. Mardee had a beautiful, fluffy, light-blue comforter, her own car, and a mother in Milwaukee who typed her papers as she dictated them over the phone. She would also send her laundry home, and within a few days, it would come back clean and pressed. Since we were not eating meals in the sorority house and were not on any university meal plan, we were responsible for shopping and cooking for ourselves. To this day, Mary and I still resent Mardee's unwillingness to let us borrow her car, either for grocery shopping or hauling our clothes back and forth from the laundromat. I remain haunted by memories of trudging through the cold and snow, carrying dirty clothes and a lot of rage about not having access to Mardee's car.

It was 1968, a tumultuous, chaotic, and frightening year. In April, Martin Luther King Jr. was assassinated as he stood on the balcony of the Lorraine Motel in Memphis, Tennessee. He was thirty-nine years old. Two months later, forty-two-year-old Robert F. Kennedy was shot to death at the Ambassador Hotel in Los Angeles. He had just won the California presidential primary and seemed on a clear path towards being the Democratic nominee for president. Those murders, the Vietnam War, and the resistance to it hovered over everything. Hundreds of organizations gathered on college campuses to oppose what, to us, was a purposeless waste of human life. The National Democratic Convention was about to get underway in Chicago in late August, and I thought it might be interesting to witness this gathering of the old guard and the war resisters. I rented a hotel room in Chicago and watched the debacle unfold from the sidelines of Grant Park. I was twenty-one and too scared to wander into the middle of the chaos of anti-war protestors. Demonstrators were met with brutality from the Chicago police. Almost six hundred people were arrested, more than two hundred injured, and clouds of tear gas drifted over all of it. Among those arrested were activists later indicted on charges related to the Chicago riots who later became known as the Chicago Seven: Rennie Davis, David Dellinger, Tom Hayden, Abbie Hoffman, Jerry Rubin, Lee Weiner, and John Froines. All seven were acquitted on charges of conspiracy, two were acquitted on all charges, and five were convicted of inciting a riot. The convictions were later overturned due to judicial bias and problems with jury selection, though I could never determine exactly what that meant.

The chaos in Chicago found its way to the typically sleepy campus at Northwestern, which probably for the first time in its history became something of a hotbed of political unrest. I remember screaming matches at political gatherings, a lot of protest signs, and cantankerous arguments in the midst of campus elections. During all of it, we three, Mary, Mardee, and I, settled into our rundown apartment and into the remaining months of our senior year.

Besides having great luck at finding friends for life, I made something of a life-changing decision by signing up for English classes with the remarkable and famous Bergen Evans, a renowned writer, wordsmith, and host of a television show on CBS, *The Last Word*. Having contended with my father's demands for perfect spelling, punctuation, and usage, I was now in the presence of a true master of the English language. I studied writing with him my entire senior year. He gave me a copy of Strunk and White's *The Elements of Style*, telling me it was the most valuable book a writer could ever have. He also told me something that went in one ear and stuck in my head: "You're a good writer with a big personality. You ought to think about going into television news."

Spring break in 1969 was transformative. I went home for what I thought would be just another quick visit before heading back to my final quarter at Northwestern. My mother's best friend, a neighbor with whom she played Scrabble on a daily basis, invited us for brunch along with the Blacklow family. Unbeknownst to me, this was bashert, a Yiddish word for destiny. My mother's friend, Jeannette, believed she was bringing possible soulmates together. She wanted the Blacklow son to meet Esther and Leonard's daughter while consuming her generous brunch of bagels, lox, and cream cheese. When Richard Blacklow walked through the door, only one thought went through my head: *This is one of the handsomest Jewish men I have ever seen.* Richard Blacklow had all the right stuff, a degree from Dartmouth, a draft deferment, and a great nose. He was handsome and smart, teaching in one of DC's most dangerous high schools during the day to avoid going to Vietnam and attending George Washington law school at night. I was smitten, and so was he. After my plane ride back to Chicago for my final quarter at Northwestern, we stayed in touch by letter.

ON RECOMMENDATION OF THE FACULTY OF THE
SCHOOL OF EDUCATION
NORTHWESTERN UNIVERSITY HAS CONFERRED THE DEGREE OF
BACHELOR OF SCIENCE IN EDUCATION
UPON
JULIE LYNN HONICK
WHO HAS HONORABLY FULFILLED ALL THE REQUIREMENTS PRESCRIBED
BY THE UNIVERSITY FOR THAT DEGREE

DONE AT EVANSTON ILLINOIS THIS FOURTEENTH DAY OF JUNE IN THE
YEAR OF OUR LORD ONE THOUSAND NINE HUNDRED AND SIXTY-NINE

PRESIDENT OF THE BOARD OF TRUSTEES

SECRETARY OF THE BOARD OF TRUSTEES

CHANCELLOR OF THE UNIVERSITY

DEAN

MY NORTHWESTERN UNIVERSITY DIPLOMA...FROM THE SCHOOL
OF EDUCATION...A DEGREE I NEVER USED FOR TEACHING.

I graduated, skipped the ceremonial pomp and circumstance, left, and never went back. I had a teacher's degree I would never use, three lifelong friends and some ability to write. I was about to do what millions of college seniors were doing, taking a much-anticipated European vacation, a gift from my parents for surviving four years of mostly discontent. Dulcie had another year at Northwestern, but decided to travel with me to Europe during the upcoming summer, months of too many museums and too many men.

IN LATE FALL OF 2018, as I was preparing to read this chapter to my former roommate and lifelong friend, Mardee died after a fifteen year battle with cancer. We are forever bound.

Chapter 10

Summer of '69

IT WAS THE SUMMER OF WOODSTOCK, the moon landing, and the height of the era of the sexual revolution, drugs, and rock 'n' roll. I was done with the wind, ice, and snow of Chicago, done with holding on to ropes to go to classes, done with term papers, final exams, sorority life, rules and regulations, parties where I had to fake being happy, and perhaps most importantly, done with feeling not quite smart or pretty enough. I was tired of anti-war protests and learning about friends being sent to Vietnam or dying there. I needed a break.

I had no idea what awaited me in Europe. The only foreign soil I had ever visited was in the Bahamas. I had my first passport, a Eurail Pass, a little bit of anxiety, but a lot of excitement about getting out of America. "Sugar, Sugar" by the Archies, "Let the Sunshine In" by the Fifth Dimension, and "Get Together" by the Youngbloods were all Top Ten hits. So was "Hot Fun in the Summertime" by Sly and the Family Stone, a perfect musical prelude to my upcoming adventure. I felt truly free for the first time in my life.

The man who helped me create fake papers in college met me in New York, his hometown, to give me a parting gift and take me to JFK Airport. The future venture capitalist gave me a beautiful Lark suitcase, made of strong, blue fabric with red leather piping. Though he was not yet the billionaire he would later become, Howard always had impeccable taste. The bag was small, carry-on size, perfect for traveling. Pack light, travel light was the advice given to the thousands of college graduates heading overseas. But as I repacked my miniskirts and bikinis from my old suitcase into my new one, I was mindful of the fact that as I headed to Europe, thousands of other young people were heading overseas as well, to Vietnam, and carrying heavier burdens and much uglier baggage. I never doubted I would come back but knew many of them never would.

The big, beautiful, Pan Am plane sat on the runway at JFK Airport, the blue stripe on each side with the globe on the tail, two jet engines on each wing, waiting to take me and another hundred travelers to London. The 707 was Boeing's first commercial jet airplane, which marked the end of propeller-driven airliners and the beginning of the jet age. Boeing was a Seattle company where this plane was built and where the career I never could have imagined would later take off. The interior of the plane was as impressive as the outside. Big, wide, cloth seats with plenty of room for legs and arms to stretch out and relax. Room to breathe. No sense of being jammed into a too small space, shoulders and thighs touching your seatmate. No elbowing for control of the armrests. No tolerating the foul smell of someone with bad hygiene. No child kicking the back of your seat. Delicious meals were served with linen napkins and real forks and knives. No plastic. And this was flying coach.

I landed in London at night, but before the iconic, black taxi took me to my hotel, I asked the cabbie to drive me to the Abbey Road Studios, so I could pay homage to the Beatles. The eponymous album named for the street where it was recorded was months away from release. The big, white stripes on Abbey Road were at that time just a crosswalk.

A few days after I got to London, Dulcie, my dear friend from college, arrived to meet me. We were a perfect match, opposites in myriad ways. She was tall with long, jet-black hair and a calm, quiet demeanor. I was shorter with long, blond hair and little ability to keep my mouth shut. We were, I think, drawn together to complete each other. I pulled Dulcie out from the quiet, safer places she inhabited, and she pulled me back from the risky places where I often ventured. We kept each other in balance. She wanted her boundaries pushed and I needed her to keep me from straying too far over the edges. At twenty-one and twenty-two years old, we loved and needed each other. We understood and appreciated our differences. She would later say I gave her a much longer leash. She shortened mine.

I think, in looking back at a trip that would last several months and include escapades in ten countries, it is important to describe not only what we saw and did but also our state of mind. We arrived on the European continent with no fear of anything or anyone. We had no planned itinerary, no exact idea of how we would get anywhere or where we would stay once we arrived. We simply knew we would find our way, whatever direction it might go. We were living in a time of sexual freedom. There was no talk of AIDS and little, if any, awareness of sexually transmitted diseases. We had heard of syphilis and gonorrhea, but those were diseases we believed were relegated to older, lascivious men and the women and men who serviced them. For two, Jewish, fresh-faced, spoiled, white girls, the realities and risks of unprotected sex did not exist.

I had one mission in Amsterdam. My future billionaire friend asked that I buy pornographic magazines for him, stash them in the blue Lark suitcase he gave me, and schlep them back from Europe. I never understood why Howard, who lived in New York City, was uncomfortable going into Times Square himself and buying his own X-rated rags in any number of porn shops. Regardless, Dulcie and I ventured into Amsterdam's infamous red-light district with beautiful prostitutes seductively posed in windows, encouraging anyone, no matter the gender, to come inside and purchase their services.

Amsterdam was known not only for legalized prostitution and drugs but also for its world-famous Rijksmuseum housing works by Rembrandt, Vermeer, and Frans Hals. Here and in every major city we visited, Dulcie's and my distinctively different patterns of behavior took root. She, the art history major, would spend hours perusing the magnificent efforts of long-dead artists, and I would find some nearby cafe, more interested in engaging those who were still alive. She studied paintings. I studied people. She had a voracious appetite for art. I drank Cokes and smoked.

Our Eurail Passes, which gave us unlimited train service throughout Europe, took us north to Denmark and Sweden and south through Germany. We found cheap but decent hotels, managing to avoid the youth hostels, which were just a little too funky for us. The scenery that rolled past us on the trains was magnificent, but what I remember most is how nervous I was as the German train conductors collected tickets, looked at passes, and eyed our suitcases. World War II had ended only twenty-five years earlier, and I wondered what the starkly uniformed men on the train with their gruff, no-nonsense accents had done in the war. Though I had not lost any family members in the Holocaust, Dulcie and I were both Jews and deeply inculcated with knowledge of the ovens, the concentration camps, and the soldiers who carried out Hitler's plan. These uniformed men on the train scared me. Just to be on the safe side, I got rid of the porn magazines I had bought for Howard.

I breathed easier when we arrived in Austria, but Vienna was dank, wet, and dreary, so we headed south to Josef Tito's Communist-controlled Yugoslavia, hoping to get away from reminders of World War II and find sun on the beaches of the Adriatic. We passed through the darkness of Zagreb and kept traveling to the coast, to the thirteenth-century walled city of Dubrovnik, a perfect place to stay for a while. It was mid-July 1969. Within a few days, Americans landed and walked on the moon, Ted Kennedy drove off a bridge in Chappaquiddick, half a million people headed to Woodstock, and we came close to being evicted from the Excelsior Hotel for flirting too much with the local help.

The Excelsior was built into a cliff side adjacent to the deep, blue Adriatic Sea. A local tourist agency directed us to the hotel saying most Americans stayed there and that it was a bargain, twenty dollars a night for both of us. The only other Americans we met were Hubert Humphrey, on vacation from the previous year's failed attempt at becoming president, and the avuncular Harry Frankel, claiming to be a prominent movie producer with more than a dozen film crews throughout Yugoslavia. My long, blond hair, skimpy mini-dresses, and flirtatious attitude caught Mr. Frankel's eye. I was twenty-two, Harry in his late fifties or early sixties. Though he seemed quite old to me, it was not enough of a deal breaker to resist flirting with him since he was paying attention to me.

With no famous art museums luring Dulcie away from me, we put on our colorful bikinis, smeared ourselves with Bain de Soleil tanning cream, and stretched out on beach towels by the pool. *Bain de soleil* is French for "sun-bathing." I remember its delicious, fruity scent and the orange jelly cream oozing out of the metal tube. It is still available today, marketed as a sunscreen, not a tanner. Fifty years ago, we did not know about the dangers of cigarettes, sugar, or suntanning. We did not want protection from the sun. The darker the better.

BOATING WITH OUR YUGOSLAVIAN BOYFRIENDS...
IN THE ADRIATIC...SUMMER OF 1969.

Two pretty, American girls in skimpy bathing suits attracted the attention of the young men working at the hotel. Dark, handsome Deso was
drawn to Dulcie, and Deso brought along his best friend, Josko, for me.
While Deso and Dulcie snuck off to the hotel massage room for some privacy, I brought Josko to my room. We met them at the end of their workday
and spent evenings in the ancient walled city, a series of round stone fortifi-
cations built in the Middle Ages to protect its citizens. The city survived all
manner of invaders, centuries of warfare and was thriving under communist rule. It was where Josko and his family now lived. He took me home,
excited and proud to show off his new friend, especially thrilled to have an
American with him because of the recent moon landing. Dulcie and I were
elevated to celebrity status only because of where we were born. Josko and
his family spoke no English, and I knew not a word of Yugoslavian. It didn't
seem to matter. Our faces and gestures conveyed most of what we wanted to
say. We danced in the streets, ate the local fare, laughed, and came back to
the Excelsior Hotel to have some privacy and sex, quite oblivious to the fact
that our antics captured the attention of hotel managers.

JOSKO, MY TEMPORARY YUGOSLAVIAN BOYFRIEND.
I OFTEN WONDER WHAT HAPPENED TO HIM.

One morning after our trysts, Dulcie and I were having breakfast in the outdoor cafe of the hotel when the manager walked up and said, "I'm sorry, but you're going to have to get out, and you have to leave by noon. We can't have women like you here. "

Women like us? What was he talking about?

He seemed cautious and quiet but deadly serious. No further reasons were given why we were being evicted. I supposed in a Communist country no justification was necessary to uproot people. They may have allowed miniskirts and a certain amount of ogling and philandering, but it occurred to us they did not approve of American girls bringing Yugoslav boys to their hotel rooms. Dulcie thought it was because we were fraternizing with the help since Deso worked there.

With only a few hours to gather our things and get out, I turned to my new, best, older, powerful friend, Harry Frankel. Dulcie and I were nervous and scared, but Harry was enraged. He tore off towards the hotel manager and was instantly assured his young American friends could stay.

"Harry, what did you say to him?" I asked.

"I told him if he makes you leave the hotel, I will pull out every one of my seventeen film crews shooting throughout his country." Whether or not Harry was as powerful as he claimed, hotel managers believed him.

Although we were allowed to stay, when Harry checked out a couple of days later, we did too. With our Hollywood mogul and protector gone, we got on a boat and crossed the Adriatic to Bari, on the east coast of Italy. Bari was gray and industrial but provided a break from boys and the threat of being evicted. We headed by train to Rome and into a sweltering heatwave reminiscent of the many unbearable summers I spent in the bog of Washington, DC.

Despite my slight disdain of museums and crowds, it was too hot in Rome to stay outside and talk to people. When in Rome do as millions of tourists do and go to Vatican City. Inside the Sistine Chapel and St. Peter's Basilica, it seemed as if a million of the annual visitors convened at once to try to escape the heat. Almost five hundred years earlier, Michelangelo painted the ceiling of the chapel, apparently with some reluctance. The thirty-three-year-old prodigy was hard at work on a marble tomb for Pope Julius II and resisted switching gears to paint. He considered himself a sculptor, not a painter, but nevertheless spent the next four years of his life completing one of the greatest frescoes in the world. The experience was so unpleasant for him he wrote a poem about it. He claims to have "grown a goiter from this torture" and that his "skin hangs loose below me." Contrary to popular fiction, he painted his masterpiece not on his back but from a standing position. And he was quite wrong about not being a good painter.

Besides the beauty of the ceilings, I remember something falling down on us. I thought it was chips of paint. I mentioned it to Dulcie, but it seemed impossible that flakes from the brush of Michelangelo would be landing in my hands. We were quickly ushered through the church and into St. Peter's Basilica to see the *Pietà*, another of Michelangelo's masterpieces carved from Carrara marble. The sculpture of Mary holding the dead body of Jesus after his crucifixion seemed alive and shimmering. It was graceful, beautiful, and overpowering in its sadness. The shiny folds of the cloths on Jesus's limp body and draping Mary's face were luminous and appeared as if they would blow away with the slightest bit of wind. They had not moved in almost five hundred years and never would. Mother and son, frozen for eternity.

As we did in every city, Dulcie and I ate, drank, and flirted with boys, some Italian, some traveling Americans as we were. After a week in the Eternal City founded in 753 BC, we threw coins in the Trevi Fountain and headed north to Florence.

More museums, more people, and some monsters.

Firenze at first was magic. The Ponte Vecchio, or Old Bridge, built in Roman times spans the Arno River and, as it still is today, was filled with little shops selling jewelry, clothes, and food. I bought a cameo with flowers carved in it for my mother and a beautiful, green-enameled gold ring mounted with a large, pink coral stone for me. I put the cameo in a little box, tucked it away in my suitcase, and put the ring on my left hand.

A day or so later, I took off the ring to wash my hands and freshen up. I placed it on a beautiful marble table outside the bathroom but I was not in our hotel bathroom and I was not with Dulcie. I was with a stranger, a young man I had met in a bar and allowed to seduce me and cart me away to a beautiful villa ten miles outside of Florence. I committed the cardinal sin of separating from my traveling companion, and I would pay a very steep price for being careless.

All of the furniture inside this strangers' home was covered with large, crisp white sheets, protecting what seemed to be antiques from dust and dirt over the summer months. Moments after coming out of the bathroom, two other young men came into the bedroom. They were three, young, dark-haired Italian men, and I was a lone, blond, foolish American woman. It happened so fast. They stripped down to their naked bodies and ordered me to take off my clothes. One pulled out a knife. They took turns raping me. I never looked at their faces. Instead, I fixed my stare on my gold, coral ring sitting on the marble table. I went to some other place in my mind and thought if only I could get away without being cut or killed, I would be okay. They finished. They laughed. They were done with me. All I could think about was getting my ring before I escaped. I got dressed, grabbed the ring, and ran out into a street I did not know, focused on somehow finding my way back to Dulcie.

It was after midnight when I staggered along the road. There were no cell phones or pay phones or homes in sight. I stuck out my thumb. A red sports car pulled over and stopped. The driver was a dark-haired, handsome man who leaned his head towards me and asked if something was wrong. I got into his car and he told me his name was Massimo. I told him what happened to me. In that moment, he decided this was not the memory he wanted me to have about that night in Florence. He was one of the managers of the Galleria dell'Accademia, the home of Michelangelo's *David*. Massimo opened the doors at two in the morning and gave me time alone with *David*.

Me and a six-ton piece of gleaming marble, carved by twenty-six-year-old Michelangelo. As the *Pietà* seemed alive and pulsing, so did *David* with his fixed, intimidating stare and rippling muscles, poised and ready to kill his enemies. Hours earlier, I was raped. Now, I was the recipient of a stunning act of kindness from a man who wanted to make me smile again. I shoved the frightening events from earlier that night into some faraway corner of my mind and chose instead to revel in my great good luck of escaping with my life and being allowed close to one of the greatest miracles of art ever created. Massimo and I found Dulcie early that morning. I told her what had happened to me, and being the logical person she was, insisted I report the assaults to the local American embassy. We went to the embassy, but there was little they could do. I did not know the names of the young men who attacked me. I did, however, get a stern reminder that I should not have gone off on my own. We moved into Massimo's apartment and spent the remainder of our time there in Florence. Not quite done making magic happen, he drove us into the Carrara hills, where Michelangelo got his massive slabs of white stone and where a group of monks had created a restaurant. Over the next few hours, we were treated to incredible food and many glasses of wine, all the while entertained by enormous peacocks strutting around and showing off their resplendent blue feathers.

After Florence, we left on a train that took us along the French Riviera. I had Massimo's address and phone number, his good wishes, and his admonishment never to leave Dulcie's side. I survived my ordeal and replaced that horror with the indelible memory of my time with *David*. Perhaps it might have been more normal to feel outraged, violated, and angry. But I never did. I just felt derelict for putting myself into a situation that made me vulnerable. Though no one deserves to be sexually assaulted and rape is never the victim's fault, I felt I had some responsibility for what happened to me. I was lucky to get away with my body and mind intact. During the assault, I prayed to the Almighty just to let me live and not be literally scarred by the knife they were holding. *Please just don't cut me.*

In the years after Florence, the assault never bothered me or disrupted my life. I somehow managed to bury the attack in a far corner of my mind. I do not know where that powerful resolve came from that enabled me to quickly move on, but I was lucky to have it. What I would learn in the decades ahead both as a woman and a journalist is that the particular kind of pain that rape can cause to any woman, man, or child is never easily dismissed or forgotten. A body taken and savaged leaves scars that change lives forever and rarely, if ever, disappear.

Bypassing Paris, we vowed someday to return with our husbands. We never walked the beaches of the French coast but headed straight for Barcelona, a hot, crowded city where we stayed in a disgusting place near the train station. Two handsome, gay men who delighted in combing their own chest hair, hung out with us as our European vacation was ending. I managed to get food poisoning and became violently ill. Dulcie got me to a doctor who gave me medicine to control the vomiting and managed to get me on a plane back to London.

My blue Lark suitcase was a little worse for wear, filled with dirty clothes and a cameo pin for my mother. It also contained dozens of letters from Richard Blacklow, the handsome law student with the perfect nose, letters that had been waiting for me at every American Express office in every city we visited. And the green-enameled, gold ring with the coral stone that held my focus on a violent night was still on my finger.

Though I lost the ring some time ago, I never lost Dulcie. We remain close friends to this day.

Chapter 11

Marriage and Migration

For all of my bravado in dealing with Nazis, racist librarians, the dystopia of college, and overcoming rape in Europe, I fell lockstep into a safe and predictable life with very little resistance. In truth, I did not know who I was. How does any twenty-two-year old ever know that? The rebel inside me quieted down as I moved back into my childhood home with my parents and into the arms of Richard Blacklow. After the previous and calamitous eighteen months with the murders of King and Kennedy and the growing furor over the Vietnam War, it felt safe to be home. Richard asked me to marry him, and it never occurred to me for a second to say no.

We took a train to Philadelphia to buy a discount diamond ring. Paying retail was not in our Jewish DNA, and the Blacklows knew somebody who knew someone in the diamond business who would give us a good deal. We settled on a small, oval-shaped diamond with a flaw in the center, but I liked that. Its imperfection, I thought, was charming and realistic. I did all the things young women on the verge of marriage are supposed to do. I registered for china, silver, and serving platters at Lord & Taylor, Garfinkel's, and Saks Fifth Avenue in Washington, DC, and argued with my parents about the guest list. In between the wedding craziness, we took time to help organize the upcoming Vietnam Moratorium March scheduled for November 15, 1969, in DC. In a crowd of half a million people, we felt part of something bigger and more important than us. But when I stopped to look around, I felt lost and confused heading towards January 24, 1970, my wedding day.

Richard and I talked about living together and not getting married, but our traditional Jewish parents would likely have become apoplectic with shame and outrage had we done that. Other young people were living together in lieu of marriage, but we were not brave enough and decided getting married was an easier and less controversial option.

I continued steadily on the bridal track. I selected five bridesmaids and their dresses, decided to get married in Richard's sister's wedding gown, chose a synagogue, booked a rabbi, and began looking for an apartment with Richard. I did all the right things but went through those rituals in a state of numbness. I was on autopilot, doing what I needed to do to please my parents who, I am certain, were thrilled their wild child was finally settling down.

Getting ready to walk down the aisle...January 24, 1970.

❧

ON THE MORNING OF JANUARY 24, 1970, the weather in Washington, DC, was cold and icy. So was I. I felt anesthetized. If I did not have an album filled with wedding pictures, I do not think I would remember much about that day. The pictures seem devoid of emotions. I look dazed and drunk. In what is supposed to be one of life's truly remarkable moments, I recall almost nothing except the cold weather. Marrying Richard Blacklow would turn out to be of great consequence, a decision that changed my life in unimaginable and wonderful ways. But on the day we married, I was slightly bewildered.

AFTER THE VOWS. HUSBAND RICHARD HOLDING MY ARM.
I AM LOOKING AT THE CAMERA, DAZED AND A LITTLE DRUNK.

Richard was handsome, loving, popular, Jewish, and in his final year of law school. I was pretty, Jewish, and had no idea what career I wanted, let alone how I might find something worthwhile to do with my life. If Richard Blacklow was hesitant in any way, he never showed it. I, on the other hand, was terrified. My immaculately attired bridesmaids, in their

Puritan-looking brown-and-white dresses, coaxed me back to a private dressing room in the downtown DC synagogue and gave me a straight shot of bourbon to get through the nuptials. I hated even the smell of whiskey, but on January 24, 1970, I held my nose and swallowed.

More than two hundred people watched me marry Richard. I know there was dancing, drinking, and good food only because people later told me how wonderful it was. Jews do know how to put on a good celebration. I left the synagogue holding onto Richard for support as snow started falling, my eyes closed as if I was unsure of my next step.

On that night, we returned to our little apartment on Connecticut Avenue, a bargain at $165 a month, number 305. We were probably too exhausted to have sex. The next morning, Richard went out for a jog. He was an early devotee of long-distance running, but I thought it was an odd thing to do. Though I did not realize it at the time, it portended things to come. Richard sometimes went away at inopportune times, choosing to go mountain climbing a week before our son was born. But I digress.

As many young men did in the late Sixties and early Seventies, Richard managed to avoid getting drafted. Instead of risking his life in Vietnam, he opted to take his chances teaching in one of Washington, DC's most dangerous inner-city schools. He survived the halls of Gonzaga High during the day and went to law school at night. The only thing I knew how to do at all was write and I took a job at the Council for Exceptional Children in Arlington, Virginia, writing articles and editing journals focused on the needs of handicapped and disabled children.

Our honeymoon was delayed because of law school and Richard's teaching duties, but we finally got away on a brief ski trip to Stratton, Vermont. Against my better judgment, I agreed to stay with a few of Richard's friends on the trip north. I remember few things about the honeymoon, but to this day, I still hear the sounds of our roommates having sex and loathed every minute of my time on skis. I hated being cold, feeling trapped in ski boots, and being humiliated in ski classes with five-year-olds who were far more adept at staying upright. I am smiling in some of those pictures from my Stratton honeymoon, but I was faking it.

ON OUR DELAYED HONEYMOON AT STRATTON, VERMONT.
I HATED SKIING AND CLEARLY WAS NOT VERY GOOD AT IT.

We were happy in those early days together. We had our routines and the security of having our families around for emotional support and Sunday dinners.

Richard agonized studying for the DC bar exam, which he passed but would never use there. Having previously dropped out of law school to be a ski bum in Colorado, he was good at taking risks and escaping from a life that did not make him happy. A year later, we were both ready for change, for something completely different. He applied for a job as a law clerk for a judge in Seattle, as far away from his parents and his DC roots as he could get and still stay in the United States. He got the job. We returned borrowed furniture, packed up our clothes, and piled into our two-door Mustang, painted in a bizarre baby-poop, mustard color, and headed on a cross-country trek to a city where we were told it rained all the time.

The billboard which greeted us
upon arriving in Seattle. *Ronald K. Edge*

We arrived in Seattle in late summer of 1971 on the Interstate 90 bridge, welcomed by the now notorious billboard: "Will the last person leaving Seattle—Turn out the lights," which we spotted somewhere as we drove around our adopted town. I had no idea what that meant, but it was quite literally not a good sign. I quickly learned it referred to the so-called fall of the House of Boeing, at that time the biggest employer in the Pacific Northwest. The workforce was reduced by more than half, from eighty thousand to just over thirty thousand employees. The city was devastated by the collapse of its biggest industry, but Richard had a job unrelated to airplanes, so we had some sense of security arriving in what seemed to me a very, very small town. Seattle's tallest building at the time, the Smith Tower, was only thirty-eight stories, barely five hundred feet tall.

I knew no one, but fortunately, Richard knew one person, a friend from law school who offered us a few nights in her home while we looked for a place to live. We found a little, yellow house to rent for $160/month, five dollars less than our DC apartment. It was extraordinarily ugly but convenient, close to the University of Washington where I was hired as a writer in the UW medical school, and not too far from a bus stop so Richard could get to the King County Courthouse and the offices of Judge Solie Ringold.

WITH RICHARD AND OUR GOLDEN RETRIEVER, DAMANI.

The house in View Ridge was owned by a creepy man named Stu. He had locked off a couple of rooms so we could not get access and locked off the basement to keep god-knows-what out of our reach. The peculiar house had a cramped kitchen, one bedroom, and a small living room, which, as poor, young emigrants to Seattle, we decorated with Marimekko fabrics and a cheap shag rug to cover the stained floors. The most wonderful addition to the house was a golden retriever puppy, a gift for Richard's birthday and, other than our son, the greatest present I ever gave him. We named him Damani, a name we thought was African in origin, meaning "little king" but apparently is a type of Pakistani goat.

PART TWO

Life and Death in Television News

Chapter 12

Destiny

THOUGH IT IS CLICHÉ, almost everyone alive knows that in a single moment life can change. Had I not gone to a brunch a few years earlier, I might never have met my husband who moved us to Seattle. What seem to be simple choices in the moment often have results of enormous consequence later in life. In the summer of 1972, I had another of those serendipitous moments. A young, blond woman who looked a lot like me stood in front of a camera delivering a story on the five o'clock news on KING 5 Television, the NBC affiliate in Seattle. A female reporter on local television. I had never seen that before. I was stunned. It was, in today's parlance, an aha moment. As I watched her on the air, I remembered what my English professor, Bergen Evans, had said to me three years earlier: "You ought to think about going into television news." When he said that, I had never imagined such a thing was even possible. I had never seen women in television news. Clearly, things had changed.

On a Sunday afternoon, just a few days after seeing that woman reporter on Channel 5, Richard dragged me, reluctantly, to a Dartmouth alumnae picnic. I was momentarily charmed by the presence of Julia and Michael Phillips. He was a Dartmouth graduate and a well-known movie producer, creator of *The Sting* and later, along with his wife, *Close Encounters of the Third Kind* and *Taxi Driver*. After running out of things to discuss with the Phillips, I was drawn to a tall, dark, young, and handsome John Lippman, a recent Dartmouth graduate with a new job as a reporter for KING Television, where I had just seen the blond girl on the air. I was on the right track, and this was the guy handing me the baton. If I was interested, he said I should contact the news director at KING. I was interested.

The next morning, a Monday, I made perhaps the most important phone call of my life to Norm Heffron. He agreed to meet me.

The enormous blue, KING building took up an entire block along the outskirts of downtown Seattle, sandwiched between Dexter Avenue with small restaurants, shops, a few retail businesses, and a bank with a huge clock that never displayed the correct time. On the other side, Aurora Avenue, busy with cars traveling in and out of downtown Seattle and a thoroughfare for young prostitutes plying less conventional trades. The building was a converted furniture store, now home to the first television station in the Pacific Northwest. KING Television began as KRSC-TV on November 25, 1948, broadcasting a Thanksgiving Day high school football parade. There were apparently a lot of technical problems, but those who had television sets were impressed. Also momentous was the person who owned KING, the irrepressible, irresistible, and indefatigable Dorothy Stimson Bullitt, the first woman in the United States to buy her own television station. She changed the name from KRSC to KING, buying the call letters from the owner of a freighter. Legend has it that she rowed out to the ship owner, bribed him with a bottle of champagne to buy the letters, which he agreed to sell if she made a donation to his church. This is an unverified version of the events that created KING Television. The station's logo for much of its history was an odd-looking, little humanized microphone creature, draped in an ermine robe and wearing a crown with "KING" written on the front. It was created by Mrs. Bullitt's friend, Walt Disney. One of the little KING Mikes sits on my desk with his frozen, goofy smile and googly eyes.

I went into the cavernous building and was escorted to the KING newsroom, filled with green metal desks, the sounds of teletype machines, typewriters, and the stench of cigarette smoke. The carpet was gray and stained, the intensity palpable and the only woman in sight was a secretary outside Norm Heffron's office. Otherwise, I saw a lot of men talking, typing, smoking, and staring at me as I walked into Norm's office.

"Have a seat," he said.

I sat down on his scruffy, well-worn, brown-leather couch.

"So tell me your name again and why you're here."

"My name is Julie Blacklow, and John Lippman suggested I come in to see you."

I handed Mr. Heffron a very sparse resume, showing the few jobs I had since graduating. My job history consisted mostly of working the holidays at my father's stores, selling handbags at the Hecht Company in Arlington at Christmastime, and a couple of unimpressive writing jobs.

"I see you went to one of the top journalism schools."

"I did," I replied, "but I never took a journalism course."

He looked disappointed and surprised.

"But I learned how to write," I quickly replied and then added, "Mr. Heffron, I am a really curious person. I want to know everything about everything, and I'll ask anybody anything about anything. I really think this is where I need to be."

I felt a little nervous, edgy about being pushy in a strange place where the only thing I knew was that I wanted to work there. It never occurred to me that I did not belong there, though there were few women in this male-dominated profession. I knew about Barbara Walters and Nancy Dickerson who were pioneering women in television. But I had never seen women in local television news where I was raised. I knew of female newspaper reporters, my favorite, the legendary Mary McGrory from the *Washington Post*. To this day, I remember her opening line about the funeral of JFK in 1963: "Of John F. Kennedy's funeral, it can be said that he would have liked it." To my mind, it was one of the most perfect and eloquent sentences ever written in the English language. I always tried to write a sentence such as that but never did.

Norm did not say much. He cleared his throat, made little eye contact, but then uttered words that changed my life.

"Why don't you come back in a couple of weeks with a five-minute newscast, and we'll give you an audition on the news set."

I went home and studied the five-minute local newscasts on the hour and half-hour of the *Today Show*, anchored by the young, blond woman I had seen on the news, Robin Groth. Other than changing the locations and some of the names in the stories she was reporting, I plagiarized every word she said. I typed it out, double-spaced on plain, white paper, and read it to Richard dozens of times. A week later, in a new, dark-blue dress, new shoes, and freshly cut hair, I went into the KING Newservice studio and sat in the anchor chair. One of the floor directors, Tom, walked over to me, pinned a microphone to my dress and whispered in my ear:

"You look beautiful . . . and you're as good as Barbara Walters."

I did not agree with his assessment, but I chose to believe him. Norm Heffron must have believed him too. A few days later, Dean Woolley, KING's head of human resources, called me to tell me I got the job.

"What job exactly?" I asked her.

"I'm not sure," Dean said, "but Norm wants you in the newsroom. Can you start next week?"

I walked into the KING Television newsroom and might just as well have wandered into a room full of robed Sumerians writing in cuneiform on tablets and speaking some indecipherable language. I did not have a clue how television news was made or what my job would be. I had neither the education nor experience that would qualify me to even be there, but I felt some deep sense of belonging and that I was where I was supposed to be. I was twenty-five years old, a stranger in a very strange land. Bold enough to get in the door, wise enough to know I knew nothing, but anxious and eager to begin doing something.

Other than a couple of secretaries and the librarian who catalogued every story and script, all the people in the room were men—reporters, photographers, editors, producers, and directors, a testosterone-rich environment. Two female reporters were there, Robin Groth and Kathy Wynstra. I was not completely alone, though it often felt that way. In the first few decades of television news in America, if there were women on the broadcasts, they were often weather girls hired to brighten up the newscasts. Anchoring and reporting duties, up until the early Seventies, were almost exclusively the domain of men. Reuven Frank, the late president of NBC News, once told *Newsweek*: "I have the strong feeling that audiences are less prepared to accept news from a woman's voice than from a man's."

By my great luck of marrying a man who moved me to Seattle, I was working at a station on the cusp of a revolution in broadcasting. I was a woman in the right place at the right time. Reuven Frank was ultimately proved wrong. We were ready to do the work, and audiences were ready to accept news from women.

The viewers were, I think, a bit more willing to listen to women than were some of the men in the KING newsroom of the early 1970s. There were a few people in their twenties like me, but most of the men were in their forties, fifties, and sixties, married to women who, for the most part, not work outside the home. We novice reporters were young, pretty, and often as uncomfortable being in the newsroom as some of the men were having us there. We would, as pioneers in television news and as women in a man's world, have to prove ourselves. We would have to work a little harder, try to be a little better, never complain, and never, ever show emotion. If we felt like crying, we went into the girl's room. Not infrequently, we were forced to tolerate the sexual overtures, comments, and occasional grabbing of our breasts and patting on our rear ends. The phrase "sexual harassment" did not exist in the vernacular of the early 1970s. The thought of suing a person or company for what is now called a "hostile work environment" was decades away from consideration. We just put up with it, ignored it, or responded with as friendly a "fuck you" as one could muster. I occasionally patted the butts of some of the men in the room. All in good fun. Sort of. We were girls trying just to be one of the boys. By 1973, a young psychopath named Ted Bundy would provide Robin Groth and me a rare, if not macabre, opportunity to prove we could handle the toughest of stories and handle them as well, or better, than any of the boys.

For the first few months on the job, I was assigned to work with the irascible, bombastic, misogynistic, and pugnacious Don McGaffin. At the time he was one of the country's first consumer reporters, in charge of KING *Call for Action*, a daily segment focused on helping viewers cut through the occasional red tape of city and county codes or people who felt screwed by some car dealer, vendor, or insurance company. Don was always able to get phone calls returned and successful in getting consumers some semblance of satisfaction. I was his research assistant and perfect accomplice. Making trouble, asking uncomfortable questions, and being persistent and pushy was in my DNA. I used to do it for sport. Now I was getting paid to do it. Though McGaffin (nobody called him Don) occasionally patted me on the ass and grabbed my breasts, he loved me. He saw a younger version of himself in me, someone who loathed injustice and inequity, a person never afraid to take on bullies. He was a brilliant, loud-mouthed thug of a journalist . . . a feisty Irishman who loved nothing more than sticking it to anyone, including the powerful people at KING, if he thought it was warranted. Everyone was fair game. Besides teaching me how to write for television news, never to waste words, and let people and pictures tell the story as much as possible, McGaffin gave me three pieces of advice I never forgot:

- Never be late to a story or miss a deadline.
- If you make a mess, clean it up.
- Never, ever bore the viewer.

"We are journalists," he often said, "but this is television. We have to educate but entertain while we do it."

Though McGaffin was well-known for his aggressive, take-no-prisoners reporting, his offscreen antics were equally remarkable and voluminous enough to fill his own book. He was once shot by a Seattle neighbor who likely had good cause to shoot him. The bullets hit him in the ass, and McGaffin sued him. The case ended up in a King County Superior Courtroom. During the trial, somehow the subject arose that McGaffin wore a wig, which made him more indignant than being shot. He leapt off the witness stand, lunged at the defendant, and pulled on his own hair to prove it was real. It was.

McGaffin traveled to El Salvador for KING Television with his cameraman to cover the war, and both were captured by rebels intent on executing them. As the rebels droned on about Maoism, McGaffin sassed back at them saying words to the effect, "Don't you guys have any ideas of your own?" They were held captive for several days, eventually released, and McGaffin returned to Seattle to continue making trouble in his hometown.

He was so nuts. After playing a round of golf with several of his colleagues, he gloated about how good he was over lunch in the clubhouse. Disgusted by his bragging, future Seattle deputy mayor Bob Royer reached across the table and ripped off McGaffin's shirt. Not to be outdone, McGaffin excused himself, went outside where the golf clubs were propped against a stand, removed Royer's clubs from the bag, and set the golf bag on fire.

McGaffin went on to great success in San Francisco, slaying crooks and cons with his acid tongue and ferocious commitment to journalism. Later, he had a massive stroke, which, in the cruelest of ironies, took away his ability to speak and continue his life's work. It was perhaps the result of too much booze, too many cigarettes, the stress of always fighting something or someone, or probably a combination of all of that.

Years later, after returning to Seattle, he died at the age of seventy-nine. I was the only woman asked to speak at McGaffin's memorial service, something he had requested. I stood in front of an enormous crowd. McGaffin was a revered journalist, loved by his colleagues, hated by those he had top-pled from power, and respected by viewers who admired his ferocity and commitment to his trade. He was the gold standard of journalism.

I paused and spoke truth about him: "To be perfectly honest, he was a pain in the ass, but I loved him, and nobody ever did this job better than he did. Nobody."

He was my greatest teacher. I vowed to make him proud.

KING BROADCASTING, WHICH HOUSED ONE OF THE
MOST REVERED LOCAL NEWS STATIONS IN THE COUNTRY...GONE.

The old, blue concrete furniture store which housed the original KING Television headquarters was demolished and replaced by a modern build-ing with large, glass slanted windows. In 2018 that building, too, was razed and replaced by a new structure with two towers. As of 2019, Facebook was leasing part of that space. KING Television is still in business and moved its location to south Seattle, a stone's throw from where the Seahawks and Mariners play ball.

Chapter 13

Julie Blacklow Reporting

THE FIRST TIME I WAS ON TELEVISION and not just watching it was in 1957 when my parents took me to New York City to sit in the audience of *The Howdy Doody Show*, one of the first television series produced at NBC in Rockefeller Center. It was an early show, in color, which helped RCA, owner of NBC at the time, sell color TV sets. There was a quick shot of me in the audience, and that was the extent of my being on camera until 1972.

After working for Don McGaffin for a few months, I was promoted from being his top researcher to the bottom of the journalism food chain when several general assignment reporters moved on to larger television markets. For several weeks, I tagged along with older colleagues as they covered daily stories, riding in the back seats of the news cars alongside film cameras, clunky tripods, lights and light stands, and dozens of extra reels of film. Videotape was still years away. My job was to help carry equipment, keep quiet, and learn as I watched the entire process of heading out the door to cover a story, watching it being written and edited, and seeing the final product on the five o'clock news. More than one of my veteran colleagues said repeatedly, "There is really never an end to the story. It is not over at six. There is always more to tell."

Beyond the technical side of television news, I was immersed in the culture of it and the ethos that was the spirit of KING Broadcasting. Those standards emanated from station owner Dorothy Stimson Bullitt and the notable cast of managers with whom she surrounded herself. Her belief in doing good and doing right was KING's reason for existing, a sacred duty. Speaking of religious references, Dean John Leffler, the head of Seattle's St. Mark's Episcopal Church, had an office near Mrs. Bullitt's where his door was open to all of us for guidance, confession, or consolation. Without the words ever explicitly being stated, if you worked there you knew what was expected—excellence, honesty, and an unflagging commitment to the people of the Pacific Northwest. Mrs. B, as everyone called her, believed it was more important to be right than to be first, best if you could do both. KING Television and Radio were there to serve the public and did not exist just to generate ratings or revenue, though KING accomplished both.

Her values and lofty standards were inculcated in all of us, not only in the news department but also in every corner and every office of the old, blue building. She did not tolerate fools, mediocrity, or too many Republicans, although she traveled seamlessly in all political and economic circles. Local and national politicians, artists, and business leaders were all her friends or wanted to be. She was a big deal and big deal maker. I was one of the very privileged people who got to know her well.

I was occasionally invited to dinner at her elegant home in North Seattle. We ate on metal trays in her TV room, and I remember admiring the unusual green paint adorning the walls of one of the smaller rooms in her large home. She said her friend Mark Tobey, one of the renowned artists of the Northwest School, painted the room for her, and in one corner of the room, he signed it in gratitude for allowing him to stay with her for a while. Despite her wealth, prominence, and power, she lacked arrogance and always remained approachable and tolerant. On one visit to the KING newsroom, she tripped over McGaffin, who had me pinned on the floor, dry-humping me. She carefully stepped over us, muttering to herself, "Oh . . . children . . . really."

On a warm, sunny, spring late afternoon, Mrs. B, now in her nineties, walked out of the new KING Broadcasting Building, the old blue, furniture store long gone, and noticed her driver had not yet arrived to take her home. She was still coming to work, if only for a few days a week. Never one to stand around doing nothing, she climbed into a large raised planting bed at least two feet off the ground, got down on her knees, and began pulling out weeds from the fancy landscaping. The legendary Dorothy Stimson Bullitt was committed to excellence wherever it was needed.

Chapter 14

Groping Gordon

READY OR NOT, I was going out on my own to begin writing and producing stories, mostly for the news anchors to read, what's known in the business as "voice-over" pieces.

Gordon Vickery, the longtime chief of the Seattle Fire Department, was holding a press conference announcing his retirement, the type of assignment considered worthy of airtime but not important enough for a full story, something simple, a good first outing for a novice. I walked into a room full of television, radio, and newspaper reporters, several dozen people in all. I knew a few of them, but all knew Chief Vickery or knew about him. He was a big shot, brusque, forceful with an occasional sharp tongue, both admired and feared. I was a nobody. He was ending his career. I was beginning mine.

Working with doctors at Harborview Medical Center, Gordon Vickery helped create Medic One, a rapid response team of firefighters with medical training to help people in crisis before being transported to a hospital. It was among the first service of its kind in the country and was so successful that *60 Minutes* once called Seattle "the best place to have a heart attack." Vickery's efforts to hire minorities and women also won him a lot of praise. Gordon Franklin Vickery was fifty-two and accomplished. I was twenty-five and had done nothing of consequence. Unless being the only woman in the room that day counted for something. Which apparently it did.

Vickery strutted into the conference room, spotted me, and did not hesitate for a second to saunter over and introduce himself. Without hesitation, he sidled up next to me, put one hand on my back, slid it down to my rear end, and squeezed it. I did not hesitate, either, to reach around in front of him and grab him by his balls . . . firmly. I leaned into him and said, "Mr. Vickery, don't touch me again . . . anywhere . . . any time . . . ever!"

We looked at each other for a moment as a few people watched our interaction.

GORDON VICKERY, FORMER CHIEF OF THE
SEATTLE FIRE DEPARTMENT...SUBJECT OF MY FIRST STORY.
MOHAI, SEATTLE POST-INTELLIGENCER COLLECTION, 2000.107.220.04.01

Chief Vickery got the message and apologized.

He was retired for less than a day. After his press conference, he was tapped to run Seattle City Light. Then in 1979, he moved to Washington, DC, when President Jimmy Carter appointed him director of the US Fire Administration, a federal organization created to improve the country's firefighting capabilities. In that position, Vickery created federal legislation requiring sprinkler systems and smoke detectors in buildings and served as acting head of the Federal Emergency Management Agency (FEMA).

Gordon Vickery returned to Seattle in 1984. Ironically, given all that he did for victims of heart attacks, he died of heart failure in 1996. His great legacy, Medic One, lives on and has, without question, saved and continues to save thousands of lives.

"I had one ruling credo," he once said, "and I made it plain to the five mayors I worked under and the City Council people. 'I don't work for you,' I told them. 'I report to you, but I don't work for you. I work for the people of Seattle.'"

We were alike in that way, serving the people first and foremost. He was tough, rough around the edges and took no lip from anyone. I would become much the same as a reporter after my intimate first encounter with the fire chief in 1972. I saw Gordon Vickery many times after that. I always got a smile and a wink but never, ever anything more.

Chapter 15

Movie Stars and a Monster

TWO OF THE GREAT GIFTS of being a reporter are that every day brings some new experience and more time is typically spent away from the newsroom than being stuck behind a desk. One day you're covering Spider-Man visiting an elementary school, and the next you are interviewing a group of child molesters or a murderer. The variety of exposures can cause emotional whiplash.

JAMES CAAN, AS HE LOOKED WHEN I MET HIM
ON THE SET OF "CINDERELLA LIBERTY."

In the summer of 1973, I was sent to the Seattle waterfront to cover a story about a film being shot in Seattle, *Cinderella Liberty*, about a sailor who arrives for a temporary stopover but extends his stay when his service records are lost. The sailor, John Baggs Jr., was played by James Caan, fresh off his star-making role as Sonny Corleone in one of the greatest films ever made, *The Godfather*. I was less interested in the plot of *Cinderella Liberty* than I was in meeting Sonny Corleone, unsure whether I would encounter a man willing to chase down his brother-in-law and smash his face with a garbage can or a charming womanizer. I met the softer side of Sonny.

Jimmy, as he preferred to be called, was in his early thirties, divorced, and handsome, his sex appeal no doubt enhanced by his fame. I interviewed him as he was lying on a bed, and he asked that I, not the cameraman, clip his microphone to his shirt. Happy to. I was young, blond, pretty, and nervous, but his relaxed demeanor had a calming effect on me. Jimmy Caan was easy to talk with, playful, flirtatious, and accessible, despite his newfound fame. I was schooled by my older colleagues just to have a conversation with people, let them do most of the talking, never ask a yes-or-no question, and absolutely never intrude on moments of silence just to fill space. Silence alone, my older colleagues taught me, is often the most powerful moment in an interview. But Jimmy was chatty as I listened to him talk about *The Godfather*, working with Marlon Brando and Al Pacino, and getting riddled with hundreds of bullets as he parked by that infamous tollbooth. Jimmy Caan was my first close encounter with a real movie star.

Ronnie Caan was my first encounter with the brother of a real movie star. Ronnie was hanging around the movie set and clearly inherited his brother's movie-star looks and flirty personality. He was also in the movie business but behind the cameras as a producer. Ronnie hinted at our getting together to mess around later that day, but fortunately I had a deadline to make, a man I was married to, and good enough judgment to know there were professional lines one should never cross, no matter how tempting. Allurements recurred many times in future decades. Mostly, I resisted, but not always.

A few months after being charmed by the Caan brothers, I was sent to the Seattle Space Needle to do a story on another movie being shot in the Northwest, *The Parallax View*, starring Warren Beatty. The plot focused on an ambitious reporter who gets in way over his head while investigating a vast political conspiracy. Photographer Doug Rives and I arrived at the base of the Space Needle only to be informed we would be escorted around, told what pictures to shoot, and were forbidden from interviewing or even talking with any of the stars. I met director Alan Pakula, who was incredibly intimidating in his insistence that Doug and I obey his rules—no contact with actors, no going off on our own to snoop around the set. Ridiculous. One of the ironies of covering movies in production or celebrities is that they want the free publicity, but on their terms, rules I found absurd and impossible to follow. As a child, I always bristled at being told what to do or what not to do, a personality trait I never overcame. As a journalist, my reaction to boundaries and being denied access to something was more than bristling. For a few minutes, Doug and I attempted to fade into the background, to convey the illusion we were content being told what to do. I waited, watched, and connived.

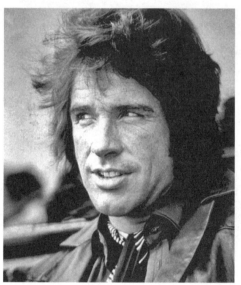

WARREN BEATTY, AS HE LOOKED IN THE MOVIE
"THE PARALLAX VIEW"...SHOT IN SEATTLE.

Warren Beatty and I had something important in common. We both graduated from Washington-Lee high school in Arlington, Virginia, where he and his sister Shirley MacLaine were raised. He was there ten years before me, on the football team, and in his senior year voted Best All Around. I have no idea what that means. Best All Around what? As a Washington-Lee graduate, I was not assigned any flattering descriptions, only known for being expelled after cursing out a racist librarian. Nonetheless, I thought our high school connection might prove useful. We were practically family.

While my cameraman remained captive in the hands of a set publicist, I wandered away, looking for Warren and spotted him outside the glass partition at the top of the Space Needle. I waved my arms to get his attention and held up a scrap of paper on which I'd written: "I went to your high school . . . please let me interview you."

He wrote back on a piece of paper: "What were the school colors?"

"Blue and Gray," I wrote back, "the Generals."

A COUPLE OF WASHINGTON-LEE GENERALS...AROUND 1965.

That was enough to convince him to give me a few moments to chat with him on camera, and it happened before the movie police could stop the interview. He was charming, handsome, and though he graduated from Washington-Lee a few years before I got there, once a W&L General . . . always a General. Though he was a star football player in high school, Warren Beatty turned down football scholarships to study liberal arts at Northwestern University, another thing we shared. Someone from the set of *The Parallax View* called KING Television to complain that we strayed from the rules. But nothing ever came of that. We got more than the story we wanted—a one-on-one interview with the star—and the station was satisfied. The movie ultimately become a classic. As did its star.

IN JANUARY OF 1974, young girls were disappearing off the streets of Seattle and vanishing from Lake Sammamish State Park twenty minutes east of downtown. Witnesses at the park recalled a light-brown Volkswagen cruising in the area, a car connected to the very handsome and seriously deranged Ted Bundy. The grim details of his life, the dozens of women he murdered, and thousands of lives he ruined are well documented in other books. But in 1974, it was the first time I ever heard the words "serial killer" spoken together and the first time I would venture professionally into a very sick, dark world.

Theodore Robert Cowell was born in Burlington, Vermont, in a home for unwed mothers, and one does not need a degree in forensic psychiatry to have some basic understanding of how Ted Bundy came to slaughter as many as one hundred women. It is unknown who his father was. Family members later told authorities they thought his mother was impregnated by her father, that he was raised by his mother's parents and grew up believing his birth mother was his older sister. It is confusing just to absorb that information, let alone grow up with that reality. When he was around four years old, his mother/sister moved to Tacoma, Washington. His mother married John Bundy who adopted young Ted. It was not until he went to college at the University of Washington that he learned the convoluted and shocking truth of his past, which experts believe triggered his staggering killing spree. People who have made a career studying Bundy believe his first victim was an eight-year-old child, Anne Marie Burr. Neighbors recall her traipsing after Bundy in their Tacoma neighborhood while he was on his paper route. Her body was never found.

By his late twenties, Bundy's victims were young, beautiful women whose remains were found brutalized, beaten, and often decapitated. Sometimes he picked up the women in his tan Volkswagen, and at other times, he broke into their homes at night and bludgeoned them to death as they slept. Bundy experts believe he occasionally went back to the places where he dumped the bodies and spent hours with the corpses, grooming them, and performing sexual acts until the extent of the decomposition made his post-murder depravity impossible.

Every murder leaves behind countless, grieving family members who, despite what some people believe, often do want to talk to reporters, both to share their grief and vent their outrage. My colleague Robin Groth and I were the designated duo to cover the monstrous Ted Bundy. The assignment editors thought victims' families would find it easier to talk with female reporters instead of men. I think the men simply did not want any part of talking to grieving families. I never liked doing it, but I was good at it. Despite perceptions that reporters always barge into homes or accost victims in the throes of misery, I never went anywhere in these circumstances without an invitation. I learned, in my early steps into the world of human misery, the art of listening, how not to intrude during silent moments, and the importance of giving people as much time as they needed to say whatever they needed to say.

Ted Bundy's hunting grounds ranged from the University of Washington campus to Colorado, Utah, California, Oregon, Idaho, Vermont, and eventually to Florida, where he murdered at least four women. He was arrested, tried, and convicted. Bundy, who once described himself as "the most cold-hearted son of a bitch you'll ever meet," was executed in the electric chair on January 24, 1989. Though he confessed to some thirty murders before he died, experts believe he may have murdered as many as one hundred women over his lifetime. He took so much from so many but left me something I never wanted, the ability as a reporter to talk with people in the saddest and most painful moments of their lives and find a way to share that pain with viewers. I ached every time I did those stories but learned how to be compassionate and professional without letting the sadness devour me. I had a job to do and I did it and subconsciously began building an inner shield that kept most, but not all, of the suffering, from getting deep inside me. The skills I learned covering Ted Bundy's savagery would be honed over the years in many other tragic circumstances. KING's chief photographer, the indomitable Phil Sturholm, said I was "always the best at asking people complicated and delicate questions in the worst moments of their lives."

What a strange thing to say. Though I never considered the truth of that as I was covering those stories, it occurs to me now that Phil was insightful. I was never taught how to conduct myself in difficult situations or how to interview grief-stricken families. I do not think you can ever be taught how to do that. I just knew.

Inevitably my beat became 'crime and suffering' with, thank God, lighter moments in between.

WHILE TED BUNDY was murdering young women in the summer of 1974, Marion Robert Morrison arrived in town to play the part of Lon McQ, a police lieutenant investigating the killing of his best friend. John Wayne, all six feet four inches of him, was holed up in the Seattle Police Headquarters building where some of the scenes were being filmed. This was a reprieve assignment, a welcomed break from the horror stories I was often assigned to cover.

THE DUKE—JOHN WAYNE—IN SEATTLE TO SHOOT THE MOVIE "McQ."

The rules on the set of *McQ* were the same as those for *The Parallax View*, shoot a few scenes and absolutely no interviews with Mr. Wayne. Do not even look at him. I obeyed at first. I knew if I could get the Duke's attention, I might be able to break the rules again. I caught his eye and waved to him. He strolled over with a bit of swagger and introduced himself as if I might not know who he was.

"Hi, little lady . . . I'm John Wayne. What can I do for you?"

He towered over me, and I was struck by how thick and solid he seemed, as imposing as a big, gnarly tree. His shoulders made him seem as wide as he was tall. In his late sixties, he was still ruggedly handsome and quite capable of charming a young, eager reporter anxious to get a forbidden interview. If John Wayne wanted to talk, no one, not even a room filled with cops, was going to stop him. He was a commanding but cooperative presence, ready and willing to chat. I asked him about his role in the movie and his impressions of Seattle. He thought it seemed small, though he loved bringing his famous yacht, the *Wild Goose*, through the Ballard locks. The converted mine sweeper was built in Seattle, overhauled by Wayne as a traveling playground for his friends and family. He seemed relaxed and at ease, so I decided to be more forward with him.

At the time, news consultants hired by the station had cooked up one of their periodic and idiotic stunts as a means to entice viewers to watch the news and discourage them from changing channels. They called these nonsensical antics "teases," where a reporter would do a quick on-camera stand-up to promote an upcoming story. The justification for these ridiculous performances lay in the wholly unfounded belief they might convince a viewer to stay tuned to the news through a commercial break. There was never any proof this technique worked, but in the early 1970s, reporters were forced to do this. I decided on the spot to ask Mr. Wayne to do one of these teases, and to my utter shock, he agreed. With our camera rolling, he grabbed the microphone, put his big arm around me, and said, "I'm John Wayne, and coming up next on KING Newservice, I'll be talking with Julie Blacklow."

That was possibly the only tease that ever did what it was supposed to do and likely the best one the station ever aired. The action movie *McQ* went on to some commercial success, with its chase scenes, a lot of cops, and the alluring drawl and mighty presence of the one and only John Wayne.

During his life, as is true for anyone as famous as he was, he had his share of admirers and critics. He was loved and loathed, a life-long Republican who supported the war in Vietnam and often made racist remarks. But he was also the guy who once said about Rock Hudson, "Who the hell cares if he's queer?" The Duke was a complicated man. One of his favorite sayings was "Each of us is a mixture of some good and some not so good qualities. In considering one's fellow man it's important to remember the good things . . . We should refrain from making judgments just because a fella happens to be a dirty, rotten SOB."

James Caan. Warren Beatty. Ted Bundy. John Wayne. Four of some two hundred stories in my first year in television news. I grabbed a prominent city official by his balls, broke absurd rules designated by movie directors, interviewed big movie stars, and covered one of the most notorious serial killers in American history. I proved to myself I could do this work and erased doubts among some of my male colleagues that women could succeed in their previously all-male club. I was off to a decent and promising start.

Chapter 16

Your Call Cannot Be Completed as Dialed

B Y FALL OF 1975, I was newly pregnant, among the first on-air women reporters in the country to try to become a mother and hold down a ferociously crazy career where you were on call all the time. Cameraman Arlo Smith and I were sent up north to the small town of Sedro-Woolley about sixty-five miles north of Seattle. The town was originally known as Bug because of the mosquito population, but some of the pioneering women in the late nineteenth century did not like the name. They implored one of the town's founders to change the name to Cedro, from a Spanish word meaning cedar and to replace the *C* with an *S*. The Woolley half of the name came from another of the town's founders, railroad developer Philip Woolley.

Sedro-Woolley High School was the setting for a public hearing on a proposed nuclear power plant to give the townspeople a chance to spout off about any concerns they might have about "unavoidable adverse impacts." The high school auditorium was overflowing with angry residents and erupted in a shouting match of impressive proportions. Arlo and I shot what we needed for our story, packed up, and left the town to head back to the station.

There were no cell phones back in the Seventies, only two-way radios in the news cars allowing us to communicate with the newsroom, but the radios worked only if you were in range. We were out of range and running late. Arlo and I pulled up next to a phone booth adjacent to Interstate 5 near a dingy 7-Eleven. I put a quarter in the slot and dialed the number for the KING-5 newsroom. A voice answered:

"KING-5 News. Can I help you?"

A PHONE BOOTH MUCH LIKE THE ONE I WAS IN
WHEN IT WAS PULLED OUT OF THE GROUND.

As I started to talk, the entire phone booth, with me and my unborn child inside, began tilting, wrenched from its foundation, falling backwards. The crunching, screeching sounds of bolts being yanked from the concrete pad underneath added to the panic I was feeling. I thought it was an earthquake. What else could it possibly be?

I began screaming. "What the fuck? Help me!"

From the phone, now dangling and banging against the glass, a tiny, distant voice was yelling, "Julie, Julie! Are you okay? What's happening?"

I was too rattled to pick up the phone, thinking only I was going to die.

I kept screaming. Then, suddenly, with a loud crash, the structure stopped falling when it was halfway to the ground. The phone booth had been torn from its foundation when a cherry picker on top of the phone company truck became entangled with an overhead line attached to the phone booth. Thrown to the back, I twisted my body around with great difficulty and saw that the phone booth with me inside was now resting on the enormous tires of a General Telephone Company truck. I began pulling on the glass door in a vain attempt to open it, but it seemed stuck. I kept pounding on it and screaming.

By this time, Arlo came running towards me from the news car. Two men in General Telephone Company uniforms rushed out of the truck . . . all three converging at the door of the phone booth. They managed to push the door inward, making an already cramped space even tighter. No longer worried I was going to die, my fear turned to fury.

I yelled at the two linemen who were trying, along with Arlo, to get me out. No easy feat. The men had to reach in, grab my arms, and gently pull me upright and over the tilted floor of the booth. Now free and realizing I was not physically hurt, I went insane. I started pummeling my rescuers while Arlo was convulsed in laughter by the side of the news car. Fearing for the safety of the phone company employees, he raced over and pulled me away from the two men.

The General Telephone guys were relieved I was not injured, but they were now faced with some harsh realities. They had failed to follow protocol by accidentally yanking a phone booth from its moorings with a person inside trying to make a call. And, worse, they realized the person inside was a television news reporter who was pregnant.

Arlo wrangled me back into the news car, and we headed back to I-5, heading south towards Seattle, leaving behind two anxious men standing next to their truck with an uprooted phone booth leaning on it. A few minutes down the road, I suddenly remembered I had left the KING assignment editor dangling on the phone, not having a clue what had happened to me or what all the yelling was about. Still out of radio range, we had to find another phone booth, preferably one without a truck nearby. I completed that call, gave a brief explanation about why I was screaming, assured them I was okay but would not be able to make the five o'clock show. We would have the story ready by the late night newscast.

The next afternoon, as I was working on another story, a tall, very distinguished-looking man with a crop of beautiful white hair, wearing an expensive-looking suit, was escorted over to my desk.

"Julie?"

"Yes sir," I answered.

He reached out his hand to shake mine and said, "My name is Al Baron. I'm the regional manager of the General Telephone Company. I came down here today just to make sure you're okay and to apologize for the inconvenience we caused you yesterday. That's not usually how we do things." With a twinkle in his eye he added, "I believe we owe you some money for the call you were unable to complete yesterday."

Mr. Baron reached into his pocket, pulled out a quarter, and handed it to me with a big smile and his very sincere apologies. Mr. Baron was glad no one was hurt, and I think he was a little nervous about my suing the company. I did not.

The nuclear power plant, by the way, never was built up in the town once known as Bug.

Chapter 17

The Nicest Felon

JOHN EHRLICHMAN OF WATERGATE INFAMY.

H E CAME TO FAME the way nobody wants to become famous. John Daniel Ehrlichman, convicted of conspiracy, obstruction of justice, and perjury, served a year and a half in prison for his crimes, all part of the Watergate scandal in the 1970s. He was disrespectfully known as one half of the Berlin Wall surrounding Richard Nixon, the only American president ever to resign from office. The other part of the wall was the notorious Bob Haldeman. Both henchmen purported to isolate Nixon and try to prevent the demise of his administration following the illegal break-in at the Watergate Hotel, location of the Democratic National Committee headquarters. Their efforts failed. They were political villains. But John Ehrlichman, a former Eagle Scout, was true to his word and honest with me.

Compared to subsequent political crises, the crimes of the Watergate era pale somewhat, but in the 1970s, the lies and cover-ups of the Nixon era were shocking. The fact that John Ehrlichman became embroiled in the political turmoil was at odds with how he began his legal career. Starting out in Seattle, he was an expert in land use and zoning, supporting efforts to clean up Lake Washington and trying to make Seattle a better place in which to live. Then he got involved in politics.

Ehrlichman, which means "honest man" in German, failed to live up to his name. As one of Richard Nixon's lawyers, he was named chief domestic advisor and, in that role, committed crimes that eventually landed him in prison. He created the notorious plumbers unit, which, along with other acts of malfeasance, concocted the plan to break into the office of Daniel Ellsberg's psychiatrist and discredit the man who leaked government documents about the Vietnam War, the man who exposed the big lie. In 1975, the not-so-honest man was convicted for the violations against Ellsberg and for his failed attempts to cover up Watergate. Ehrlichman was sentenced to a maximum of eight years in prison.

On my way to work one morning in the early spring of 1976, I heard on the radio that John Ehrlichman was in his home in Hunt's Point, a very pricey neighborhood east of Seattle, enclave of the rich and occasionally famous. Kenny G had a home there. Ehrlichman had not yet started serving his prison sentence and remained mostly out of sight from the public and press following his conviction. I finished anchoring the five-minute newscast on the hour and half-hour of *The Today Show* and decided to hunt for John at his Hunt's Point house.

I grabbed photographer Lou Avery, and we took off in a large, blue news car with the words KING Newservice emblazoned on the sides, making it impossible to disguise who we were. The station saw this as free advertising, but I thought it was an impediment to hide our identity and something that made us as an easy target for anyone who wanted to yell or throw things at us. On this particular day though, I put it to good use.

As we approached John Ehrlichman's home, I asked Lou to drop me off a block from the residence. I assumed, correctly, someone might be outside guarding the house. I sent him ahead in the not-so-subtle news car to draw the attention of anyone who might be deflecting visitors.

Seven months pregnant, I snuck around to the back of the house and knocked on the door. Almost immediately, the door opened and standing in front of me was the newly convicted felon himself, the former head of the plumbers unit who, in his own words, had "abdicated my moral judgments." The man heading soon to prison invited me inside for a cup of coffee.

"Hi, Mr. Ehrlichman, I'm Julie Blacklow with KING TV. May I talk with you?"

"Hey, I just saw you on the news! Come on in. Have a seat. When's your baby due?"

"Sometime in June," I answered as he pulled out a chair for me.

I momentarily forgot about Lou still standing outside and, as I would later learn, being interrogated by a couple of federal marshals.

It was surreal, sitting in John Ehrlichman's kitchen chatting over a cup of coffee. But I wanted to talk with our cameras rolling. He hedged a little, as if he wanted to let me interview him, but eventually said he could not. A judge had ordered him not to speak with the media before serving his time in prison. I remember looking at him, words coming out of my mouth with other thoughts pouring through my brain—*I am sitting across from a criminal, a man guilty of multiple felonies, a man who tried to protect Richard Nixon. I am having coffee and being utterly charmed by him.*

My usual techniques of cajoling, pleading, and praising people were not going to work on this particular day. After breaking the law and being convicted of his crimes, he was resolute in following the judge's directives and doing the right thing. Disappointed, I got up to leave.

"Julie . . . that was quite sneaky of you to come in through the back door. I admire your initiative . . . something I might've done myself. How 'bout this? I can't talk with you on camera now, but I promise you'll be the first reporter I talk with after I get out of prison."

Dripping with sarcasm I responded, "Oh yeah, I'm sure I believe you!"

"Really," he said, "I promise."

I walked around to the front of the house where Lou was leaning against the news car and, fortunately, not in federal custody. We drove back to the station without the interview but with a promise. It was a promise I never expected would be kept. I wrote a thank-you to John for the coffee, the chat, and for not having me arrested for trespassing on his property.

Less than a week later, I received a handwritten reply sent from New Mexico.

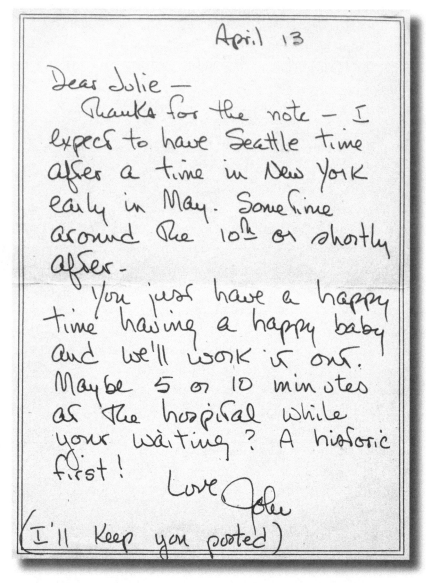

April 13

Dear Julie —
Thanks for the note — I expect to have Seattle time after a time in New York early in May. Some time around the 10ᵗʰ or shortly after.
You just have a happy time having a happy baby and we'll work it out. Maybe 5 or 10 minutes at the hospital while your waiting? A historic first!
Love John
(I'll keep you posted)

A SURPRISE LETTER SENT FROM JOHN EHRLICHMAN
PROMISING A FUTURE MEETING.

April 13

Dear Julie –

Thanks for the note—I expect to have Seattle time after a time in New York early in May. Some time around the 10th or shortly after.

You just have a happy time having a happy baby and we'll work it out. Maybe 5 or 10 minutes at the hospital while your [sic] waiting? A historic first!

Love,
John
(I'll keep you posted)

Jeremy Isaac Blacklow arrived later that spring of 1976. In the fall, former Eagle Scout John Daniel Ehrlichman departed for prison.

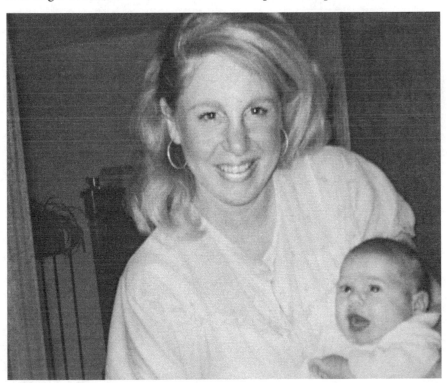

WITH BABY JEREMY, 1976.

⊗⊚⊚

EIGHTEEN MONTHS LATER, a smiling John Ehrlichman walked out of the Swift Trail Federal Prison in Safford, Arizona. He was fifty-three, a lot thinner, and followed by dozens of reporters and photographers. He posed for pictures but gave no interviews. Watching this scene unfold on national television, I remembered a promise he had made to me in his suburban Seattle kitchen, "You'll be the first reporter I talk with after I get out of prison." Reporters were shoving microphones in his face, trying to get him to comment about prison, Watergate, anything. But he declined, saying only, "Sorry . . . I have a promise to keep in Seattle."

He was talking about me.

A few days later, my phone rang in the KING newsroom. I was away from my desk, and someone picked up the phone and started yelling my name.

"Blacklow, there's some guy on the phone. Says he's John Ehrlichman and he wants to talk with you."

No one believed the call was for real. But I did. The most famous man in America that day agreed to come to KING Television for our on-camera interview.

The newsroom, typically blasé about celebrities of all kinds passing through, was silent and stunned when John Ehrlichman, dapper looking with his salt-and-pepper beard, walked through a side door and came over to my desk. Everyone stopped what he or she was doing and stared. As the cliché goes, you could hear a pin drop. I got up to meet him, shook his hand, and we headed down to the KING 5 Studio to videotape our long-awaited conversation.

He was in a reflective mood as he talked about his regrets, the pain the country suffered, and the suffering he caused his family. He said he thought he was a better man after serving his time and talked about losing his "moral compass" in the service of the president, themes he often repeated in his post-prison life.

"Never ever defer your moral judgments to anybody: your parents, your wife, anybody," he was quoted as saying.

In a somewhat lighter moment, he later wrote in his book, "I don't miss Richard Nixon very much. Richard Nixon probably doesn't much miss me either."

Permanently disbarred from practicing law, John Ehrlichman settled for a while in Santa Fe, New Mexico. He wrote books, was an occasional television and radio commentator, and eventually moved to Atlanta where he served as vice president of Law International, a firm specializing in the handling of hazardous waste. He had come full circle, starting his career focused on land use and ending his career in much the same way. He died at the age of seventy-three on Valentine's Day 1999 of complications from diabetes.

It is likely most people alive during the Watergate fiasco will remember John Ehrlichman as a convicted felon, an architect of one of the country's most notorious political scandals, one that took down a president. But he was more than that. He was an Eagle Scout, a war hero who flew twenty-six missions over Germany in a B-24 bomber, and a man who regained his bearings after losing his moral compass. He was also, to me, a man who kept his promise and the most charming felon I ever met.

One more story about John Ehrlichman. In 1987, he was hired by Dreyer's Grand Ice Cream to make a commercial for one of the company's products. In the ad he says, "When I said I never knew a thing about the Watergate break-in, you probably didn't believe me, did you? Well, to show you what a good guy I am, I'll give you another chance. This Dreyer's Grand Light Ice Cream is 93 percent fat-free, and it tastes great. So even if you didn't believe me last time, you'd better try this stuff."

Public outrage forced Dreyer's to pull the ad. The company received hundreds of letters and angry phone calls from customers who did not like the idea of using someone of such low moral character to sell ice cream. John Ehrlichman and Watergate left a residual bad taste in the minds of many Americans. Even ice cream could not sweeten the memory.

Chapter 18

The Lost Child

A T FIRST THE SCREAMS sounded like a child playing, but the howls were the terrified shrieks of a child dying. A man who heard the racket looked down from his second floor balcony and saw the attacker holding a small child huddled in the alley below. He recognized the young girl as someone who lived in his building, a beautiful, blond eight-year-old, kicking, shouting, and trying desperately to escape. The man with shaggy, brown hair put his hand over the child's mouth trying to muffle the noise she was making. The witness ran downstairs and found the assailant holding the child, her clothes covered with blood, ripped away from her body. She had a slash on her hand and a large stab wound in her chest penetrating her heart. She was pale, quiet, and dead. A bloody butcher knife lay nearby, the weapon that finally silenced the young girl. It was September 28, 1976. Her family has asked that I not use her name.

The attacker holding her was nineteen-year-old Michael Charles Green, his shirt and pants soaked with the child's blood. He was arrested at the scene and taken to a Seattle police station where it was noted that the fly of his pants and his underwear were smeared with blood in such a fashion, according to police reports, "as to expose his genitals." Green was charged with aggravated first-degree murder, "aggravated" because the crime, according to prosecutors, was committed during "furtherance of a rape or kidnapping." A change in the death penalty statute just a year earlier called for a mandatory death sentence for aggravated murder. The state wanted Michael Green to die for what he had done. So did many others.

WITH JEREMY, AROUND 1978.

I came back into the newsroom in late September after a calm, sun-filled summer with my new baby. Dealing with child killers was the last thing on my mind and the last kind of story I wanted to investigate. But having covered the Ted Bundy murders and other assorted horror stories, I had become the "crime and misery" reporter. I never tried to avoid dealing with the dark side of the human experience. It fascinated me. The who, what, where, when, and how of these tragedies are often readily known, but rarely the why. I always wanted to know why. Why does one human being kill another? Why does someone rape a child? Why such brutality?

I knew his name. I knew what he had done. I knew where he did it. I knew when and how. But why did Michael Charles Green slaughter this little girl? Why did a nineteen-year-old become a kidnapper, rapist, and murderer?

I became obsessed with finding answers.

IN SEATTLE, the worst killers sometimes got the best lawyers. Michael Charles Green certainly did. Anthony "Tony" Savage made it his life's work defending murderers and rapists with a particular focus representing those facing the death penalty. Michael Green was a perfect match for Tony, a giant in the courtrooms of King County, Washington, literally and figuratively. He was six and a half feet tall, bearded, and brilliant and quite the opposite of the killers he represented. Tony was gentle, soft-spoken, humble, and gracious. I once asked him how he could represent such terrible people, a common question often posed to criminal defense lawyers. He was resolute in his answer. Everyone, no matter the crime, deserves at least one person on his or her side. He thought good lawyers needed to be on both sides of a case, that it made the criminal justice system better and more honest. It was a cornerstone, he said, of our democracy, and he opposed the death penalty with unmatched ferocity.

Perhaps one of the luckiest things that ever happened to Michael Green was having this towering and much respected lawyer represent him, and I was lucky to know Tony from other criminal trials I had covered. I revered him. He did not admire all the media, which typically surrounded him during his high-profile trials, but he respected us and thought the press too was a vital pillar of democracy. Tony always returned my phone calls, chatted with me during trials, and to my complete surprise, allowed me to interview Michael Green before his trial began. That was highly unusual, giving a reporter access to an alleged killer before a judge or jury was able to meet him.

Photographer Bill Fenster, assigned to cover the Green trial with me said that I "had an uncanny ability to convince people to do things they really did not want to do and . . . somehow managed to be aggressive without making people angry." Most of the time, I believe that was true. But not always. No one could convince Tony Savage to do anything he did not want to do. At the time, I thought he had his own agenda in giving me access to Michael Green before the trial. I suspect he wanted to try to put a human face on a tragedy that stunned a city still reeling from the crimes of Ted Bundy. Perhaps he thought it would be difficult, if not impossible, to generate sympathy for a man accused of kidnapping, raping, and killing an eight-year old child.

Tony's ground rules were simple. No questions about the child, the killing, or the blood on Green's clothes. Anything else was fair game. Some of my colleagues wondered what else there was to talk about if not the crime itself. I knew the details of the murder would come out during the trial. I wanted to know more about Michael Green's past, less about his present—who raised him, what life was like for him before he arrived in Seattle and butchered a little girl.

We set up our cameras and lights in a small, dank room in the King County Jail, painted in what I thought of as prison green, a color I rarely saw anywhere other than in government institutions. I sat in an uncomfortable chair next to a metal table and waited. Thirty minutes later, Michael Charles Green, wearing a standard issue orange jumpsuit with the words "KING COUNTY JAIL" written on the back shuffled up to meet me, his ankles in shackles, accompanied by his gentle giant of a lawyer. Tony shook my hand, smiled a little, and conveyed with a wink and without uttering a word: *You know what to do and what not to do.*

Michael reached out his hand as well. I shook it, reluctantly, as close as I would ever be to a murderer. I noticed there were no wrinkles by the knuckles on his hands, which seemed almost claw-shaped. Michael was ashen, pale, and unhealthy looking with disheveled, brown hair. I do not know what I expected him to look like, given the crime he was accused of and the circumstances of where he was now living. He seemed sad, weary, and limp, almost as lifeless, I thought, as the child he had murdered. It occurred to me he was deformed in some way, perhaps physically and mentally. But I was there as a reporter, not a doctor and not a psychiatrist. I asked him about everything but the murder.

In a soft-spoken voice, Michael talked about growing up in Ellensburg, Washington, about two hours east of Seattle, a college and cattle town famous for its annual rodeo and its unrelenting winds. He told me about one brother, a doctor, and a sister who was an opera singer. His father was head of the Education Department at Central Washington University, and his mother was a teacher. He said, "I was a misfit . . . a black sheep born into a family of overachievers."

Eloquent and insightful words, I thought. Both the facts of Michael's comments and the way he expressed them startled me. I never expected such expression from a young man accused of such horrific crimes. He was reflective and intelligent. He considered his life in Ellensburg unremarkable. He went to school. He once had a girlfriend. Michael Green was telling me the story he wanted me to hear. Later, I discovered many things he did not share.

My interview aired on the news that night, less remarkable for its contents than the fact we interviewed a man charged with murder before his trial began. Our viewers got to see him and listen to him. That was enough of an exclusive for the moment. He had not really said much, but it was, in my mind, what he did not say that intrigued me and left me still wanting to know why. Why did a man from this obviously successful family turn into a rapist and killer? Why did he become a monster? I expected to hear a story of child abuse, of alcoholic or drug-addicted parents, of a child bounced around the foster care system from one home to another. But his story defied all my assumptions. None of it made sense to me.

The morning after the interview was televised, I went to our news director, Norm Heffron. "Norm, I need permission to follow up on this story. I need to go to Ellensburg and try to find out more about Michael Green."

"What are you looking for?"

"I want to try to talk to people who knew him . . . how he grew up . . . because his story doesn't make any sense. There has to be a lot more going on here."

"How long do you think you'll be gone?"

"I don't know. I guess we'll be back when we're done. I don't know who to call to set up interviews ahead of time. I just need to go."

"Okay . . . take Fenster . . . but stay in touch and let me know how things are going."

Bill Fenster and I loaded up the yellow Ford Maverick with KING Newservice painted boldly on the car. Two hours later, we arrived in Ellensburg, ravenously hungry and pulled into a drive-in hamburger joint. We knew no one in the town and had no plan how to begin our investigation. An attractive, young waitress brought our food to the car, a girl who looked about the same age as Michael Green, and we asked if she was local and grew up around here.

"Yes," she said.

I asked, "Did you by any chance know a Michael Green? He's from Ellensburg, and I think he went to school here."

"Yes," she answered immediately. We went to school together, and he used to follow me home. He called me the apple of his eye, but he scared me. He always made me nervous."

I do not remember what we ate or even if we ate. We were stunned that the first person we talked with in Ellensburg was a former neighbor and classmate of Michael Green.

She allowed us to interview her on camera where she repeated that same story. When we were done, she directed us to Michael's childhood home. A favorite Bill Fenster motto was "Dare to be lucky!" We were.

Fenster, the name everyone called him, and I walked up to the Green family home and knocked on the door, leaving the camera in the car. A thin, white-haired man answered the door. It was Michael's father. He and his wife were shocked to see us there, acknowledging with a nod that they knew why we were there. I told them I wanted and needed to talk with them about their son, but they were not ready to share anything. They were devastated by what had happened, though perhaps not as crushed as the family of their son's victim. Fenster and I left for a time, but I was determined not to leave Ellensburg without interviewing Dr. and Mrs. Green. There had to be some explanation why Michael had killed this child, and I believed his parents had some of the answers.

Going door to door, Fenster and I talked to neighbors, all of whom recalled a very troubled young boy. They remembered Michael sometimes shooting at them with a BB gun and killing small animals. One woman, a next-door neighbor, said he shot at her through her back screen door. Her parting words to us: "I knew someday he was going to kill someone."

We then headed to the Ellensburg Police Department. The chief agreed immediately to allow us to interview him on camera. He knew Michael Green all too well, as a kid in and out of juvenile court dozens of times. He said he was deeply frustrated with the entire handling of Michael Green and echoed what the neighbor said: "I always knew he was going to kill some-body someday. We did our job to the best of our ability."

After Michael fired a handgun at a woman in a passing car, Ellensburg was done with him. Prosecutors and judges, who'd been dealing with him for years, sent him to a psychiatric hospital in Yakima, an hour south of where we were. We headed there, racing to arrive before it closed for the day. An official from the facility confirmed Green had spent time there, had gone through their program, and had been thought eligible for release. When he was discharged, he was sent to a halfway house in Seattle for continued rehabilitation. We returned to Ellensburg. It was the end of a twenty-hour day for Fenster and me. Instead of drive-in food, we opted to have a steak dinner on the company before finding a motel room. I fell asleep in my salad and never touched the steak.

The next morning, we went back to the Green home and walked up to the front door, once again leaving the camera in the car. This time, for some reason, Michael's parents invited us in and allowed us to set up our camera and lights as they sat down next to each other on a living room couch. The same rules applied here as they did when I interviewed their son in jail, no questions about the crime. They expressed shock at hearing of their son's arrest and learning about the charges of kidnapping, attempted rape, and murder. He was born later in life, some years after their other children. They called him "their lost boy," haunting words. I wanted to know what they meant by that, but they only said he was a loner, isolated, and seemed troubled.

There was more silence than sound in our interview with Michael's parents. I thought to myself what could they really say? I think they felt somehow responsible as they looked away from me and the camera, their minds wandering, perhaps trying to make sense of this horrific tragedy. We recorded the devastation and pain on their faces, the powerful sounds of silence from a mother and father who could not fathom what happened to their son and the child he murdered.

I wanted to ask why they had not done more to help him. He clearly showed many signs of abnormal behavior. They had seen it, as had their neighbors. But I kept quiet. That question, perhaps justified, would only cast blame on them. My job was not to judge them, only to meet them and try to understand why it happened. Their son's judgment day in court was coming.

Bill and I left Ellensburg with an unsettling collection of stories about a young boy seemingly destined to kill. A kid bounced around the justice system, passed from police to prosecutors to judges and psychiatrists, but none with the knowledge or power to stop him. Believing he successfully completed the psychiatric program in Yakima, prosecutors sent Michael to a halfway house in Seattle where the goal was to help him re-enter society, a mission that was an abysmal failure. The house where Michael Charles

Green came to live was across the street from an apartment building, the home of his eight-year-old victim who, according to prosecutors, he had been stalking for weeks. It is where he would graduate from killing small animals to killing a small child. The why of how it happened was slowly coming into focus. The only explanation in my mind was that he was born to kill, a lost boy from the very beginning of his life.

This story was my first close encounter with a truly evil act, the random slaughter of a young girl by a teenager born into a good family. I thought of my toddler son at home and wondered if he were ever to exhibit signs of malevolence, would I notice? Or would I ignore them? Would I make excuses for him? And in this close brush with the darkest side of human behavior, I put on another layer of my 'interior armor', that shield which kept the depravity from getting inside of me and permitted me to tell these stories without allowing them to destroy me.

STATE V. MICHAEL GREEN was one of the first trials where cameras were allowed inside a courtroom. We were not permitted to show the defendant's face or to film witnesses or jurors, but we were allowed to record the audio testimony and show the faces of the victim's family and the faces of Dr. and Mrs. Green as they watched. The trial was short, as was the time it took the jurors to find Green guilty of aggravated first-degree murder. They deliberated just ninety minutes. It was a conviction that carried with it the death penalty.

It was harrowing for everyone watching the trial, but particularly the family of Green's young victim. I remember vividly the child's mother and Michael Green's mother embracing at the end of the trial. This crime had shattered the lives of both families. Both mothers lost their children. One was dead. The other was heading to prison. Watching them holding each other was wrenching, powerful, and profoundly sad. Bill and I edited all the images and interviews gathered over the previous months, from the time of the murder to the trip to Ellensburg and through the trial. It was a real-life horror story of a crime that should never have happened, about a tormented and dangerous teenager who should not have been free to kill. When we were done editing, we went into the daily, morning editorial meeting and announced we had a fifteen-minute piece that needed to be shown uncut and without a commercial break. "We've never run a story that long on the five o'clock news," said one manager.

"Yeah," replied the show producer who had previewed the story and typically wanted to shorten everything, "but this one's interesting."

The story aired as edited with no commercial break.

News director Norm Heffron, the very reserved, taciturn manager of KING 5 News, decided to send the story to his friend and former colleague in New York, Tom Brokaw, co-host of NBC's *The Today Show*. Norm never mentioned he was doing that. I think he did not want us to have any expectations or be disappointed if they decided not to run the story. On Friday, February 11, 1977, it aired on *The Today Show* as it had run on KING in Seattle. Unedited. Unprecedented. Unbelievable.

A couple of weeks later, I received letters from NBC executives. From *The Today Show* executive producer Paul Friedman:

Dear Ms. Blacklow:

This is just to say what you must have guessed by now. I thought your reporting and production work on the Michael Green story was excellent. You should be very proud. Please feel free to contact us, through Ed Planer, whenever you've got something that might be of interest.

Good luck—and thanks.

NBC News   A Division of   Thirty Rockefeller Plaza
              National Broadcasting Company, Inc.   New York, N.Y 10020   212-247-8300

Paul E. Friedman
Executive Producer, TODAY

February 11, 1977

Ms. Julie Blacklow
KING-TV
320 Aurora Avenue North
Seattle, Washington 98124

Dear Ms. Blacklow:

This is just to say what you must have guessed by
now: I thought your reporting and production work
on the Michael Green story was excellent. You
should be very proud.

Please feel free to contact us--through Ed Planer--
whenever you've got something that might be of
interest.

Good luck--and thanks.

Sincerely,

Paul E. Friedman

From *The Today Show* producer Ed Planer:

NBC News   Thirty Rockefeller Plaza
                            New York, N.Y 10020   212-664-4444

Dear Norm,

The Michael Green murder story had everybody's
eyes bugging out this morning. It was a great piece
and we consider ourselves very fortunate to have had
it on the show.

Thanks again for everything and I hope to
see you soon.

Best regards,

Ed Planer

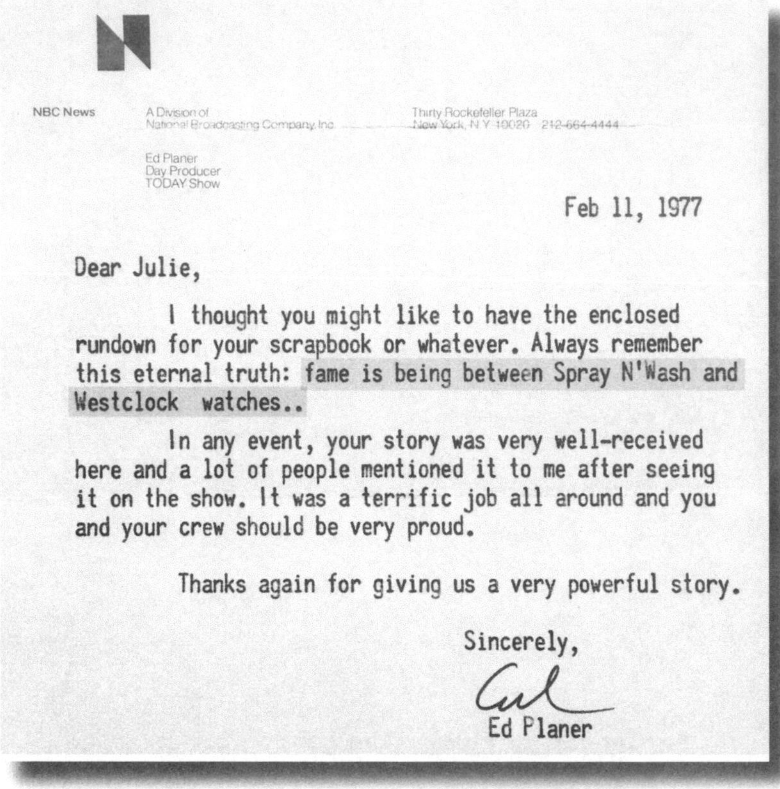

N

NBC News   A Division of   Thirty Rockefeller Plaza
           National Broadcasting Company, Inc.   New York, N.Y. 10020   212-664-4444

           Ed Planer
           Day Producer
           TODAY Show

                                                    Feb 11, 1977

Dear Julie,

    I thought you might like to have the enclosed rundown for your scrapbook or whatever. Always remember this eternal truth: fame is being between Spray N'Wash and Westclock watches..

    In any event, your story was very well-received here and a lot of people mentioned it to me after seeing it on the show. It was a terrific job all around and you and your crew should be very proud.

    Thanks again for giving us a very powerful story.

                                    Sincerely,

                                    Ed Planer

Dear Julie,

I thought you might like to have the enclosed rundown for your scrapbook or whatever. Always remember the eternal truth: fame is being between Spray N' Wash and Westclock watches. [These were the commercials on either side of our story.]

In any event, your story was very well-received here and a lot of people mentioned it to me after seeing it on the show. It was a terrific job all around and you and your crew should be very proud.

Thanks again for giving us a powerful story.

```
7:24:15      ( :45)    STATION BREAK
7:25:00      (4:15)    CO OP:
7:29:15      ( :45)    STATION BREAK
- - - - - - - - - - - - - - - - - - - - - - - - - - - - - - - - - - - - - - - - - -
7:30:00      (1:00)    ANNOUNCE SCRIPTED
7:31:00      (3:00)    KALBER: B NEWS
7:34:00      (1:30)    KALBER LEADS LIPTON CUP A SOUP/LITTON MICROWAVE OVEN
7:35:30      (2:15)    KALBER INTROS WOOD: WEATHER
7:37:45      (1:30)    WOOD LEADS  VASELINE PETROLEUM JELLY/PRINCE MACARONI
7:39:15      (2:15)    WOOD: SPORTS
7:41:30      (1:30)    WOOD LEADS HIGH PROTEIN DOG MEAL/SPRAY N WASH
7:43:00      ( :10)    TEASE
7:43:10      ( :45)    STATION BREAK
7:43:55      (11:00)        INTROS KING-TV/MICHAEL GREEN EJ: SEATTLE
                       MURDER. RUNS 10:23 SOT
7:54:55      (1:30)    OC LEADS WESTCLOCK WATCHES/FASTEETH (SCRIPTED)
7:56:25      (1:15)    CLOSE. NOTE CUT
7:57:40                CART/MINI/CHR: TOMORROW/BW SLIDE
7:58:24                STATION BREAK
```

THE ACTUAL RUNDOWN FROM *THE TODAY SHOW*.

NBC forwarded other letters they received from viewers around the country, some from parents who has seen the story and made what must have been gut-wrenching decisions. In our story, they saw in their own children the kinds of behaviors Michael Green exhibited at an early age and, after seeing the story, decided to put their children in institutions or seek immediate medical help early in their children's lives.

It was then, only five years into my career, that I began to understand deeply the power of journalism. I knew we reported the news, we covered events, we were daily visitors in homes of the people we were there to serve. I never realized we could influence parents to make life-changing decisions. It was a lesson I never forgot.

The story also caught the attention of Eric Ober, a CBS executive who would soon become president of CBS News. He flew out to Seattle, took me to dinner at the Mirabeau restaurant, and asked if I might be interested in coming to work at *60 Minutes*, the gold-standard of investigative reporting. At that time, there were no full-time women correspondents on the program. He thought I might be a good candidate for that position. But I had a new baby, and I was moving my parents from Washington, DC, to Seattle to help me care for Jeremy. I had no desire to live in an airplane traveling from story to story. I thanked Mr. Ober for his interest, for the dinner, and for his compliments about the work. I stayed put. It was where I thought I needed to be.

Michael Green's conviction with the death penalty attached was eventually overturned. The higher courts in Washington State determined there was insufficient evidence that a kidnapping or rape occurred, though King County prosecutors vehemently disagreed. Green was granted a new trial, facing only the murder charge, and was convicted in one hour. He was given what is known as an indeterminate sentence, meaning his case comes up continually for review by state parole boards. Now more than four decades after the murder, prosecutors and the victim's family condemn the continuous review process allowed to Green, believing there was overwhelming evidence of attempted rape, justifying a sentence of life without parole.

Michael Green's most recent review was held on February 23, 2016, before the Washington State Department of Corrections Indeterminate Sentence Review Board. The board raised the issue that Green was not participating in the rehabilitation program at his prison. Why, they wanted to know, was he not cooperating?

He read from a letter he had written: "I was all of the things I have been accused of and so much more, but I no longer am that man. That is why I have not fulfilled your recommendation to continue to participate. It would be disingenuous of me to say otherwise. Disingenuousness was part of that old man. I have thrown it away. I like who I am and I like who I am becoming . . . rage has been replaced with love and purity of heart."

When he was asked what was behind his rage the day he murdered the young girl, he told the board about the impact of seeing his sixteen-year-old brother sexually assaulting his ten-year-old sister when he was four years old. He said he became angrier over the years, and by the age of eighteen, he felt "powerless and like a victim."

A board member asked him directly, "Why did you want to rape that little girl on that day?"

He replied, "She became my sister. I wanted to end all the pain and heartache I had felt."

Green later admitted that he, too, was involved in sexual activity with his sister and experienced shame about that. He also said that when he heard his young victim scream, the thought that entered his mind was "Shut up! That rage I had been building came out. I pulled the knife out and killed her."

The review board determined that, as of 2016, Michael Green was "no way ready for release." Green's claim that he had become a Christian and that his sexual deviancy issues and rage were conquered "through God" did not convince the review board.

King County, Washington prosecutor Michael Hogan, who is also a member of the young victim's family, summed up the tragic story with these words: "It's never going to be right. We will take this to our graves and the only emotion I have about this is that we need to do everything that we can to make sure he never gets out. I'm proud to work in the office that helped incarcerate him. My only consolation is that Michael Green will be disappointed in his quest for release for the rest of his life."

Michael Charles Green remains in prison in Eastern Washington, not far from the town of Ellensburg where he grew up. He is up for review again in 2024.

Tony Savage, the bearded giant who helped Michael Green avoid the death penalty died in 2012 at the age of eighty-one.

FOR MOST OF MY CAREER, even on long and complicated stories, I often worked with different photographers. I went through the entire journey about Michael Green with Bill Fenster. He was as transfixed as I from the very beginning of the tragic saga. What echoes most and haunts us are the words we heard repeatedly: "I knew someday he was going to kill somebody." With all the signs along the way, all the warnings from Michael Green's childhood, all the predictions from neighbors, cops, and prosecutors, it still happened. A tragedy so many predicted, but could not prevent.

Chapter 19

Ambushing Richard Nixon

O N SATURDAY, MAY 9, 1981, a typically slow weekend news day, photographer Laddy Kite and I returned from covering a mundane and utterly forgettable event as many weekend stories often were. This particular assignment was the dedication of a stoplight in a rural suburb of Seattle. Residents petitioned for some time to get a stoplight installed at a hazardous crossroads plagued by accidents. They were ecstatic having won the fight and thrilled at the prospect of having their efforts recorded and shown on the five o'clock news.

We turned over the video of the new stoplight to an editor, walked over to the assignment desk, and asked if there was something else, perhaps a bit more newsworthy, going on anywhere within driving distance that might be more exciting than a traffic light installation.

"Well there really isn't much going on. Richard Nixon's in town . . . I think . . . for a wedding or something, but who cares? Nobody wants to see that."

"What? When?" I shouted back at her.

"Probably right about now," she replied.

I was flabbergasted! How could a person purporting to be an assignment editor regard the appearance of even a disgraced former president as not worth a mention? Despite her claim that "nobody wants to see that," Laddy and I did.

"What else do you know about this?" I asked her.

"Nixon's in town for his niece's wedding . . . it's his brother's daughter . . . his brother Ed, I think, who lives up in Lynnwood."

At that moment, our only purpose in life was to find Richard Nixon somewhere in the Seattle area.

I called a police officer who was a friend and occasional mole and, conveniently, head of the Seattle Police Department's security detail. Even infamous ex-presidents still had Secret Service protection, and if anyone knew where Nixon was, it would be this cop.

"He's headed to the Rainier Club downtown, but you'd better hurry."

I ran to get Laddy, told him to stop whatever he was doing, and head with me to the news car. We did not ask permission from the misguided assignment editor to try to find Richard Nixon. We had no time to waste, and fortunately, it should be noted, Mr. Kite had a well-earned reputation for ignoring speed limits.

We parked up the hill from the toney Rainier Club and got out of the car. Laddy grabbed his camera and recorder as two shiny black limousines pulled up to the front entrance of the building. Still putting his equipment together, I yanked Laddy towards the limos, dragging him down the street. We plowed through some plants and brush, crossed over a lawn, ran along the sidewalk, and closed in on our prey. Two dark-suited men wearing sunglasses and carpieces stepped casually out of the first car and headed toward the second car to open the door for their special passenger.

But the Secret Service agents never made it.

Before they could react, I pushed one of them to my right against the front car and shoved the other agent to the left. They had no time to pull out their guns or employ their well-honed skills of protecting their charge. I barged towards the second limo when the back door began to open.

Laddy shoved the microphone into my hand as a foot emerged from the car onto the sidewalk. There sat the only man forced, in disgrace, to resign as president of the United States. He seemed annoyed, surprised, and shocked at the intrusion by a woman he did not know. Then he caught sight of Laddy and his camera, and his whole demeanor changed. His skeptical grimace was replaced instantly with a smile, morphing from a look of disgust to one of delight that television cameras still showed up for him.

The befuddled Secret Service agents backed off once they saw Mr. Nixon was not upset by our presence.

"Hello, Mr. Nixon," I said. "My name is Julie Blacklow with KING Television News here in Seattle . . . the NBC affiliate."

"Oh, I have a daughter named Julie."

"I know, sir."

WITH A GAGGLE OF REPORTERS, AGAIN SHOVING A MICROPHONE IN
RICHARD NIXON'S FACE AT A POLITICAL FUNDRAISER IN SEATTLE.

We did a quick interview with him, asked about his niece's wedding, how life was going in San Clemente, and other idle chatter. How did he like Seattle? Nice town. Probably too much of a Democratic state for him. I considered telling him in that brief encounter that my aunt—my mother's sister Pauline—was on the Watergate Grand Jury which led to his downfall, but I kept that tidbit to myself.

We had an exclusive for what was typically a boring Saturday newscast. Good enough. Mr. Nixon stayed in town for another day to attend a fundraiser, spending the night at a downtown hotel where, among a horde of reporters and photographers, I shoved a microphone to his face again.

He left to return to California the next day. The stoplight, installed the day before, remains in place.

Chapter 20

Divine Intervention

IN THE WINTER OF 1978, after starring in the John Waters film *Eat Your Makeup* where he was dressed in drag to portray a fictionalized version of Jackie Kennedy, Harris Glenn Milstead made a stop in Seattle. Better known as Divine, the character in that film begins kidnapping models, forcing them to eat their own makeup. If not famous on the big theater screens, Divine was, quite literally, a big, big star. Obese, outrageous, and over the top.

Harris was born and raised in Baltimore to a conservative middle-class family, which, I am guessing, did not see all his movies. He starred in another Waters film, *Pink Flamingos*, and would finally make it onto the big screen in the unforgettable *Hairspray*. Idolized by the LGBT community, Divine was described by *People* magazine as "the Drag Queen of the Century." The twentieth century.

He arrived in Seattle in the late 1970s for some personal appearances and to make the rounds at some very private parties, which I attended because of my friendship with fashion photographer Billy Bernardo, a friend of Divine's. Billy was trying to do a photo shoot in Seattle and needed some young kids to pose as models. He called and asked if he could borrow my two-and-a-half-year-old, Jeremy. Though it had snowed quite a bit the night before, Billy was intent on coming over, taking Jeremy shopping, buying him some too-expensive clothes, and taking pictures in the snow at various locations in Seattle. Never one to take a cab or rent a car, Billy said he was coming over in a limousine to pick up Jeremy in about an hour.

The doorbell rang . . . and rang . . . and rang. I didn't hear it, but Jeremy did. He opened the door, and unable to process what was standing there, he called upstairs to me in his toddler voice, "Mommy there's something at the door, but I don't know what it is!"

DIVINE...AN UNFORGETTABLE DRAG QUEEN.
STEPHANIE CHERNIKOWSKI/COLLECTION/GETTY IMAGES

"It" was a portly adult, resplendent in pink tights, a fluffy pink tutu, a massive blond, curly wig, arched black eyebrows, too much lipstick, and dangling earrings. It was Divine in drag. Having Divine come first to my door was Billy's idea of a great prank. He anticipated I would answer the door, not my child. Billy came out of the limousine, and he and Divine came into the house for a few minutes. After some coffee and a quick chat, they left . . . without Jeremy. I was not a particularly overprotective parent, but I was concerned about the possible lasting effects on a two-year-old as a result of being with Divine for more than a minute.

Before leaving, Billy invited me to a very private party later that evening where I was escorted by a couple of my gay friends. Needless to say, the "drag queen of the century" arrived exquisitely dressed and was, inevitably, the center of much attention. I sat on his ample lap for a few minutes eschewing many offers of cocaine and other assorted drugs. Bowls of cocaine were everywhere, big Chinese export bowls filled with white powder that was not confectioner's sugar. I was the only biological woman there, though I was no competition for Divine, who wore better clothes, had better make-up, and was far more entertaining than any other guest in the room.

In 1973, he said of himself: "Divine. That's my name. It's the name John [Waters] gave me. I like it. That's what everybody calls me now, even my close friends. Not many of them call me Glenn at all anymore, which I don't mind. . . . You always change your name when you're in the show business. Divine has stuck as my name. Did you ever look it up in the dictionary? I won't even go into it. It's unbelievable."

I looked it up in the dictionary.

"Heavenly. God-like. Extremely good. Unusually lovely."

In other words, Divine.

Chapter 21

Serenity and Silence

IN LATE SUMMER OF 1979, the forty-four-year-old spiritual leader of millions of Tibetan Buddhists around the world made his first visit to the United States. The Dalai Lama, Tenzin Gyatso, was fêted in New York City and everywhere he went, visiting churches, cathedrals, and Tibetan monasteries along the way. He stopped in Newark, Houston, Los Angeles, San Francisco, and Seattle, with other stops at colleges and universities. The US government, trying ever so hard to be diplomatic and not offend China, asked His Holiness to say he was visiting America as a Buddhist religious leader, not as an exiled head of state.

Tenzin Gyatso became the head of state in Tibet in 1950 at the age of fifteen, the same year that Chinese troops occupied Tibet. After a failed uprising against Chinese rule, the Dalai Lama fled Tibet to Nepal but never stopped urging China to allow Tibetans to preserve their culture, language, and religion. Since being exiled from Tibet, he has endlessly traveled the world giving speeches, attending meditation conferences, meeting with heads of state, and continuing to rattle the Chinese government, which considers him a troublemaker. The Dalai Lama claims he does not want Tibetan independence. The Chinese are unconvinced.

The most beloved exile in the world landed at Boeing Field in Seattle on a clear, sunny day, walked down the stairs of the plane, followed by his entourage of monks and a coterie of friends and followers traveling with him. A throng of local newspaper, radio, and television reporters gathered by a nearby gate, straining to see him, hoping to have a brief moment with him. I was among the pack.

Some years earlier, I began studying Buddhism, questioning the tenets and dictates of my own religion, Judaism. I was starting to believe most organized religions were too restrictive, judgmental, and the cause of too many wars. In Buddhism, I found a path much easier to follow with its core philosophy of kindness, tolerance, and love, a religion based on inclusiveness, not condemnation. The man walking towards me was the living, breathing embodiment of those tenets, the spiritual leader of more than five hundred million people around the world.

As he got closer, I felt a sense of calm and serenity. Always smiling, he exuded an aura of palpable happiness and gentleness. I held out my microphone, but for once in my life, I could not think of a single question that might be worthy enough for this man. I was frozen, in a state of complete awe, mesmerized by this humble monk.

Looking directly at me, he said, "And what question do you have, young lady?"

"I can't think of anything to ask," I said.

"Well, that's fine," he replied, "because I really have no answers."

THE DALAI LAMA IN SEATTLE, 1979 AT THE KEY ARENA.

Chapter 22

Pregnant . . . with Something

EVERY WEEK IN THE TELEVISION NEWS BUSINESS is a smorgasbord of experiences. It can run the gamut from interviewing murderers to a moment with the Dalai Lama, from covering a forest fire to hanging with musician Patti Smith or Jackson Browne . . . or with Cindy Crawford, the supermodel with the famous mole on her face. I once spent a day with her driving around in a chauffeured limousine going from one personal appearance to another. At a stoplight, Cindy uttered a rather memorable comment, saying she was sometimes insecure about her looks. I found that fascinating. Clearly, even the most beautiful people see flaws imperceptible to the rest of us. I could not see a hint of what she was talking about. In any case, despite my own imperfections, which I am certain others saw, my professional and personal life were moving along fine. But as John Lennon famously said, "Life is what happens to you while you're busy making other plans."

In 1980, with a toddler at home, I was trying to get pregnant again without success. I went to the doctor for what I thought would be a routine physical. The exam included a vaginal probe, a pap smear. I felt the cold speculum and the latex-gloved fingers of my doctor poking around inside me. He wanted to make sure everything felt right. It did not.

"Julie, are you pregnant?"

"No," I said. "I just had my period."

"Well, you're four months pregnant with something."

"*Pregnant with something*? What does that mean, 'four months pregnant with something'?"

"I'm not sure, but I need to send you downstairs right away for an ultrasound exam."

I instantly had that sinking feeling when you know your life is about to take a dramatically and dangerously sharp turn, one that will either leave you dead or mangled by the side of the road. The moment reminded me of a scene from John Irving's *The World According to Garp*. The title character's son, when warned to be careful about the undertow in the water, hears the word "undertoad" instead, believing a scary amphibian is hiding in the water waiting to pull him in and drown him. In the book, the word "undertoad" conveys an expression of anxiety, a reference to life's unseen events that will, in essence, pull you under. I believed the undertoad was coming to drown me.

I went down into the bowels of the hospital to the diagnostic imaging department. I removed my clothes and donned one of those thin, hideous green hospital gowns that rarely cover your entire body and always destroy any sense of privacy or dignity you might have possessed. I handed my paperwork to a nurse who could barely be bothered to look at me.

"Take a seat . . . we'll call you when we're ready."

When "*we're ready*"? I thought to myself. I wasn't ready but had to follow orders, something I rarely did well. I could not sit down or calm down. I was sick with fear and anxiety. The undertoad was getting closer.

A young, male technician led me down a hallway to the ultrasound room. I felt as if I was walking to my own hanging, to the electric chair, or to be burned at the stake. To me, it was the walk of death, and no matter how slowly I walked, I could not avoid the inevitable. I lay down on a metal table as two young men slathered a glob of cold, wet jelly onto my abdomen, spreading it around from the middle of my belly to the top of my thighs. As one of the men slowly moved the probe over my belly, blurry black-and-white images appeared on the screen. I had no clue what I was looking at, but one of them said, "Hey, Mike . . . come take a look at this!"

"Whoa!" the other technician replied.

"What are you seeing?" I asked.

"Sorry, miss. We really can't say anything."

"But you just did!" I replied . . . in a voice filled with panic and frustration.

"Well, we're done with the test, and we'll send the results upstairs to your doctor, and he can tell you what's going on. We're not allowed to say much. Please go ahead and get dressed."

The undertoad now certainly had me in its grips, and there was no way to escape.

Dr. Allen said it looked as if I had a very large tumor in my abdomen, so large it made it impossible to see most of the uterus or anything else down there. He scheduled me for surgery the following week, for a hysterectomy. There would be no second child. The only question was would Jeremy lose his mother.

"Do you think it's cancer?" I asked the doctor.

"Probably not," he said, "because if it was, you would've been in a lot more pain and probably have died from anything that size."

How comforting.

A week later, I walked, haltingly and terrified, into the main entrance of Group Health Hospital in Seattle. I filled out all the necessary forms, including one indemnifying the doctors if, by some chance, I died in surgery. As I was lying in my hospital bed the night before the surgery, I turned on the news—KING 5 of course—and saw the irrepressible and outrageous Don McGaffin announce to our viewers I was about to have my uterus extracted. Un-fucking-believable! I was mortified. Shortly after the newscast, Dorothy Bullitt, the owner and matriarch of KING, walked into my room to apologize for McGaffin's transgression and wish me luck with the operation. She was sorry about McGaffin's revelation, but the damage and embarrassment were done. I needed to get some rest.

The next morning, surgeons filleted me with a seven-inch slice to my belly, exposing one of the biggest fibroid tumors they had ever seen, a three-pound mass, which had enveloped my uterus and cervix. They removed all of it, but left two lonely ovaries, preventing me from entering menopause at the age of thirty-one. It was a five-hour procedure, much longer than anticipated, mostly due to the fact that I lost a lot of blood, which stopped my heart for a minute or so. For a moment, I died on the operating table but remembered later during regression therapy that I had an out-of-body experience, hovering in an upper corner of the operating room near the ceiling, watching the surgeons shout at me and tell me to stop bleeding. I did not see any light, go down a tunnel, or have a conversation with God. I left my body for a few seconds and returned to it quickly. After being sutured and bandaged, I was wheeled into the ICU and eventually back to my room for a few days before being sent home. My ability to make more babies was gone, but also gone was the burden of menstruation. No more periods or cramps. No more sanitary pads or tampons. I once calculated I saved hundreds if not thousands of dollars on feminine products. This was the only bright spot in a very dark time.

Before I was discharged from the hospital, I suffered one more indignation. A psychiatrist came into my room to talk about any sadness I might be feeling due to the loss of my menstrual cycle. Only a man would conjure up such a ridiculous thought. I never missed having periods. I thought perhaps my mood swings and general annoyance with the world would disappear with the end of my menstrual cycle. I was wrong. I was released from the hospital, but the undertoad still had me in its grip.

After a week at home, I was getting worse, not better. I could barely walk or hold a toothbrush, let alone pick up my young son. The pain in my belly was unrelenting. When my temperature peaked at 104 degrees, my husband and parents helped me into a car and drove me back to the hospital.

I was given a private room since the doctors were unsure what was wrong and did not want to take any chances that I might infect someone else. The first round of antibiotics proved useless. My fever hovered around 102, and I had to be helped to the bathroom and back again, then resort to a bedpan when I could no longer support myself at all. I was diagnosed with a pernicious and potentially deadly post-surgical infection. An abdomen open for five hours proved irresistible to bacteria. Some very nasty bugs had infested my belly.

Because traditional antibiotics were ineffective, doctors turned to the big medical guns, Keflex and Clindamycin, relatively new drugs used mostly as a last resort in the early 1980s. A nurse told me they were tested in the Vietnam War to treat wounded and dying soldiers but rarely used in hospitals. Two IV's were set up next to me, Keflex in one, Clindamycin in the other, a hanging plastic bag on each side. My only entertainment was watching them slowly drip into me. Antibiotics have been around thousands of years. The Egyptians used to apply moldy bread to infected wounds until Alexander Fleming accidentally discovered penicillin when he noticed a fungus creating bacteria-free zones wherever it grew on a plate. I was lucky to be past the era of the moldy-bread approach.

Drugs, no matter their benefits, often carry with them unpleasant side effects. In pharmaceutical ads, the list of disclaimers is typically longer than the drug's therapeutic value, sometimes including the mention of death, a bit more than a side effect. In my case, the medicine dripping into me was killing the nasty bacteria but also destroying all the good bacteria in my intestines. Any liquid I drank immediately went through me. To replace the missing flora in my gut and provide nutrition I wasn't getting since I couldn't eat real food, I was forced to eat a wretched concoction of live flora, a vile-tasting, sour, green glob of goo. That was tough medicine.

After days of watching antibiotics dribble into me and eating unsavory meals of good bacteria, I was not showing any lasting signs of improvement. I did not want to talk or see anyone. But one friend convinced the nurses to let him in my room—Rabbi Moses Londinski, a rabbi with whom I had studied the Talmud, the central text of mainstream Judaism. He was an Orthodox Jew, and while a brilliant and animated teacher, he was never permitted to shake my hand or touch me in any way other than with his intellect. Physical contact with women, other than with their wives and children, is forbidden for Orthodox men. At the time, Moses Londinski was the rabbi of the Bikur Cholim Synagogue in Seattle's Seward Park neighborhood, just south of downtown. Its name, Bikur Cholim, translates to "visiting the sick," and Rabbi Londinski was being true to his synagogue's name. I do not know who called him or told him of my illness, but someone thought I needed a religious intervention since traditional medicine was not working.

With as much energy as I could muster, I smiled at him as he took a seat on the edge of my bed. He said prayers on my behalf, first in Hebrew, then English, and in one dramatic gesture, he leaned forward and embraced me. I was shocked. He was touching me and holding me, clearly a violation of Jewish law.

"How can you touch me?" I asked him. "I thought you weren't supposed to touch other women."

He replied, "*Pikuach nefesh.*" Translated, "to save a life." There are, the rabbi said, exceptions to even the strictest laws in Judaism. Nothing is more important than life itself.

Whether it was drugs or divine intervention, my fever broke the next day. My gut was working, my body was stronger, and I went home. It would take a few more months to get my full strength back so I could return to work.

But the undertoad finally released me.

Chapter 23

His Ding-a-Ling

IN THE FALL OF 1983, a rock and roll reunion tour made a stop at the newly completed Tacoma Dome. At the time, it was the world's largest wooden-domed facility. The timbers used to frame the roof were harvested from trees blown down during the eruption of Mount St. Helens in 1980. The Dome's first event was a David Bowie concert, part of his Serious Moonlight tour. Over the years, the arena hosted Bull Riders, Billy Graham, and Bruce Springsteen, along with Monster Jams, RV shows, Christmas festivals, wedding expos, and World Champion Wrestling. The Tacoma Dome offered something for everyone.

THE TACOMA DOME...SCENE OF AN ALMOST SEXUAL ENCOUNTER WITH CHUCK BERRY.

It was an impressive roster of Sixties rock stars. Danny and the Juniors were scheduled to perform, along with the Coasters, the Shirelles, Bobby

Vee, and headliners Jerry Lee Lewis and Charles Edward Anderson Berry, commonly known as Chuck. With "At the Hop," "Searchin'," "Will You Still Love Me Tomorrow," "Rubber Ball," and "Maybelline" indelibly etched in my brain, this was an irresistible opportunity to see, hear, and meet some of the authentic legends of early rock and get paid to do it.

THE EXTRAORDINARY CHARLES EDWARD ANDERSON BERRY...AKA CHUCK.

These titans of music all gathering in one arena on a single night required more than one camera to do justice to this event and more than a minute of television time to tell the story. In a decision that would likely never be made today, KING Television management allowed five talented news photographers, with more than a quarter million dollars' worth of equipment, to go with me to cover a story featuring aging rockers. The only concession they said was not to put in for overtime.

Our caravan of news cars pulled into the back entrance of the massive, bubble-shaped Tacoma Dome and we hauled our paraphernalia into the backstage area. We gathered around a large, circular table as musicians, technical crew, lighting people, and stage hands scurried around us. The audience was lining up outside, as excited as we were inside. We talked about how we were going to cover this event, surrounded by cameras, audio equipment, tripods, batteries, videotapes, microphones, and cables. It was a mountain of hardware, all the things needed to make a television story. It was impossible not to notice us, and Chuck Berry noticed. He had recently returned from a European tour, still fuming that bootlegged copies of his albums were sold with no compensation to him and no authorization from him. He saw us and our cameras as more rip-offs in the making. Though the promoter had given us permission to be there and record some portions of the concert, Chuck was not told of the arrangement and was clearly not happy about our presence.

"What the hell is all this shit?" Chuck asked with unmasked hostility.

"We're going to make you famous!" I replied, trying and failing miserably to make light of the situation.

"I'm already famous," he said, completely unamused at my remark.

"If I walk out on the stage and I see any of those goddamn cameras anywhere, I'm leaving . . . I'm gone . . . I'm done!"

This was not going well.

I needed to resort to my tried and true techniques, honed over many years, of cajoling, humoring, and pressuring people to bend to my will. This challenging moment would require a level of charm I did not possess. I was face to face with one of the first musicians inducted into the Rock and Roll Hall of Fame, voted one of the one hundred greatest artists of all time, considered the father of rock and roll. This living legend, standing just a few feet away, was fuming.

I tried to charm him. I told him how much I loved him and told him his songs helped get me through the Fifties and Sixties. In that moment, I was less reporter and more a fan. I was also desperate to salvage our story. He smelled my fear, but also sensed my admiration for him. At some point in my performance, one of the photographers watching this exchange saw Chuck's angry face begin to soften. His displeasure turned into amusement with a hint of a slight smile. I successfully stroked his ego, and for a moment, he considered allowing us to shoot a small portion of his performance. First though, he wanted to make a deal with me. Before he gave us permission to record him onstage, Chuck reached into his own bag of tricks, also undoubtedly perfected over many years. He put his hand into the pocket of his bright red, bell-bottomed, double-knit pants, which rested on top of his bright white shoes. It is important to note Chuck Berry demanded he always be paid in cash before any performance. When his hand came out of his pocket, it was filled with a large roll of hundred-dollar bills. He peeled off bill after bill after bill, and offered them to me with a shocking but tantalizing quid pro quo deal: "These are yours, mama, and you can shoot some of my show if you give me a little head before I go on."

Wow! Chuck Berry is offering me money to give him a blow job!

I took a breath. So did my colleagues.

Few things shocked me. This did. I thought about it. I considered it. He was one of my teenage idols and the success of our story was in jeopardy. A lot of things went through my mind. Is this a bad career move or a good one? This would be a decision with far-reaching repercussions. To blow or not to blow, that was the question. After a minute or so, I declined Chuck Berry's tempting offer, but that choice cost us the chance to capture his performance. We were allowed to videotape the other artists, including a backstage moment with the Shirelles, gracing us with an a cappella rendition of Carole King's "Will You Still Love Me Tomorrow."

Before Chuck Berry took the stage, we pulled back and shut down all our cameras so he would not see them. But one photographer, too far away for him to see, kept rolling. We captured a few moments on the sly of "Johnny B. Goode" and more than an hours' worth of some of the best music from the Sixties. We packed up our mountain of equipment and were done.

My story of Chuck, his ding-a-ling, and the offer of personal contact with it would entertain countless friends in the coming years. How many people ever get to meet their teenage idols, let alone the opportunity to see them up really close? I would occasionally tell the story in ethics classes I sometimes taught in local journalism schools, both for shock value and to make a point about doing the right thing when temptations are dangled in front of reporters. Whether it is an offer for a free meal or a proffer of sex for access, the answer should always be no. Sometimes in the news business, there are gray areas, but most of the time, the choices we have to make are black and white. Most journalists know where the lines are and when not to cross them, no matter who or what is standing on the other side.

> *My ding-a-ling, my ding-a-ling,*
> *I want you to play with my ding-a-ling!*
> —Chuck Berry, 1972

Chapter 24

Tracking Tina Turner

ANNA MAE BULLOCK from Nutbush, Tennessee, made an impressive comeback in the mid-1980s from a lull in her career. She was half of the Ike and Tina Turner Revue with a legacy of amazing songs, "A Fool in Love," "Proud Mary," and "River Deep–Mountain High." But in 1984, Tina was divorced, on her own, and about to release her biggest hit. "What's Love Got to Do with It" won four Grammy awards, including record of the year.

In my mind, Tina Turner never faded. The legs, the face, the hair, the powerful, gravelly voice. In the fall of 1984, coming off a hugely successful European tour, she was scheduled to perform at the Tacoma Dome as the opening act for Lionel Richie. Lionel was the headliner, but to me, Tina was the star of the show. Talking to Tina required knowing someone who could help get us backstage, but getting behind the scenes does not necessarily guarantee an interview. You have to know somebody. I did.

Stan Foreman was the Northwest regional promotion and marketing manager for Capitol Records, responsible for nine states, a big deal in the music business. Before working for Capitol, he was a disc jockey, booking agent, bandleader, and musician. Stan's whole life was music, and he loved musicians, none more than Tina Turner. I called him and asked if we could get an interview with her. Stan told me, "Tina's management said before she even started her tour that she was not going to do any radio, press, TV, or any interviews . Absolutely not . . . sorry."

That was as firm a no as I had ever heard, but I never took any no for an answer, however many times I heard it.

A couple of weeks later, I called Stan again to let him know we were coming down to the concert with or without the interview. I reasoned if we were there, we still had the possibility, no matter how remote, of talking with Tina. Stan said nothing had changed. Tina would absolutely not do any interviews.

KING News photographer Laddy Kite and I headed to the Dome on the night of the concert and arrived at the backstage entrance.

This is Stan Foreman's memory of what happened next: "I got to the backstage entrance, and there you were with Laddy, right? As I recall, I told you I would find her road manager and ask one more time if we could do an interview. When I found him, he said, 'Absolutely no interviews.' About that time, Tina walked in the room, gave me a big kiss and a hug and said to the manager, "This is my Capitol Records friend Stanley. He came to see me when nobody else cared. We'll do whatever he wants."

Stan led Laddy, hauling a camera and tripod, and me into the bowels of the Tacoma Dome, through back hallways and private elevators, on a quest to find Tina. She was in a small room, meeting and greeting record executives and a few fans who won a chance to meet her. When she saw Stan, she broke away for a moment and came right over to him. He told her there was a television crew in the hallway hoping for an interview. Would she be willing to step outside for a few minutes and talk with them? The smile on her face was radiant, and she beamed at him, clearly ready and willing to do anything he asked. She finished her business with her guests and came out into the hallway with a big smile.

In front of an audience, Tina Turner was bigger than life, a dynamic, prancing, commanding presence. Standing next to her, I thought she seemed petite, even fragile, but her sparkle belied her size. She was gracious, kind, and warm. As she began chatting with us, she glanced over at Stan, giving him a wink as if to acknowledge she was doing this as a thank-you to him for the friendship and unflagging support he had given her over the years before she became an international star on her own. We had just minutes with her, but moments that no one else would get. She thanked us for coming to see her and for our interest in her, which was endearing, surprising, and a reminder that she never forgot where she came from. Despite her fame and talent, Tina Turner was still Anna Mae Bullock from Nutbush, Tennessee.

On stage that night, she was a giant once again, a thrilling and dynamic force of nature, belting out songs with ferocity. It never occurred to me that this icon and I would ever have anything in common. But we did. Stan Foreman.

"And that," Stan said, "is how you got the only interview of the entire tour."

Tina Turner, standing next to the wonderful Stan Foreman. Courtesy Darrell Westmoreland. www.darrellwestmoreland.com.

Tina Turner's last tour was in 2009. She dazzled sold-out audiences across Europe and North America. After fifty years in show business, at the age of seventy-eight, she gave up her American citizenship, retired, and moved to Switzerland. In 2018, the woman considered the Queen of Rock and Roll worked with a team of producers and helped create *Tina: The Tina Turner Musical* based on her remarkable life.

Stan Foreman is still in the music business leading his band, Stan the Man and the Road Runners, performing regularly on the West Coast, playing classic rock and roll.

The Porn King

A LOT OF PEOPLE WATCH PORNOGRAPHY. According to the US Bureau of Labor Statistics, porn sites attract more visitors each month than Amazon, Netflix, and Twitter. An estimated 30 percent of all internet content is pornography. The industry generates more money than football, baseball, and basketball, combined. That was not always the case.

Back in the 1980s, there was no pornography on the internet because there was no internet. If you wanted to watch it, you rented videos or went to an X-rated establishment to see live shows or to a theater showing sex films. In any case, people have always loved sex and loved watching other people having sex. Some very savvy business folks made their fortunes from pornography.

One of those men was Seattle "Porn King" Roger Forbes. That is what we in the media dubbed him. It was not a title he liked, but it made for convenient headlines. Roger did not make sex films but owned X-rated movie houses. He bought the land and theaters that showed them. For research purposes, I went to his theaters back in the Seventies and Eighties and witnessed both porn on the screen and in the audience when a male patron masturbated in front of me.

Roger Forbes was as elusive as he was infamous, which inevitably made him more interesting. I tried repeatedly to meet him and to learn more about the man who would not be found, but without success. In the early 1980s, Roger was forced out of hiding. He bought two theaters in downtown Renton, Washington, back then a quiet suburb of Seattle known for family-themed entertainment, more Disney than *Deep Throat*. Mr. Forbes shook things up, deciding to show sex films in one of the theaters, but ran into a massive roadblock in the form of Renton city Ordinance 3526.

THE RENTON THEATER, WHERE THE JURY IN THE ROGER FORBES' PORNOGRAPHY
TRIAL CAME TO WATCH X-RATED FILMS, FULFILLING THEIR CIVIC DUTY.

The ordinance, passed in 1981, was itself explicit, prohibiting adult motion pictures within one thousand feet of "any residential zone or single or multiple family dwelling, any church or religious institution, and any public park . . . or within one mile of any public or private school." The code left little doubt about what types of videos or films were prohibited, including those displaying the following:

- Human genitals in a state of sexual stimulation or arousal
- Acts of human masturbation, sexual intercourse, or sodomy
- Fondling or erotic touching of human genitals, pubic region, or female breast
- Human male genitals in a discernible turgid state, even if completely and opaquely covered

There were additional restrictions, but this makes the point.

Safe to say the movie fare Roger Forbes intended to offer displayed some or all of the above images within the restricted areas outlined in the city's ordinance. His plan was a bit out of Renton's comfort zone, and the city filed a lawsuit, *City of Renton vs. Playtime Theaters.*

With litigation underway and now a matter of public record, Roger Forbes was forced out of hiding and became more of a public figure and finally agreed to an on-camera interview. I am unsure what his motivation was, but I had been bugging him for months, if not years, to talk with me. He invited photographer Bill Fenster and me to his home. If I expected some gaudy display of a porn king's home, my assumptions were mistaken. While Fenster was transfixed by the most lavish collection of cowboy boots perhaps ever assembled, I was mesmerized by a wall of shelves filled with Lalique glass, some of the most beautiful pieces I had ever seen. Roger encouraged me to touch them. I just ogled them.

Roger was circumspect and more reserved than I expected him to be. He was clean-cut and soft-spoken, not the personality I expected from a man in the porn business. He saw himself as a businessman, not a pornographer. He emphasized he owned buildings . . . which showed sex films. He did not produce them, and he calmly and forcefully made the point that he saw this battle as a First Amendment freedom of speech case. He was not intentionally making trouble, just trying to conduct his business, which he felt he had the right to do. Fenster stared at the cowboy boots one more time, and I stared at the glass collection. We packed up our gear, left, and aired our interview with Roger Forbes before the trial began.

Roger sauntered into the courtroom, tall, elegantly dressed, looking self-assured and debonair. He might just as well have been a Wall Street mogul as a titan in the world of pornography. Though he loathed the publicity he was now getting, he felt committed to fighting for the right to conduct his business.

To combat the City of Renton and challenge Ordinance 3526, Forbes brought in Robert Eugene Smith from California, a well-known champion of the First Amendment, a lawyer with years of experience in the porn industry. If Roger was a dapper, well-dressed man, Mr. Smith outshone him. Dressed head to toe in what looked like very expensive clothes, he had a pink, silk handkerchief tucked perfectly into his suit pocket and carried himself with a Cary Grant–like swagger. I remember his shiny, light-brown, buttery-leather shoes, which appeared to be hand-tooled, unlike anything you would find in a department store. He came over to meet the assembled press inside the courtroom and extended his perfectly manicured hand, adorned with a Rolex watch with semaphore flags for numbers.

"Nice to meet you folks. I'm Robert Eugene Smith, Mr. Forbes's lawyer. If you have any questions, please just direct them to me, and I'll be happy to talk with you."

LAWYER ROBERT EUGENE SMITH, WHO REPRESENTED
ROGER FORBES IN THE COURTROOM AND LATER COURTED ME.

Did I mention the silver-flecked hair and iridescent light-blue eyes? Roger Forbes bought the best of everything, including legal representation.

As a journalist, I was interested in the issues, but as a woman, I was captivated by the debonair Mr. Smith. If anyone thought this would be a routine lawsuit, and I am uncertain whether anyone did, it was clear from the beginning nothing about this trial would be normal. In most legal proceedings, evidence is presented in the courtroom, but this was not like most trials. Because the US District Court could not provide the equipment to show the X-rated evidence, the lawyers, reporters, photographers, along with the judge and jury, had to take a field trip to Renton to watch pornography on the big screen on a beautiful, sunny afternoon.

Among the twelve jurors was a former neighbor of mine, Stuart Fountain. He was young, in his thirties at the time, and gay. During the voir dire, when lawyers question prospective jurors to determine if they are suitable for service, Stuart recalls being asked about prejudices regarding pornography and whether he might have a problem looking at X-rated films. He did not. He later told me, "If you're going to be making a decision for or against the City of Renton about pornography, you really need to see what the problem is."

The jurors and alternates walked into the shabby-looking theater and were asked to take seats away from one another lest any gasps or comments exert undue influence on other jurors. They settled in to do their civic duty. For Stuart, it was a chance to finally learn about straight sex. He had, he said, experimented with women back in his days in the navy, but that was the extent of his knowledge about heterosexual sex. He said, "I was concentrating on trying to figure out how, as a gay man, I was going to make a civic judgment, how to be objective about this because being gay puts you in a different perspective about pornography. Many, if not most, gay men go to X-rated movie theaters to either masturbate or get blowjobs. We are not thinking about where the theaters are located."

Over the next couple of days, Stuart and his fellow jurors, along with the judge, a few federal marshals, and a cluster of reporters and photographers watched a lot of turgid penises, fondled genitalia, and a bevy of bare breasts. There was a lot of moaning on screen, an endless parade of sweaty bodies, and heterosexual intercourse. The production values, as Stuart recalls, were "inferior to modest at best."

We were not permitted to bring our cameras into the theater and, in any case, would not have been able to air portions of the film on our newscast. We were able to watch people watching the films, which seemed to display basically everything the city ordinance did not want shown on Renton movie screens. Stuart remembers going home after each viewing and telling his partner, "They're showing this stuff to the wrong person."

As I was watching the movies, I felt a warm hand on the back of my neck and warm breath behind my ear. Both belonged to the estimable Robert Eugene Smith. This gesture, even more than the graphic images on the screen, shocked me. I doubt I said much more than words to the effect of "what are you doing?" But it was not enough of a rebuff to stop his whispering to me and asking if I wanted to meet him for dinner later. No, I did not. I was married, but I was smitten—seduced in an instant by a man who was part of a story I was covering. Everything was wrong about this. I was flattered, and he was irresistible.

The next day, a dozen red roses were delivered to my desk in the KING 5 newsroom with a note: "With great admiration and affection, Robert."

The following day, another dozen roses arrived, along with a card professing his continued admiration for me and an invitation to meet him for dinner at Seattle's Sorrento Hotel. I did. It was delicious and the food was good, too.

Despite the best efforts of Robert Smith, the City of Renton won the first round of the case in district court. Playtime Theaters' request for a declaratory judgment that the ordinance violated the First and Fourteenth Amendments was denied.

Stuart, who considered himself the likeliest to dissent, went along with the other eleven jurors and ruled against Playtime Theaters. He remembers vividly the discussions in the jury room leading to the verdict. The word "prurient" dominated the debate. What did it mean, the jurors wondered. Did these films meet the definition? "Prurient," a word originating in the sixteenth century, comes from the Latin word *prurire*. It conveys a sense of itching or longing, a wanton feeling, according to *Merriam-Webster*. The films, they decided, definitely met that standard.

They wrestled with the definition of pornography. Stuart was reminded of the famous comment from Supreme Court Justice Potter Stewart as he considered whether Louie Malle's film, *The Lovers*, was hard-core pornography. The justice wrote: "I shall not today attempt further to define the kinds of material I understand to be embraced within that shorthand description ["hard-core pornography"], and perhaps I could never succeed in intelligibly doing so. But *I know it when I see it*, and the motion picture involved in this case is not that."

To the Forbes's jury, though, it *was* pornography, and it was more. Stuart remembers the prevailing concern in the privacy of the jury room was the feeling that the women in the films seemed coerced, browbeaten, and manipulated, as if they had no choice but to serve the domineering men. It was the undertone of violence, says Stuart, that informed the decision against Roger Forbes.

After losing the first round, the case wound its way through the judicial system, a process that would take the better part of two years. Meanwhile, I went to California to spend time with the captivating Mr. Smith. My marriage was on the verge of divorce, but it was still wrong. Unethical. Immoral. Stupid. Dangerous. Intoxicating.

Robert picked me up at the Los Angeles airport in his dark-blue Mercedes convertible, a car as impeccable as his clothes. As we headed towards Encino, I noticed the enormous homes, which seemed built into the hillsides, and wondered who lived there. He did. His residence was covered with white carpeted floors, art on every wall, large bedrooms with silk bedspreads, and nothing out of place. It was immaculate, ornate, and lush, and it was abundantly clear that the legal arm of the porn business was also quite profitable.

We went to dinner at the Beverly Hills Hotel, accompanied by Robert's perfectly coiffed, white-haired mother. We were seated next to Tom Selleck and his wife. Other celebrities were scattered around. Robert glided from one table to another, smiling, occasionally shaking a hand, with an air of prominence as if he too expected to be recognized. In a city of movie stars and moguls, he fit right in.

Besides his impressive home and perfect car, Robert owned a beautiful, sleek, wooden sailboat and took me for a cruise around the Channel Islands. There was champagne, caviar, and kissing, but nothing more than that. Odd, I thought. He acted the part of a great libertine but could never manage to give me more than a kiss. He slept alone and sent me off to another bedroom.

The next day, a Saturday, Robert wanted to take me for another sailboat ride, this time on a friend's boat, but he needed to make a quick stop in the San Fernando Valley to check in with another client. The Valley, home of the multi-billion dollar porn industry, is known in the trade as the San Pornando Valley. He parked his Mercedes in a lot filled with even fancier cars, an impressive assortment of Ferraris, Bentleys, and BMWs. The building itself was a drab, cement structure as big as a football field, the outside providing no clue about the business inside.

"I'll wait outside," I told Robert.

"Absolutely not," he replied. "I want you to see this."

We entered through a non-descript side door and immediately heard the sounds of moans and groans. We were in one of Porn Valley's massive duplicating facilities, endlessly churning out countless VHS copies of sex films headed for stores and homes throughout the world. A few images were on screen. I could barely bring myself to look . . . but could not look away. Robert introduced me to his client, one of the biggest pornographers in the industry. Just a businessman, he could have been anyone's dad, uncle, or brother.

My final boat ride with Robert was, to say the least, memorable. We walked down the ramp, once again at the Channel Islands, toward a huge, two-masted ship with maroon tanbark sails, more resistant to rot and mildew, a stunning display against the powder-blue sky. The owner was another porn mogul who invited a dozen bikini-clad film stars to join him. If I expected some display of sex frolicking and lewdness, it did not happen. Everyone was polite, gracious, and curious how a reporter from Seattle happened to know Robert Smith and end up in California. I wondered the same thing and was filled with shame, uncomfortable about where I was.

Robert and I went home for our last night together in his hillside mansion. Good food, good chats, no sex. I was relieved in a way that our friendship never went beyond talking, sharing meals, and sailing. He continued to write letters scented with his aftershave and send flowers from time to time to my home, not to the newsroom.

In 1986, two years after the first court proceeding, the caviar and the kissing, *City of Renton v. Playtime Theaters* was on the docket of the US Supreme Court. In a 7-2 decision, the court held that "zoning regulations that control the areas where adult movie theaters are located do not violate the First Amendment." The court said the law was not aimed at the content of the films shown but, rather, "with the secondary effects of adult theaters on the surrounding community." The court found the ordinance was "unrelated to the suppression of free expression. The ordinance, by its terms, is designed to prevent crime, protect the city's retail trade, maintain property values, and generally protect[t] and preserv[e] the quality of life of [the city's] neighborhoods." Two justices dissented, concluding in essence, that the city of Renton just did not approve of the contents of the films.

Renton prevailed. Roger Forbes lost. This most curious case, as well as a very brief, unconsummated romance, was over. The dashing Robert Eugene Smith passed away some years ago. Roger Forbes, now in his mid-seventies as I write this, still has a thriving adult entertainment business with clubs throughout the country. After many attempts to find him, he finally returned my call in late January of 2017. He had just had knee-replacement surgery and did not have the time or inclination to talk. He was on his way to physical therapy and said only, "I wish you the best, but include me out."

I asked him if he remembered the titles of the films shown in the Renton theater during the first proceeding more than thirty years earlier. He laughed and said he could not recall what they were but uttered one parting and enigmatic thought: "It's bad enough to show the films . . . even harder to watch them."

At that point in my career, *City of Renton v. Playtime Theaters* was the most unusual story I had covered. Assignments would get even more bizarre.

Chapter 26

Holy Smokey

The incomparable, talented and kind Smokey Robinson.

WE LITERALLY WALKED INTO THE MUSIC as we opened the doors to Seattle's magnificently refurbished Paramount Theater. In front of us, seated in metal chairs in the marble lobby, a full string section was rehearsing a familiar and unforgettable song, "Tears of a Clown," written and sung by William Robinson Jr., known throughout the world as Smokey.

We did not know why they were in the lobby since the concert was still hours away, but we knew it sounded fantastic and were compelled to record some of the magic. Laddy Kite wasted no time setting up his video camera and tripod. Though we had permission to cover the concert later and inter-view Smokey, we started shooting immediately. No one stopped us as the conductor and musicians continued playing.

Our usual two-person crew was a three-person crew for this story. Laddy and I were accompanied by my six-year-old son, Jeremy, whom I pulled out of school to meet one of my musical idols. Smokey Robinson was credited with writing hundreds of songs that were the soundtrack of my life and millions of other lives as well. Jeremy was a rock-and-roll baby, growing up, as I had, listening to "Shop Around," "Tracks of My Tears," "Mickey's Monkey," "My Guy" recorded by Mary Wells, "I'll be Doggone" and "Ain't That Peculiar" by Marvin Gaye, and perhaps Smokey's most famous song, "My Girl," for the Temptations. Smokey was Mr. Motown, a stunningly prolific, much-honored, and talented writer with an unmistak-able voice and surprisingly green eyes, which he said he inherited from his French grandmother.

He got his name, originally Smokey Joe, from his godfather who took him to see western movies and gave him that cowboy moniker. By age three, whenever anyone asked him his name, he never answered "William." He was Smokey Joe. Over time, the Joe disappeared. Smokey remained.

We were led up several floors to the top level of the venerable old the-ater. Smokey was sitting in a chair in a small room with one large window. Daylight was pouring into the room, so we did not have to set up our lights for the interview.

Smokey got up from his comfy chair to greet us. "Hi, I'm Smokey," he said, a man needing no introduction. "I'm sorry. I have a bit of a cold, and my voice is a little creaky."

Laddy and I introduced ourselves, thrilled to be in the same room with him, no matter how he sounded.

As Laddy started setting up his equipment, six-year-old Jeremy Blacklow stepped forward and reached out his little hand to Smokey and said, "It's nice to meet you, Mr. Robinson. I've been listening to your music my whole life. Mommy plays it all the time. I like it too."

Mr. Robinson smiled. We did a quick interview and let this superstar tend to his throat and get dressed for his performance.

When he came on stage an hour later, he spoke to the audience before he sang: "I have to apologize. I'm fighting a cold. It's affecting my voice. Please bear with me. I'll do the best I can."

While Laddy was out in the audience with his camera, Jeremy and I were privileged to watch Smokey sing from the wings of the stage, just thirty feet from him. I smile every time I remember that story. Jeremy, standing in front of me, my arms around him, looked up at me as Smokey entertained the crowd and said, "Mommy, this is great!"

I looked down at him with a very big smile, my hands on his small shoulders, and thought to myself, *I second that emotion.*

Chapter 27

Thank You, Johnny Rivers

ONE SUNNY DAY IN THE 1980S, Johnny Rivers, born John Henry Ramistella in New York City, made a stop in the foothills of the Cascade Mountains in Enumclaw, Washington, a town whose Salish Indian name translates to "a place of evil spirits." Enumclaw, formed from a volcanic mudflow six thousand years earlier, is the last town on the way to Mt. Rainier and the site of the annual King County Fair. I was sent there to produce a light feature on the display of quilts, canned peaches, and the yearly parade of farm animals that always looked bored, confused, and hot. Johnny Rivers, a pop singer from the 1960s, was booked as one of the human entertainers.

On the drive southeast from Seattle, Laddy Kite and I decided Johnny Rivers, rather than the produce displays and assorted farm animals, would be the centerpiece of our story. We met Mr. "Secret Agent Man," who had agreed earlier to do an interview with us. Towards the end of the interview, I asked Johnny to sing a few bars from one of his hits, his choice. He impolitely declined our request and was resolute in not singing for us. I had musician friends and understood that singers do not take kindly to being ordered to sing on command. But I reasoned we were there giving him free publicity and thought he should cooperate. He disagreed and was done with us, and we were done with him. So much for the farm animals, quilts, and famous fair scones. We left without a story.

This decision was not without consequence. The five o'clock news still had a three-minute slot with my name on it, and the producers were unaware we had abandoned our day at the fair. At that moment, we had nothing with which to replace it. I called the assignment desk, blaming the whole fiasco on Johnny Rivers but guaranteeing we would come up with some suitable feature story, though I had no idea what that might be. Laddy had always wanted to check out a little store in Enumclaw that advertised used vinyl records and Indian books. An odd combination, I thought, that warranted a visit.

"It's right at the end of this block. Do you want to go take a look?"

"Why not?" I said, having no other options and nervous about filling my time shot.

Ken MacRae's book business was in an old bank building, painted a washed-out green at the corner of Cole Street and Griffin Avenue. Once a repository of the old town's money and site of its financial services, it no longer served the area's monetary needs. Its currency was now traded in thousands of used records, a bounty of books about all aspects of Native American culture and history, and a secret not yet available to the public.

While Laddy wandered off to look at the vast collection of music and photography books, I walked over to Mr. MacRae. I needed to find out if we could create a story here and salvage our day after bailing on Johnny Rivers. If I thought Mr. Rivers was unwilling and uncooperative, Ken MacRae was unyielding in his resistance to talk about anything, on or off camera. I wanted to know how a bank became a bookstore, what brought him to the "town of evil spirits," and how he gathered his inventory of old records and books. Why set up shop in a bank? As far as Ken was concerned, I could ask anything I wanted, and he would refuse to answer. This guy was a tough sell, but I was desperate. He was intractable. As I continued politely badgering him, he dropped little hints that there was some hidden treasure out of our sight, a secret out of anyone's sight who wandered into MacRae's Indian Bookstore.

"All the stuff you see . . . this is nothing," he said. "It's just here to support my collection."

"Collection?" I said. "What collection?"

"The one you're not going to see . . . the one I never show anybody. The one I've spent decades and a lot of money assembling. It's downstairs."

That was all I needed to hear. No way was I leaving this place without seeing what was off limits to the rest of the world. I verbally pummeled him in the nicest way possible. I begged, pleaded, and flattered, and eventually Ken started to smile and surrender. Finally, after a thirty-minute struggle, he led us down steep, dark stairs into a long hallway to his hidden chambers of secrets.

"These are my vaults."

Three old bank vaults with heavy metal doors and complex locking mechanisms, each filled with an immense collection of priceless Indian artifacts. There were clothes, jewelry, and paintings—deerskin clothing and beaded pouches, moccasins and dresses—all museum quality. It was, in a word, astonishing.

At the end of the hallway was the biggest vault. As we entered it, we saw shelf after shelf of tableaus, intricately detailed three-dimensional scenes of Native American life, people as they once lived and were still living. Each depicted daily activities from different locations in North America. Scenes showing Northwest tribes included men fishing for salmon on the coastal rivers and in another women gathering shellfish from the ocean beaches. The tableaus were roughly twelve by eighteen inches in size. What was as impressive as the art was the fact that all the materials used to create each of these scenes were gathered from the locations they were illustrating. It was extraordinary.

"These are not old," Ken said. "They're being created today. It takes weeks to do each one, and only a couple of people are doing this. I buy all of them. You'll never see these anywhere else."

Except on the news, I thought to myself.

Now we understood why Ken MacRae needed a very secure building with impenetrable vaults. He had traveled up the West Coast from California looking for a safe place, an available bank building, which he finally found in the old town of Enumclaw, Washington. We felt honored and privileged to be allowed access to his secret world, but were on a deadline and still had to fill that slot for a feature on the five o'clock news. We were so excited to be able to share this story with our viewers, something never seen before. It also served as a reminder that detours often lead to wonderful and unexpected places.

Ken MacRae passed away in 2005, and the faded-green bank building no longer houses his records, books, and priceless art. I do not know where his collections traveled after his death, but I choose to imagine them still in pristine condition, amazing others, somewhere.

Thank you, Johnny Rivers.

Chapter 28

Bringing the Devil Home

UNTIL THE MORNING OF MAY 30, 1984, Seattle's Windermere neighborhood along the shores of Lake Washington was safe, elegant, expensive, and quiet. Just before noon that day, the calm was shattered along with the hopes, dreams, and happiness of a large, prominent family. When a housekeeper and member of the Gill family could not get into the house or awaken the mother and daughter who lived inside, they called a nearby resident for help. The neighbor climbed a ladder, looked inside, saw a bloody body on the floor, and called police.

The body of fifty-six-year-old Mary Colleen Gill, a mother of nine, was lying in a pool of blood. In another bedroom lay the corpse of her sixteen-year-old daughter, Katy, her eyes still open, her throat slit. Both mother and daughter were beaten around the head, strangled, and bruised. Mrs. Gill had been stabbed. A tool handle protruded from her right eye socket, a penknife shoved under her left eyelid. A knitting needle stuck out from the back of her neck. Her daughter suffered similar atrocities, a pencil and screwdriver were imbedded in her head. A knife protruded from her side, and the killer left a bite mark on her left breast, evidence that would, in time, help convict a sadistic killer. On the floor next to the bodies was a blood-spattered game of Clue.

According to Seattle police detectives, it was not an ordinary, run-of-the-mill murder, if any such crimes can be considered routine. Everything—the location, the victims, and the brutality—seemed uncommon. To veteran Seattle police detectives, it seemed intentional and methodical. Dresser drawers were pulled out, and clothes scattered around, as if made to look like a burglary, but there was no evidence of forced entry into the beautiful home or signs of anything stolen but the lives of a mother and daughter.

By 1984, I became good at reporting bad news stories. I had covered Ted Bundy, the Green River Killer, and too many child murders to count. It was inevitable that when the news broke of this particularly awful crime, I would be assigned to cover it. Crime scene tape was draped around the home in the previously quiet cul-de-sac where the Gills once lived. Police were everywhere, letting residents and family members in and keeping the media out. Veteran Seattle police homicide detective Sonny Davis could not say much, but with no evidence of a break-in, he was certain one of the victims knew the killer.

On the early news on May 30, all we could report were the names of the victims, some details about the murders, the fact that Colleen Gill's car was missing (although we didn't know if it had been stolen or just left somewhere by Colleen), and no one had yet been arrested. A dangerous and particularly vicious killer was on the loose somewhere in the Seattle area. The car was discovered the next day in a north Seattle parking lot, the keys still in the ignition. Someone had wiped the door handles clean, leaving no fingerprints.

Two days after the murders, the medical examiner determined that both victims died in the early morning hours of May 30. Neither was sexually molested, so police were able to rule out sexual assault as a motivation for the crime. The autopsy echoed what was obvious to police. Colleen Gill was repeatedly stabbed and cut with a knife. A knitting needle was pushed through her head, and a screwdriver pierced though her eye socket into her brain. Her blood alcohol level was twice the amount defined as intoxication. Katy Gill suffered similar horrors but was not intoxicated. I was, once again, stepping into the middle of a human nightmare and having to recount the facts of a family now destroyed. Once again I reinforced my invisible protective shield and steeled myself for whatever controversy might come my way. I reported what happened and kept most of the darkness at bay.

I began calling some of my contacts in the Seattle Police Department. One of my friends told me they were working on a lead, that Colleen Gill often frequented bars in Seattle's North End, one in particular, Shay's Bar. It was located on Aurora Avenue, a miles-long stretch of commercial businesses, fast food places, with one haphazard shopping mall after another. Shay's was easy to spot with its notable external décor of neon-green shamrocks. Two nights after the murders, a KING photographer and I headed there.

I went inside while the cameraman shot exteriors of the building. Holding a photo of Colleen Gill, which I brought along from a newspaper picture, I started talking to people in the bar. Though they did not know her name, several recognized her face and said they had seen her at Shay's on several occasions and saw her leave with a dark-haired young man the night she was murdered. One person remembered a woman matching Colleen Gill's description standing by the open passenger side of a silver Mustang, waiting for someone to get in. Others recalled both Gill and the dark-haired man seemed drunk.

Seattle detectives who had been to Shay's ahead of us learned quickly who they were looking for. The dark-haired man was identified by a bar employee as Brett Kendrick, and I learned that name from one of my cop friends. As the police began an intensive search for Kendrick, I went on the air that night with a picture of his face and his name and mentioned the possibility, which later proved to be true, that Colleen Gill picked up her killer at Shay's and brought him home. I expected the story would cause a storm and I was right.

By the end of the newscast, members of the Gill family were in the lobby of KING Television, arriving to scream at and wanting to kill me. I walked down to the lobby accompanied by then KING anchor Aaron Brown and the show's director. I understood their rage. We had just aired a story about the deaths of their mother and sister and implied with little subtlety that the mother brought the killer home. Most murder victims are either women in the wrong place at the wrong time or wives of abusive husbands and have little or no control over their deaths. This was different, crimes apparently committed as a result of dreadful judgment by one of the victims.

Twenty-two-year-old Brett Allen Kendrick should never have been at Shay's Bar that night or any other night. He should not have been working as a roofer north of Seattle or living with his girlfriend. Kendrick was a wanted man in Colorado on a parole violation after serving time for aggravated robbery when he took off for Seattle. He had a juvenile record of kidnapping, aggravated robbery, and aggravated assault. Police learned from one of his Seattle relatives that, on the night of the killings, Kendrick stayed at his girlfriend's house, told her to pack up his things, and told friends he planned to leave the state.

He never left. On June 5, less than a week after the Windermere murders, Kendrick was arrested on the Colorado fugitive warrant and booked into the King County Jail. He tried, unsuccessfully, to waive extradition to Colorado, hoping to get out of Seattle as quickly as possible. A search of one of Kendrick's residences in a nearby county turned up five hundred marijuana plants, which gave police and prosecutors enough reason to keep him in custody and enough time, police hoped, to do crime-lab testing searching for evidence linking him to the brutal murders. The bite mark on Katy Gill's left nipple and a pair of tennis shoes would be his undoing.

Armed with a court order, detectives were able to get bite-mark impressions from Kendrick, along with hair, blood, and fingernail samples. Crime scene investigators told police that a bloody shoe print found at the scene was left by a Jox tennis shoe. But there were no signs of bloody tennis shoes in any of the places where Kendrick lived. His girlfriend later told police she had been with him when he bought an identical pair after the murders were committed. The ones he wore the night of the murders were never found. To prosecutors and police, this was an obvious sign of a cover-up.

By mid-summer 1984, Kendrick was acquitted of the marijuana charge and about to be sent back to Colorado on a parole violation. Meanwhile, King County prosecutors charged Kendrick with murder, relying on hair and fiber evidence linking him to the Gill home and on the upcoming testimony of three respected forensic dentists who would testify that the bite mark on young Katy came from the Colorado fugitive.

On January 15, 1985, the trial began. Six men and six women were sworn in. The trial lasted for weeks. Almost two hundred pieces of evidence were submitted, and dozens of witnesses took the stand. The jury deliberated just three hours before reaching a verdict of guilty on two charges of first-degree murder.

"It was the worst." Those are the words of prosecutor William Downing, remembering the case now more than thirty years later. "The Gill homicides were the extreme . . . in terms of the burden it places on you for being intimately involved in a case. The gratuitous mutilations done to the bodies were something that I had never seen before . . . or thankfully have ever seen since. A routine shooting or a stabbing case, as awful as it is, is relatively sanitary compared to what happened here. Once you've seen the autopsy photographs—of implements, corkscrews piercing someone's head—you can't shake those images; they stick with you forever."

Downing showed me photographs of tattoos, pictures taken of Kendrick's arms. One shows a creature of some kind with a needle-like projection piercing a woman's head. The other, a needle going through a skull, both reflective, Downing said, of what Kendrick did to Colleen Gill and her daughter.

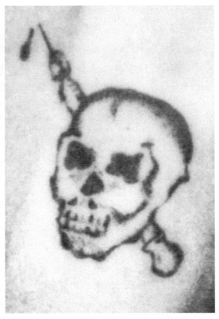

LEFT: A TATTOO FROM THE ARM OF KILLER BRETT KENDRICK, DEPICTING AN INSECT PENETRATING THE HEAD OF A WOMAN...MUCH LIKE THE WAY HE MURDERED COLLEEN GILL AND HER DAUGHTER. PHOTO PRESENTED AT TRIAL. RIGHT: A SECOND TATTOO ON THE ARM OF BRETT KENDRICK...A NEEDLE AND A SKULL.

"The depravity of man is a fact, and it's our job to toughen up and to deal with those facts so the consequences fall where they should. It's important that it's done. It has to be done, but it extracts a toll to those who are given the responsibility to do that." Downing added, "At your core, you are angry, but that emotion is counterproductive. As a professional you very carefully make sure that your emotions are not interfering with your responsibilities."

Downing took some satisfaction in the Kendrick case of just leveling the score. "You never really win. There is no sense of producing a net gain for society; you're just evening the slate." He said he used to hate it when colleagues would sometimes ask him, "How goes the battle?" "It was such a medieval phrase to me, and I was always resistant to that because it seemed like a militaristic sort of thing. I wanted to be able to do something more creative . . . to forge justice. That is how I wanted to think about the job we were doing."

Downing and his prosecution team did forge justice. From my perspective, though he might not agree, he did produce a net gain. He took a killer off the streets and, in some way, hopefully gave the victims' families and friends some peace knowing the crime was solved.

The man who should never have left Colorado or been at the bar that night was transferred from a Washington State prison years ago. As I write this in 2018, Brett Kendrick is in his mid-fifties. Under what is called the Interstate Compact, his whereabouts are known only to authorities, but he is in a prison somewhere in this country and has a projected release date of June 3, 2069.

Chapter 29

The Jumper

FEW STORIES WERE OFF LIMITS to journalists in Seattle, the twelfth largest television news market in the United States. By the late 1970s, NBC affiliate KING Television News held its dominant lead over both the ABC and CBS affiliates, but all three stations delivered solid newscasts and typically had the same stories in the first segment. It was only after the first commercial break that the content and quality of the newscasts changed. KING had a roomful of talented reporters and photographers who were unusually creative with impressive skills at making even the most inconsequential event worth watching. That ability of journalistic alchemy, to make something compelling out of nothing, was the result of managers who discovered one of the secrets of great management: Give your people freedom, let them create, and intervene and try to manage only when they fail to perform.

There was, however, one type of event we did not cover, suicides. It seems obvious why. Self-inflicted tragedies were seen as the private domain of the victims and their families, not the business of reporters and television stations. We also worried about the possibilities of copycat suicides, concerned that people in distress would mimic these tragedies as a way to become famous. Those sad types of events became newsworthy only if, somehow, they had an impact on the public. I remember one person died of a self-inflicted gunshot wound on Interstate 5, backing up traffic for many miles and many hours, an event that necessitated reporting it on the news.

On what must have been a very slow news day, there was police chatter on the newsroom radios about a man teetering on the rails of the Aurora Bridge, north of downtown, one of the most heavily traveled roads skirting the downtown area. Dozens of people called the station, mentioning the man on the bridge and police boats hovering under the bridge on Lake Union, looking up and apparently waiting for an obviously troubled man to come down. Police closed off both sides of the bridge to traffic, and drivers were blocked from crossing it.

SEATTLE'S AURORA BRIDGE...SCENE OF A THWARTED SUICIDE ATTEMPT.

Somewhat reluctantly, I followed orders to go see what was happening and got into one of the old, big blue news sedans with KING Newservice emblazoned on both sides. We headed north from the station towards the Aurora Bridge, bypassed confused and angry drivers, and were permitted to go past the police blockade. We parked on the south side of the bridge. My photographer stayed with the car as I hopped out and rushed over to the bridge railing. I looked down as the cops in their police patrol boats were looking up. Dozens of spectators were gathering along the bridge railing, unsure what was going on.

Curious myself, I looked at the man standing next to me and said, "Has he jumped yet?"

Pause.

"No," he said, "I haven't."

For one of the few occasions in my life, I was speechless.

I turned towards the cameraman still sitting in the news car, held up my left hand, attempting to cover my face, and pointed my finger towards the man. I mouthed the words "that's the guy!"

My cameraman attempted no such subtlety. He just yelled at me, "Well, grab him!"

I took a few steps toward the man who was trying to kill himself and talked with him until police showed up to take him to a psychiatric unit at Seattle's Harborview Medical Center.

The story of the man on the bridge never made our newscast, but the Seattle Police Department thought the story worthy of coverage in their monthly journal. For many years, every time I ran into cops, they came up to me and asked, "Has he jumped yet?"

"No," I'd say, "he hasn't."

Chapter 30

Final Exit

THE ONLY QUIET THING my second ex-husband ever did was die. He performed that uncharacteristically silent act in the early hours of a rainy Seattle morning in 2011.

Dramatic entrances and exits defined Ted D'Arms's life. He was an accomplished actor who thrilled audiences every time he came on stage. After our divorce, we remained close. And my dear friend, Ted, bestowed on me the questionable privilege of putting his dead body in a bag and struggling to load it into a cramped elevator.

I SAW MY FUTURE HUSBAND in 1964 at the age of sixteen, when my mother took me to the Arena Stage in Washington, DC, to see the play *Billy Budd*. The cast included an impressive roster of actors, many who later became quite famous: Ronny Cox, Rene Auberjonois, Ned Beatty, and Robert Prosky. One other name in the Playbill caught my eye, Ted D'Arms, a big man in every way it is possible to be big, in talent, personality, voice, and stature.

Ten years later, we both migrated to Seattle. He wanted to get as far away as possible from his disapproving and tyrannical father, who rarely bothered to watch him perform and felt any career outside academia was an embarrassment to the family. His father was chairman of the Classics Department at Princeton, and his brother, dean of the Graduate School at the University of Michigan, in addition to dozens of other academic accomplishments. Ted was the errant child, no matter his decades of artistic successes on Broadway and in regional East Coast theatres. I was in Seattle with my husband at the time who, like Ted, wanted to get as far away as possible from an overbearing parent, his mother.

Ted arrived in Seattle in the late Sixties, and I, in the early Seventies. It was on a stage I saw him again, performing this time for the Seattle Repertory Theatre, a renowned regional company, which Ted joined as a regular cast member. I remembered his quirky name from seeing it a decade earlier, and I was mesmerized by the man on the boards. Anytime Ted D'Arms was in a play, I went to see it. Though I wanted to, I could never summon the nerve to go meet him. I was married, the mother of a young child, and more than a little worried that if I met him, touched him, or spoke with him, I would fall in love with him.

By the mid-Eighties, I was divorced from Richard Blacklow and deep into my career at KING Television when Ted D'Arms swaggered into the newsroom to meet with his friend, the station's arts and entertainment critic, Greg Palmer. All six foot three inches of him with his mane of silver hair headed downstairs, and I suddenly felt an urgent need to visit Greg as well. Ted stood up, reached out his hand to shake mine, and everything I feared might happen, happened. I fell in love in an instant.

Greg grabbed a camera and documented that moment. I had just been given two tickets to the upcoming Washington State Fair and asked Ted if he would like to go. That is how we began, the genesis of a crazy thirty-year friendship and marriage, a pairing of belligerents who fought as much as they loved. Two people, each capable of sucking all the oxygen out of a room, now together. It was both magic and catastrophic.

THE DAY I MET TED D'ARMS, 1984.

TED D'ARMS IN THE GARDEN OUTSIDE OUR SEATTLE HOME.
BIG AND BURLY WITH ONE OF THE BEST HEADS OF HAIR IN SEATTLE. *MARY RANDLETT*

Ted was impossible to miss with his deep, booming voice and powerful physical stature. He was a man who took big bites out of life, literally. He was the only person I ever saw finish a twenty-four-ounce porterhouse steak at Smith & Wollensky in New York City, along with a side of mushrooms, spinach, and an obscene slice of cheesecake to finish off the meal. It was, again, a noteworthy performance, which drew stares and applause from other diners. Those trips to New York are among my happiest memories of our time together; hundreds of hours at the Met, at MOMA, at the Whitney and the Guggenheim, devouring the paintings of the abstract expressionists with the same gusto as he consumed that gigantic steak. Ted's appetite for music was equally voracious with his collection of thousands of CDs, from Bach to Bluegrass, from Stravinsky to the Allman Brothers Band. He loathed Beethoven, though he could never convincingly explain why. He also hated pineapple. Every other type of food and every other kind of music sated and delighted him.

He consumed literature the way many of us wish we did, reading the books we often lie about reading, everything from Homer to Heller, from esoterica to erotica. He had the impressive ability to simultaneously read a range of complex works. Dozens of dog-eared books with pieces of paper stuck inside were strewn everywhere, in his bedroom, bathroom, office, and studio. Nothing was as precious to him as his collection of art books. Their titles numbered in the hundreds, all of the great masters of abstract expressionism—Franz Kline, Jackson Pollock, Willem de Kooning, Joan Mitchell, and Helen Frankenthaler—alongside books of all of the great American and European landscape painters, big, beautiful books that others might use as décor on a coffee table. To Ted, they were inspiration, not ornamentation.

His love of painters led him from his work as an actor to a more reclusive life to try painting and continue his work as a photographer. His portraits of actors are legendary, and his photographs of flowers, trees, and the natural beauty of the Pacific Northwest stand up to the best of them.

Julie Blacklow

A PUBLICITY SHOT FROM TED.
THE ONLY PHOTO TAKEN OF ME THAT I'VE EVER LIKED, 1986.

A landscape photo by Ted. 1975.

Our relationship worked best when we lived ten miles apart. Once we married and moved in together, there was often not enough space for our egos and pathological need to be right. Divorced, we remained good friends until his death at the age of seventy-four. Even with diabetes, he ate too much and exercised too little. He was the reincarnation of Shakespeare's Sir

John Falstaff . . . robust, good-natured, witty, bawdy, and the only person I ever saw stop a play.

I had given two tickets to a friend and his wife who were sitting in the front row. During the first act, Ted heard her popping her gum, stepped out of character, went to the edge of the stage, and asked her to stop chewing. She did. He picked up where he left off and went on with the play.

A PUBLICITY SHOT OF TED. HE WAS MY FALSTAFF.

On the day he left this world, his caretaker called and asked me to find a funeral home to come retrieve Ted's body. They sent over a tiny woman with very big hair who needed help moving him from the hospital bed in his apartment and into a body bag. Since she was going to be of no use lifting him, I called our dear and aptly named friend, Jolly, to help with this task. When he arrived, we looked at one another and broke into fits of inappropriate laughter, knowing that Ted would be laughing with us at the absurdity of the moment. Dead and cold, we could still feel him with us.

We removed the blanket covering his naked body and with some difficulty hoisted him onto the shaky metal table. In life, Ted was a very large man, but in death, as with most people, he seemed shrunken and withered as we zipped what remained of him into the body bag. We rolled him down the hall and had to tilt the gurney into an almost upright position to squeeze him into the elevator. Think Hannibal Lecter propped up, being wheeled in to meet the mother of a kidnap victim. After several wobbly attempts, we jammed Ted into the elevator, rolled him out the front door and into the funeral home van, and off he went, making his final exit.

Had he been directing this scene instead of starring in it, I think he might have asked for another take, suggesting the actors be a bit more serious, given the circumstances. On reflection, though, maybe not.

PAPA ISAAC'S CHERISHED SAMOVAR WHICH MADE THE TRIP TO AMERICA WITH HIM.

BUBBA FANNY'S TREASURED CHINA, BROUGHT FROM RUSSIA TO AMERICA.

Julie and Dulcie in Copenhagen...Summer of 1969.

Off skis and upright with Richard in Vermont.

The KING 5 bobblehead microphone. Dressed in an ermine robe and wearing his crown.

Gordon Vickery sitting in a mini version of a Medic One truck, created to help him celebrate the beginning of Medic One.

In the KING 5 Newsroom, 1976. Very pregnant, but still agile enough to trespass on John Ehrlichman's property.

A copy of Chuck Berry's "My Ding a Ling."

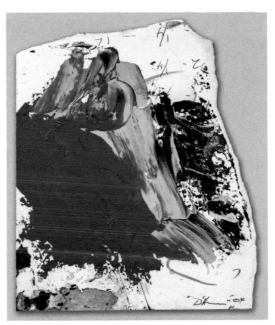

One of Ted's abstract paintings, 2004.
He tossed it away in his studio. I picked it up off the floor.

Another of Ted's bold abstracts, 1998.

COVER OF BUD KROGH'S BOOK:
"THE DAY ELVIS MET NIXON." *FAMILY OF EGIL KROGH*

THE WATERGATE CAKE.

JZ KNIGHT IN HER HOME IN YELM, WASHINGTON
WITH HER FRENCH BULLDOG. 2018.

LOVE ISRAEL AND ME.

PARTNERS. 2019. *Carrie Crawford*

THE RANCH...TO ME THE MOST BEAUTIFUL PLACE ON EARTH.

Chapter 31

A Christmas Story

I F YOU WERE JEWISH, you worked on Christmas Day. It was a nice gift for your Christian colleagues, and you earned double pay. Both good. There were very few Jews at KING Television, but I was one of them, and on Wednesday, December 25, 1984, I went to work.

It had been a relatively quiet month in local news. The only story of some interest was that the band Heart, from Seattle, saw its album go to number one on the billboard charts. In national news, the Dow Jones average peaked over 1,500 for the first time, Phoenix got three inches of snow, and Congress managed to balance the national budget without shutting down the government. Great local news stories on Christmas were few and far between.

On that Christmas Day in 1984 we got a rare gift. A large four-legged creature escaped from a back yard in a Seattle residential neighborhood, a present for a young girl, far too big to wrap or put under a tree. By the time we arrived in the Montlake area near the University of Washington, we drove slowly, looking for the address when something caught our attention. It was a horse running across a street in front of us, a full-size, brown, furry horse darting from one house to another, a big red ribbon tied around its neck.

The man whose well-intended idea was to give his little girl an unforgettable Christmas present was frantically scouring the neighborhood hoping to catch it. We got out our camera and joined the search for the runaway gift hoping desperately to get video. While we were all trying to find the escapee, a beige Seattle Animal Control truck with an officer inside arrived and started his own search. On the side of the truck, in big, brown letters was "Uncle Al, the Puppy's Pal."

All of us scattered in different directions, sometimes crossing paths and sharing information:

"Did you see it?"

"I saw him down the street!"

"I saw him in the alley."

About an hour later, we saw Dad leading his dejected looking Christmas present, the ribbon still on, his moment of freedom passed. Uncle Al, meanwhile, sat in his truck and watched the sad-looking present walk toward him. Uncle Al knew there was no way this thousand-pound animal was going to fit into his truck with compartments designed for transporting cats and dogs and other smaller creatures.

What would Uncle Al do? Would the horse be hauled away? Would the child not get her Christmas present? Would Dad be detained?

In the true spirit of Christmas, Uncle Al decided just to inform the generous dad that horses are not allowed in residential neighborhoods, even on Christmas morning. Dad got a friendly warning, the young girl got her present, and we got a great story with a happy ending. Christmas stories never got better than that.

But they did get worse.

Chapter 32

Another Christmas Story

"I would like to tell you the facts that bring us together in this courtroom this week. Up until a few short months ago, the family of Annie and Charles Goldmark had a wonderful home overlooking Lake Washington. The house is still there, but the family has been destroyed. That home was invaded by an army of one and the family was sacrificed to the desires of that one . . . to his need for action, cash and a target for unfocused anger."

—Opening statement at trial from
Prosecutor William Downing,
May 27, 1986, 9:30 a.m.

ON CHRISTMAS DAY 1985, I was sent to Seattle's Children's Hospital to cover the annual "giving of the toys" to young patients from the beloved and philanthropic Phil Smart, owner of a Mercedes empire, a man as generous as he was wealthy. We never had a chance to see Phil Smart or the smiles of the eager, young patients that day. I got an urgent call from the KING newsroom to go immediately to a typically quiet Seattle neighborhood perched above the shores of Lake Washington, tree-lined streets with beautiful homes and immaculate landscaping. On that day, the calm was shattered. Yellow crime scene tape was draped around one house with Seattle police cars parked in the streets.

My longtime friend, homicide detective Sonny Davis, saw me. "Julie . . . you'd better sit down in my car for a minute . . . this is the worst thing I've ever encountered. I've never seen so much blood, and I think you might know the people who lived here."

Lived here, I thought to myself. What is Sonny talking about?

On Christmas Eve day, Charles and Annie Goldmark were getting ready to host a dinner party for close family and friends. They planned to open presents the next morning under a Christmas tree that reached all the way to the high ceiling in their home. The stockings were hung by the hearth. Before the party, Charles Goldmark went to the nearby home of some friends to pick up the Christmas present he had bought for his wife, a new bicycle.

David Lewis Rice had his own Christmas list . . . in his own handwriting. Among the items:

BASIC ARMAMENT FOR ONE
MAN MISSION (DOES NOT INCLUDE
SPECIALIZED WEAPONS)

KNIFE
ROPE (50 FT.)
GRAPPLING HOOK W/ 25 FT. ROPE
SILENCED .22 AUTO
.38 OR .357 REVOLVER
4 FRAGS.
2 INCENDIARIES
2 PAIRS HANDCUFFS
ETHER
GLOVES - 3 PR.
BLACK UTILITIES & BOOTS
BLACK TENNIS SHOES
BLACK JACK
GARROTT
4 SMOKE BOMBS
5 H.E. CHARGES (2 LBS. EACH) W/ 5 MIN. FUSES
2 TEAR GAS GRENADES
LC-1 PACK & HARNESS

DAVID LEWIS RICE'S LIST OF ARMAMENTS FOR HIS
MURDEROUS MISSION TO KILL PEOPLE.

In all, he had twenty-eight items and his bizarre statements:

1. *I must be mobile & fluid, so that, if I am attacked, I can retreat or counter-attack, whichever I deem suitable.*
2. *I must have the ability to attack any target, regardless of size . . .*
3. *My targets must be chosen by the weapons available (I certainly wouldn't take on Ft. Lewis with only a knife.)*
4. *I must have a place that I can go to, [ocasionally] to relax and to {recouperate.} Such a place should have a space of at least 500 yds between the living area & the nearest possible attacking position.*

RICE'S NOTES TO HIMSELF ABOUT HOW HE SHOULD ACT DURING AT ATTACK.

Guests started arriving at the Goldmark home a little after 7:00 p.m. on Christmas Eve. It was dark inside the house, and no one answered the door. The guests left, went back to their homes, and tried calling the house, but no one answered the phone. Neighbors returned and entered the Goldmark home using a spare a key they had, but nothing could have prepared them for what they saw at the top of the stairs.

From official documents:

> There were their friends, Annie, Charles, Derek and Colin
> Goldmark, all lying on the floor of the bedroom, their
> heads soaking in their own blood. Charles and Annie had
> their wrists handcuffed behind their backs where they lay
> on the floor. Annie appeared to be nude at the time. Only
> Chuck was able to speak at all, and all he could say was:
> "Cold, cold," and "It hurts."

Firemen and police officers arrived and tried to do their jobs, beginning futile attempts to save the lives of the three "males who had their skulls
fractured and their heads stabbed and the one female who had been stabbed
in her chest and neck." While the medics worked, the police looked for evidence and quickly found some of the weapons used in the attacks, a bloody
steam iron used to bludgeon the victims' heads and a bloody fillet knife used
to stab them. The Goldmark family never saw Christmas Day 1985.

From official documents:

> Annie Goldmark was pronounced dead at the scene that
> night. Four days later, her youngest son, ten-year old Colin,
> died. Two weeks after that Charles Goldmark died. Three
> weeks later twelve-year old Derek also succumbed. In the
> case of all four, death came without anyone regaining con-
> sciousness and as a direct result of the injuries inflicted on
> them in their own home on Christmas Eve.

Why this family?

On December 26, Seattle police got a call from a man saying he believed
an overnight guest in his apartment was involved in the Goldmark murders.
Robert Brown had opened his guest's notebook, without the knowledge of
his guest, and read a letter saying: "To whom it may concern, I am the person you are looking for in the Goldmark case."

It deeply concerned police and prosecutors. Brown told police the
guest's name was David Rice. While waiting for detectives to arrive to talk
to Brown, police saw a man matching Rice's description come down the

apartment stairs and head towards the street. David Rice turned and ran. A few blocks later, he stopped running and was arrested. A detective showed Rice the letter Brown had given to them, and Rice admitted he had written it. This is what he wrote.

> *To whom it may concern, I am the person you are looking for in the Goldmark case. I know that what I did was a very terrible thing. That is why I am as you see me now. I want it perfectly understood that no one else had anything whatsoever to do with what I did. I went to great lengths to make sure of that. . . . I did not use the rifle that I purchased a few weeks ago, instead, I fooled them with a toy pistol which you will find in the storage locker. . . .Again, I want it understood that no one knew anything about this, so please do not cause any unnecessary suffering to innocent people. I think that I've already done enough. I guess I should tell you why I did what I did. That way, you won't have to ask other people about it. My life is a mess.*

David Lewis Rice was deep in debt with no place to turn. And according to prosecutor's notes: "Rice wanted to have some action in his life, action of a violent nature. He had long been fascinated with weapons . . . explosives . . . and talked of killing communists."

He had seen the Goldmark name in a book, which referred to an accusation of Communism in the 1930s involving Charles Goldmark's parents. That was enough for Rice to search out his targets on Christmas Eve. Anyone named Goldmark must be a Communist.

In a subsequent confession, Rice told of his meticulous preparations for the murders. He had been planning to kill Charles and Annie Goldmark for six months. He did not intend to kill the children and said if he had known they were there, he would not have gone to the house on Christmas Eve.

David Lewis Rice was charged with four counts of aggravated first-degree murder, and the prosecutor gave notice that he would be seeking the death penalty. Rice entered the general plea of not guilty, as well as a plea of not guilty by reason of insanity.

As is typical in a death penalty case and one of such magnitude and shock, there were trials and appeals and countless professional witnesses for both prosecutors and defense lawyers. To add another level of grotesqueness to the whole spectacle, David Rice conducted an unprecedented series of jailhouse interviews, inviting in one reporter after another to speak with him. I was one of them. I was always fascinated by what makes people do what they do, whether acts of great kindness or unspeakable evil.

I waited in a gloomy, little room inside the King County Courthouse. The camera sat on a tripod, the lights set in place. A door opened, and the devil himself walked into the room. If any human ever exuded malevolence, it was David Lewis Rice. His hair and beard were black, as were his dark, dead eyes. He looked the part. He acted the part. And he was standing just feet away from me, a confessed killer of an entire family including two little boys. By the time I met this murderer, I had faced dozens of serial killers, murderers, rapists, and child molesters. I was often surprised at how insipid most criminals looked, as if they could be your neighbor or relative. This monster was different. He looked unlike any human I had even seen. He terrified me.

His dark, soulless countenance was palpable, oozing out of him like a menacing, putrid cloud of smoke, which, if inhaled, would poison me. When he stared at me, I felt sick to my stomach. He was ready to talk, but I was not ready to listen. Over many years covering the worst of humanity, I always relied on that interior shield I had constructed to protect myself from all the darkness I encountered. But in this seedy, little room, just a few feet away from this evil creature, my armor cracked. All I knew was that I had to get out of the room quickly. My ability to separate myself from a criminal's actions crumbled.

I turned to the cameraman I was with and told him to pack up our equipment, that we were not going to do the interview and that I would explain to the managers at KING that we could not put this murderer on television. Other stations and other newspapers would talk to him and show his evil face, but I could not do it. It was the only time I ever ran away from a story. Maybe it was the cold-blooded, calculated nature of the crimes, or perhaps it was the little boys who were murdered. Maybe it was the slaughter on Christmas Eve. Or all of that.

David Lewis Rice was convicted in 1986 of four counts of aggravated murder in the deaths of the Goldmark family and was, himself, sentenced to death. The case dragged on for twelve years when, in 1998, Rice pleaded guilty to the crimes in exchange for avoiding the death penalty. He is serving life without parole at the Coyote Ridge Corrections Center in Connell, Washington.

He once said, "Believe it or not, I really hold human life as a precious thing."

Chapter 33

Exile/Resurrection

It's a law that every challenge, fear or loss you encounter,
bears gifts far more valuable than the price of the trouble they
cause. . . . And . . . no loss ever goes unsettled in the long run.
—MIKE DOOLEY'S 'NOTES FROM THE UNIVERSE' TUT.COM

HOW DO YOU WRITE ABOUT the worst day of your life? Worse than being raped. Worse than having a three-pound tumor that gutted your belly and took a year of your life. Worse than losing your parents. Worse than cancer. Where are the words to describe an event you never saw coming, like a car crash, hurricane, or heart attack? A cataclysmic shock that would tear your life apart. A day when people you trusted betrayed you. A calculated and vengeful act that would steal your job, destroy your reputation, and turn you into a drug addict. It was a crisis that created a dark, fetid pile of rage that festered inside me and hurt so badly I wanted to kill myself. Death would have been a relief, but this was worse than death. I lived. The worst day. Ever.

IT WAS MONDAY, APRIL 21, 1986. I was finishing a story about Spider-Man visiting a Seattle elementary school when news director Don Varyu walked over to my desk in the back corner of the old, musty KING newsroom, a sprawling expanse of metal, gray-green desks, covered with file folders, newspaper clippings, ashtrays, and typewriters. There were no computers. I was typing on an IBM selectric.

"Hey, Julie, when you're finished with your story, could you come to my office, please?"

When a news director or any boss asks to see you alone, it is almost never good news. I heard a sense of urgency and nervousness in his voice, finished my story, and walked across the newsroom to his office. I had a strong sense of foreboding and imagined the undertoad was coming back to pull me under the water and drown me.

"We need to go up to Sturges's office," Varyu said.

Sturges Dorrance was the general manager of KING Broadcasting, and now I had no doubt I was going to drown.

The chaos leading to that day began six months earlier, on October 24, 1985. A ten-year-old child was kidnapped from her Bellingham home and held for ransom for almost a week by work-release inmate and convicted murderer James Vincent Miller. All the local stations knew of the kidnapping and were aware multiple police agencies were involved. At the request of the FBI, we agreed not to air anything about this for the time being. It was only on the final day of the child's captivity, on October 30, that increased chatter on our police scanners indicated something big was happening. We did not know exactly what it was other than a police chase underway. Assignment editor Bill Baker called the FBI to find out more and asked pointedly what areas we should avoid. Baker was told to keep all news crews off Interstate 5, along the entire corridor from Bellingham to Olympia, a one-hundred-fifty-mile stretch, an unreasonable request. At any given time, we had as many as a dozen crews driving on I-5 covering different news stories, including sports and weather. For the kidnapping story, KING and other local stations sent teams both north and south on the interstate. Though most of the action was thought to be south of Seattle near Olympia, Baker sent photographer Mark Anderson and me north towards Bellingham.

"I just want you to go, just go . . . go . . . go!" he said.

He rushed us out the door with no specific information as to what was going on or what we should do. He gave us some radio frequencies, including an FBI channel, and told us to listen to the scanner as we drove. We heard nothing. We were still clueless as to what we were doing. We talked about our kids, the challenge of finding good day care and babysitters. We expected to be called back to the station because nothing was happening in our direction. Then we started hearing some unintelligible static and the words "Rabbit" and "Charlie" but no entire sentences and no context for any of this.

Then this came over the radio: "Two twelve. Exit 212."

That was the exit we were approaching. We got off the freeway and headed west, looking around for anything unusual, any police activity, something that might catch our eye. We turned right, then left, and spotted a large silver van with two men inside. We drove down the road, turned our news car around, and pulled up next to the van with an antenna on top and a government license plate on the back. I rolled down my window and asked, " Are you police officers?"

"No," they said. "Who are you?"

I identified myself and said, "Why don't I believe you?"

I knew these men were law enforcement officers, and I knew they were lying. They abruptly rolled up their window.

We pulled away, and within minutes, we heard on our radio scanner: "There is a KING-TV crew here. Get them out!"

We left the area on our own, headed south back to Seattle, confused. We were trying to do our job but were unable to learn anything. Typically, in a crisis situation, police set up command centers which accomplishes two things. First, the police can direct the press to a location of their choosing, which keeps the media out of sensitive areas. And second, the media have a place to go for updated information so they can report to the public. That is how things are supposed to work. On October 30, 1985, that did not happen.

By the time we returned to KING, it was almost dark. We never took our camera out of the car or shot a single frame of videotape. We encountered a couple of lying law enforcement officers. That was the extent of our efforts.

The young kidnap victim was released later that day at an Olympia, Washington hospital after being held for six days. The kidnapper freed her after a ransom of $250,000 was paid. The following day, October 31, police traced the kidnapper to an address near Olympia, based on a license plate spotted when the ransom was picked up. As police searched the home, James Miller approached the house, spotted police, and took off with police chasing him. After crashing his car into a fence, he ran, firing two shots at police who then shot him with a machine gun. The coroner later said it appeared that Miller killed himself with a shot to his head to avoid capture. The official cause of death never was established. The ransom money was found in his house.

The kidnapping of the young girl, whose picture he spotted in a bank where the child's father worked, was not the first crime committed by James Miller. He was a convicted murderer, in Washington State prisons since 1962 and sentenced to three consecutive life terms for setting a fire that killed his three children and almost killed his wife, who had refused to give him a divorce. Though he was not yet eligible for parole, Miller was put on work release in 1978 by mistake due to a mix-up in the prison system. He went to work for his wife's company as a rehabilitation counselor and was still on work release when he abducted the young victim.

In any case, he was free to wreak havoc again, setting in motion a series of calamitous events that outraged a community, tarnished KING Television's reputation, and almost destroyed me.

On November 1, 1985, the day after James Miller either was killed by police or committed suicide, Bellingham Police chief Terry Mangan went into a rage, accusing KING Television of "blatant and repeated interference in the investigation." He called our actions "reprehensible." Initially, KING News director Don Varyu threw Mangan's words back in his face, saying Mangan's own remarks were what was reprehensible. Varyu rejected Mangan's attacks saying we did nothing but cover the news and if there was any failure it rested on the police who failed to set up a command post. But the verbal attacks intensified, including criticism from the Whatcom County prosecutor, who agreed we crossed the line. The barrage of criticism went on for more than a week. Besides being accused of endangering the life of a child, police claimed we had flown our helicopter over one of the crime scenes, though at that time our chopper was in the shop for scheduled maintenance.

Mangan did not let up, fueling public opinion, resulting in newspaper coverage criticizing KING's actions. Station management, figuring they had to do something to quiet the growing outrage, decided to hold a press conference in Bellingham. On November 8, 1985, a week after the child was released, news director Don Varyu rode up to Bellingham with station manager Sturges Dorrance in his old Peugeot.

Varyu remembers they did not talk much on the trip north. Varyu told his own bosses at KING he thought this press conference was a "seriously flawed idea" and thought to himself, *How dare you mess with my newsroom.* He said, "Sturges knew how I felt. I told all of them I thought this was a very bad thing to do."

But Varyu was pressured to go to Bellingham where Sturges Dorrance said, "KING-TV is "deeply sorry it had unwittingly interfered" in the Bellingham police operation. KING reporters had intruded on the police investigation. "We didn't mean to be there, but we were."

D2 Seattle Post-Intelligencer Saturday November 9 1985

KING admits erring in kidnap case

By Alice Noble
P-I Reporter

BELLINGHAM — Executives of KING-TV yesterday admitted the Seattle station's news crews made a couple of big mistakes in covering the kidnapping of a 10-year-old Bellingham girl.

Station Manager Sturges Dorrance told a news conference that the station is "deeply sorry" it had unwittingly interfered in critical police activities surrounding the

Among other developments yesterday, Bellingham Police Chief Terry Mangan said his department has effectively closed its investigation into the kidnapping.

Meanwhile, Attorney General Ken Eikenberry announced his office is beginning its own investigation into whether kidnap suspect James V. Miller, 61, or his relatives had violated the state's prison work release program.

observed picking up the ransom. KING News Director Don Varyu said the news crews unwittingly intruded upon the operation and had no intention of jeopardizing either police activities or the victim's safety.

His comments were an about-face from last week, when Varyu said, "We find it reprehensible the comments made by the Belling-ham police chief that King 5 News in any way threatened or obstruct-

could have been mistaken for a police vehicle, pulled up next to a police surveillance van that was watching the girl's father in the middle of the ransom run.

A woman in the van began asking questions, the police documents said. When she received no answers, she "made the statement that she would just sit right alongside us until she did find out what we were doing." However, the van did leave a short time

al because it covered a large geographic area from Bellingham to the drop site near Fort Lewis and because police were not giving out information about the operation.

"I know for a fact our people felt uncomfortable working in the field not knowing what was going on," Varyu said.

Dorrance, in a later telephone interview, also confirmed the station had erred in including several

ARTICLE FROM THE SEATTLE POST-INTELLIGENCER, NOVEMBER 1985 WHERE KING MANAGEMENT ADMITS ERRING IN THE BELLINGHAM KIDNAP CASE.

With those words, KING Broadcasting capitulated, surrendered, and apologized for doing its job. Reporters, photographers, editors, and news managers back at the station watched this pathetic display with disgust, shock, and anger. Those who should have had our backs chose instead to betray us. They sold us out, groveled, and tried to appease law enforcement in a gratuitous public display. It was a watershed event in the history of a station that built its reputation on truth-telling, honest investigation, and fair reporting. It was a moment that, in many minds, changed the way KING Television News was perceived and subsequently treated.

Many times, as we covered other stories, we were accosted by people furious that we had endangered the life of a child and enraged that we had disregarded the consequences of our actions. That was not who we were, but by bowing to the pressures of a reckless police chief, KING management created that impression. The attacks continued for months. If KING management believed its capitulation would calm things down, they were mistaken. It only made things worse.

The apology did more than sully the reputation of the newsroom. It also opened up KING to a lawsuit from the family of the kidnap victim. They sued the station for what is called a "tort of outrage," claiming that the actions of KING's employees jeopardized the safety of their daughter. The suit was settled for an undisclosed amount of money, but the legal process ignited a tedious round of depositions for anyone who had anything to do with the story. Inquisitions that were depressing, disheartening, and for me, disastrous.

"SIT DOWN," Sturges said.

I took a seat in his small, dark office on April 21, 1986, some six months after the kidnapping debacle. News director Don Varyu sat down next to me.

"We have some things we need to go over concerning your depositions," Sturges said.

"What kinds of things?" I asked.

He rambled on about discrepancies in statements I had given months earlier. Both men shoved papers in front of me. They seemed nervous and edgy.

"Here," said Dorrance. "See this . . . and now look at this."

They accused me of changing my story. Of lying. I had no idea what they were talking about and failed to see any discrepancies. I said I told the truth every time I was asked about my role in covering the story. We saw nothing except two lying policemen, interviewed no one, and had less involvement than any other crew assigned to cover the story that day.

Minutes later, Sturges said, "I'm sorry, but we're letting you go."

"Letting me go? What are you talking about?"

"You're fired. We really have no choice here. We have to let you go. Please go back to the newsroom, gather up your things, and leave."

Dorrance said I was fired because of false statements in my depositions. I asked him for copies of the transcripts, but he refused to give them to me. He handed me a final paycheck dated and signed on April 18, three days earlier.

I was devastated and almost unable to speak but for one last comment. I stood up, my heart pounding, my body reeling. Looking back at the two men before heading out the door, I glared at them and said, "You have seriously fucked with the wrong person!"

I staggered back to the newsroom alone and told my colleagues what had happened to me. I wept and asked someone to find a cardboard box so I could pack my notebooks and pictures. My friends were almost as stunned as I was. A couple of them stormed up to Sturges Dorrance's office to confront him and Don Varyu. I am certain they demanded answers and just as certain they did not get them. I called my parents. It was the first night of Passover and, as usual, my mother had prepared a feast for my friends and me. Her first thought was to cancel the Seder dinner, but I insisted we go ahead with this ancient ritual.

More than a dozen relatives and friends feasted on my mother's matzoh ball soup, gefilte fish, brisket, and lemon chicken. Her flour-free brownies were legendary. It all seemed so normal. My body was at the dinner table but my mind was elsewhere. We read through the Haggadah, the story of the banishment of the Jews from the Promised Land by an evil pharaoh, forced into the desert for forty years to suffer in exile, hoping and praying they might return some day. It echoed my story.

As I tried to get through the Seder dinner without collapsing, news director Don Varyu was presiding over a hastily called meeting of the confused and furious newsroom staff. He said, "The News Department did not fire her." His words did nothing to calm things down.

Firings for kidnap coverage stunKING newsroom

by Ross Anderson
Times staff reporter

When veteran TV reporter Julie Blacklow...

Bellingham officials publicly accused KING of 'blatant and repeated interference in the investigation.' KING first rejected those charges, then publicly apologized.

After almost fifteen years of hard, award-winning work, building a good reputation, and earning the trust of the public I felt privileged to serve, it was all stripped away. I was branded a liar and accused of endangering the life of a child. My job, my good name, my ability to support myself and my child were gone. Wiped away in an instant.

Ten-year-old Jeremy and I headed home from the Seder. He knew what had happened but could not comprehend or absorb what it meant for us. Neither could I. I tucked him into bed and I collapsed. He woke me up the next morning, reminding me I needed to get dressed for work, that we were running late. But there was no work to go to. In a daze, I packed his lunch, he walked to school, and I went back to bed with a throbbing headache and the sickening realization I no longer had a job.

The phone rang. It was Hal Green, the lawyer for my union, AFTRA, the American Federation of Television and Radio Artists. Hal, from the Seattle law firm of MacDonald, Hoague and Bayless, had just gotten off the phone with the executive director of the local AFTRA office, the spunky, indomitable Mathis Dunn. Both had heard I was fired and knew from the moment it happened a clock began ticking for the union to file a grievance on my behalf. Contrary to the station's belief that they had every right to fire me, Hal Green and Mathis Dunn begged to differ. They believed none of the procedures for termination as delineated in the union contract had been followed, and they did not think the reasons for my firing were credible.

"Julie," Hal said, "we have a deadline in which to notify KING of our intent to grieve your firing."

"Oh God, Hal . . . I can't go through this. I don't want to deal with this."

My outrage in the moment they fired me vanished days later. Now I just felt weak and terrified.

"We'll deal with it for you . . . that's what unions are for," Hal said. "We'll take care of this. You just have to agree to let us do it."

On April 29, 1986, a little over a week after my firing, Hal crafted a letter on AFTRA stationary giving notice to KING Broadcasting that a fight was underway:

Dear Mr. Varyu:

Pursuant to Article IV of our Agreement, Julie Blacklow and the Seattle Local of AFTRA believe a question has arisen concerning whether Julie Blacklow was discharged from her employment with KING-TV without due process and without just cause.

*Please consider this letter as the initiation of a grievance as
a first step of the contractual procedure and a request for a
meeting at your convenience.*

Signed,
Mathis L. Dunn, Jr.
Executive Secretary

AFTRA   SEATTLE LOCAL

American Federation of Television and Radio Artists
Affiliated with AFL-CIO

April 29, 1986

Mr. Don Varyu
News Director
KING-TV
333 Dexter Ave. N.
Seattle, WA 98109

Dear Mr. Varyu,

Pursuant to Article IV of our Agreement, Julie Blacklow and the
Seattle Local of AFTRA believe a question has arisen concerning
whether Julie Blacklow was discharged from her employment with
KING-TV without due process and without just cause.

Please consider this letter as the initiation of a grievance at
the first step of the contractual procedure and a request for
a meeting at your convenience.

Sincerely,

Mathis L. Dunn, Jr.
Executive Secretary

Julie Blacklow

It was a shot across the bow, and the fight was on, a fight that would
last almost a full year. As Mathis Dunn later said, "We could not foresee the
uphill battle in trying to prevail, but it was simply the right thing to do. One
of our members was seeing her livelihood taken away unfairly. The light was
dim, and we had to help brighten things up."

Instead of covering the news, I was now a news story. The headlines sickened me:

> "KING journalist fired for actions during kidnapping..."
> —*Seattle Times*

> "Television station fires reporter over kidnapping coverage..."
> —Associated Press

The AP story was picked up by all the local papers and some national papers as well. Local television stations ran the story too, though not KING. Every story regurgitated the allegations that I had interfered in the ransom drop and endangered the life of the young girl and never failed to mention I was fired for lying in my depositions, presumably changing my story to protect myself. In one accounting, station manager Sturges Dorrance called me "stupid."

In several private meetings with some of my colleagues, Dorrance said I was "wholly unbelievable," that I "perjured" myself and "breached the trust of the company." Reporters demanded proof of his allegations, but he said he "was not at liberty to reveal details." He said if they only knew what he knew, they would see that "Ms. Blacklow was not to be believed or trusted." No one believed or trusted anything he was saying. It all got back to me, a full-bore smear campaign. KING's pathetic public apology and its decision to fire me still did not quiet things, especially inside the newsroom. My co-workers wanted the truth, but knew they would not get it from their managers.

ANGRY LETTERS FROM VIEWERS FOLLOWING MY FIRING.

If some viewers were outraged at our coverage of the kidnapping, it seemed an equal number were also furious about what happened to me. Within a few weeks of my firing, KING Television and I started receiving angry letters:

I looked and looked, but I guess card manufacturers haven't made cards for unjustified releases of professionals.

I'm really outraged at what KING has done to you! One of their best reporters! I can't believe it!

After so many years of excellent service at KING and in our community, it is a shame that Ms. Blacklow's fine work will no longer be associated with your organization.

To Ancil Payne, president of KING Broadcasting:

This is to voice my extreme protest of your firing of Julie Blacklow from your news staff. To fire your employee over this disagreement before it has been settled through the courts is a complete breach of professional standards. It is obvious by your action that you are not supporting your news staff in the duties which you assign them and in my mind is a severe blemish on your editorial policy. Please register my complaint along with many others I am sure you have or will receive from many viewers who feel that your action places the integrity of your station in serious jeopardy.

Here are excerpts from a few of the hundreds of letters sent to me:

I still can't believe this happened to you. I know you'll keep your spirits up because that's the kind of person you are. I'm glad you're a fighter! Keep up the fight! I'm pulling for you!

I hope you clean their clock on how they handled this.

I feel this is a dirty deal you got. If a person doesn't do their job they catch heck . . . and when they do they still don't win!

There is no question that you became the sacrificial lamb that KING used to avoid legal entanglements.

> *It terrifies me to think that reporters might be intimidated from doing what they must do if we are to have a free press and TV News system. Our democracy needs all the help it can get.*

> *KING 5 News will be missing an intelligent and credible reporter and KING 5 viewers will also be short-changed in your leaving.*

> *I was shocked to read in the paper about your troubles with KING. It's clear you got a raw deal from them. After all the great work you've done for them, they sure treated you shabbily. Don't let the assholes get you down.*

The assholes did. I went into a tailspin of depression. I was afraid to go out, afraid to answer the phone, and terrified to answer the door. I stayed in bed and relied on my parents to bring food and help me take care of Jeremy. I was a divorced, single parent. How would I be able to pay my mortgage? No one in the Seattle television market was going to hire me with this dark cloud hanging over me and a legal fight underway.

My union repeatedly tried to settle the dispute without going to trial or arbitration. It sent a letter to KING:

> *Ms. Blacklow has been employed as a News Reporter for KING-TV for over 12 years, has had no prior disciplinary action, is one of the highest, if not the highest paid News Reporters at KING and in this market, has won numerous awards for the quality of her performance as a professional journalist. The remedy sought is reinstatement with full back pay and benefits.*

KING dug in, unwilling to bend and refusing to admit any kind of mistake or wrongdoing. AFTRA also dug in. KING would not even agree to an arbitration where a judge would decide my fate, a decision both sides would have to honor. After months of both sides inundating the other with legal documents, AFTRA and KING agreed to go to arbitration. In July, the date was set. November 11–14, 1986. I would have to wait an interminable and very lonely five months before my case was heard. All summer long and well into the fall.

My son was off to Camp Orkila in the San Juan Islands for the summer, so he did not have to witness his mother's unraveling. I felt ashamed, paranoid, depressed, and frightened. I let my beautiful garden I had spent years cultivating rot away, allowed the aphids to devour the roses, and gave free range for the weeds to grow. I did not care about anything. I did not want to eat. I could not sleep. The only person I called persistently was Mathis Dunn, the head of the union, trying to find out what, if anything, was happening. He always took my calls, even though I became a pest. Mathis tried to bolster my spirits telling me repeatedly over those many months he was certain we would win. I never believed him. How could I or anyone prevail against KING Broadcasting and its cast of corporate lawyers? Mathis had no doubt, but doubt and fear were all I had. I wanted to disappear. I wanted to die.

I understand fully the urge to take one's own life. There is a darkness that descends over you and into you. A palpable, thick, and all-consuming sadness that obscures all feelings of happiness, safety, and love. It is a blackness that blocks the ability to think about how such an act might affect the people who love you. All you can think about is ending the pain.

On a late summer afternoon, I drove my car to a gas station, filled it up, drove to a hardware store to buy a rubber hose, and went home to commit suicide in my garage. I connected the hose to the exhaust pipe and ran it through the back window. Life slammed me into what seemed like an impenetrable, dark, and deadly wall with a force so powerful I could hardly breathe or see any path out of the gloom. I was not thinking of my son, parents, friends, or family who loved me. I was just desperate to stop the pain. I started the motor, rolled up the windows, and waited.

My doorbell rang. I ignored it, but it did not stop. I heard pounding on the front door and then on the garage door. I tried to ignore that. Then someone called my name. Again and again and again. I turned off the engine, left the garage, and went to the door. My dear friend, Linda Farris, stood there holding a bouquet of flowers.

"Hi, sweetie. How are you doing?"

I hugged her and thought for a moment I should tell her the truth. I was trying to kill myself. I lied instead. "I'm okay. Come on in."

Linda, owner of the renowned Farris art gallery and Seattle style maven, said she was thinking about me and decided today would be a good day to stop by. It was a very good day. Without knowing it, Linda saved my life when I did not want to save myself. After she left, I took her visit as a sign from the Universe that it was not yet my time to go. I was going to have to get through this personal crisis somehow and be the strong woman I once thought I was. Tough, indefatigable Julie was almost broken. Almost.

Several months had passed since my firing, and I started going out again, to shop for food, prepare meals, and see friends. I cashed in IRAs to pay bills, borrowed money from my parents, and applied for unemployment benefits. Then something quite unexpected and wonderful began to happen. Almost every time I went out in public, whether to a gas station, a grocery store, or shopping mall, strangers came up to me to wish me luck, give me a hug and a smile, and let me know they were rooting for me. It gave me hope and courage when I had none.

The arbitration was still a couple of months away, and with the end of summer came the inevitable Seattle rain. To calm my nerves, combat my depression, and help me sleep, my doctor prescribed Xanax. It was, he said, very addictive but necessary to help me through this ordeal. "When this is behind you," he promised, "we'll put you on a withdrawal program, but you need it now."

I was in a deep sleep one night when, around three in the morning, I heard the sound of water, not hitting the roof of my house but dripping inside. I ran downstairs and saw water pouring onto my kitchen floor. I grabbed the largest pots I could find and spent the rest of the night emptying the pots as they filled up. The next morning, I called a good friend who owned a real estate company, thinking he might know someone reliable in the roofing business. Within a couple of hours, Colonel G. M. Pembrook showed up at my door.

"Just call me Colonel," he said. "I've already sent my guys up on your roof, and it looks like you need a new one."

"Yes, sir . . . I was afraid of that. How much do you think this will cost?"

"Well, I'm not sure, but probably around five thousand dollars."

"I don't know what to do," I said. "I don't have the money for that."

Without hesitation, the Colonel said, "No problem. I'm gonna get my guys to put tarps up there today to cover the spots where the water's coming in, and we'll replace the roof when we get a break from the rain."

"No problem?"

"No," he said. "I know who you are and what that goddam station did to you. Didn't like it one bit. So just give me a dollar down and an IOU . . . and you can pay me back when you win your case."

Another stranger who believed in me.

I grabbed a dollar from my purse, quickly wrote out a promissory note, and handed them to the Colonel. Within weeks, I had a new roof on my home, a new friend, and an arbitration set to begin in a week.

In the weeks leading up to the arbitration, Hal Green and AFTRA executive director Mathis Dunn met with me and a dozen of my colleagues from KING scheduled to testify at the proceeding. They prepared us for the kinds of questions we were likely to be asked, certain that KING's lawyers would try to confuse or intimidate us. I was inspired by the bravery of my co-workers willing to take a stand against the company that paid their salaries.

Blacklow: Hearings open today in firing of KING-TV reporter

From Page C1

operation.

Many of the top names in local news will testify about those events or as character witnesses for Blacklow starting today. Those expected to be called include KING anchors Jean Enersen and Mike James; former KING anchorman Aaron Brown (now at KIRO-TV); KING reporters Jack Hamann and Larry Cali, who also worked on the story in question; and the members of KING management who fired Blacklow.

The missing depositions are those from KING general manager Dorrance and news director Donald Varyu. They were among several statements made to the attorneys at the time the Mauceri family sued. The suit, for unspecified damages, was settled out of court July 14.

Last week, arbitrator Kane reportedly ordered KING to do whatever was necessary to provide the statements by Dorrance and

Julie Blacklow — TED D'ARMS

KING claims Blacklow was fired only for those alleged discrepancies the news staff has since been

by those rotten reporters," Hamann said. Hamann said KING has not changed its policies governing coverage of crime stories since that event.

But assignment editor Randy Partin, who also worked on the story, said local news now seems more reluctant to pursue kidnapping cases (there have been two more Seattle-area kidnapping cases in the past year), and he thinks that's a change for the better.

"I don't think you can send a crew out to chase a kidnapping without endangering" those involved, Partin said. He believes no news crews should have been sent to the Mauceri story, because, unlike a contained fire or shooting scene where reporters know where police lines are drawn, there were no guidelines to go by in the Bellingham case. And, Partin said, the question of whether mistakes were made in that case has not been resolved.

Partin says news departments

I HATED BEING THE NEWS AND NOT COVERING IT.

A FRIEND DROPPED ME OFF at 9:00 a.m. on Tuesday, November 11, 1986, outside the Westin Hotel in downtown Seattle. I took a Xanax and headed for the Glacier Peak room. Mathis Dunn and Hal Green were there to greet me and show me to my seat directly across the table from the men who seven months earlier had destroyed my world. The distinguished, white-haired Joseph S. Kane, a respected lawyer, was selected to serve as a judge and preside over the arbitration.

KING Broadcasting presented its case first with witnesses still maintaining the proceedings were not arbitrable, that:

> the station had the unfettered right to judge the competency and ability of its employees. What is unique about the television industry is how people are perceived by an audience. How reporters and anchorpeople are perceived by one audience varies greatly from one person to another. It is highly subjective.

> Blacklow is no longer competent and able to perform her job as a reporter after her dishonest testimony. Her credibility was destroyed.

KING witnesses testified the station could do whatever it wanted—hire and fire whomever it chose, that "management had the freedom to make quick uncontested decisions regarding on-air personalities. . . . Any time the station's ability to transmit truth in an unbiased matter is called into question, the integrity of the entire operation is threatened."

Sitting in this drab, airless little room, listening to these abhorrent accusations against me was infuriating and sickening. I wanted to scream at them and defend myself against the lies Joseph Kane was hearing. But all I could do was sit there. During its two-day case, KING lawyers put witnesses on the stand who agreed with the station's assertion that I had interfered with the police proceedings. They submitted copies of several statements I had given . . . taken months apart . . . dissecting sentences and phrases to help build their case against me.

I was thinking, as I had for months, *Why did KING managers ever go to Bellingham to apologize in the first place, a sniveling, senseless response to a police chief trying to make a name for himself? If they had done the right thing, stood by their reporters and defended us, I would not be sitting in this cesspool.* At the end of their deceptive presentation, KING summed things up by calling me an "incompetent liar, unworthy of trust either from the station or the public." In conclusion, KING attempted to block AFTRA, the union, from even presenting its case:

> The Arbitrator must apply the terms of the Agreement and find that AFTRA's claim is not arbitrable. Even if the claim is considered, the evidence taken at the hearing made it plain that Blacklow's repeatedly inaccurate deposition testimony was not inadvertent. Facts convincingly show that KING properly discharged Julie Blacklow for intentionally making false statements under oath. KING TV's news operation depends upon credibility—and Blacklow can never again credibly report the news because of her dishonesty. The discharge must stand.

I was many things. I was pushy, confrontational, aggressive, persistent, sometimes abrupt, intolerant, impatient, and sarcastic. But one thing I was not was dishonest. I was not a liar. I was not deceptive, and I was absolutely credible.

KING told its story. We had our own.

Witness by witness, union lawyer Hal Green unraveled KING's allegations. He showed that at no time had any of KING's attorneys showed any concerns about my statements or mentioned any inconsistencies. My account of what happened on that fateful day of October 30, 1985 was identical to my photographer's statements. Other reporters' and photographers' depositions were similar, and all had occasional inconsistencies in statements given months apart. One KING lawyer, testifying for us, took the stand and recalled complimenting me on how well my deposition had gone. He later called me after I was fired to say he was shocked at my discharge and wanted me to know he had nothing to do with it.

Green argued that the just cause clause in the union contract had not been proved, that there was no substantiation of intention to deceive, as required in the contract, and that I was never told I was sent to cover a story involving a life-and-death situation. Green countered KING's claims that I was fired for being a liar, saying KING had no proof of that. KING's allegation that I had engaged in "a carefully calculated pattern of deceit in a sworn deposition," Green said, "was equally false."

Co-workers to testify on KING reporter's firing

Several KING-TV reporters are expected to testify in an arbitration hearing set to open next Tuesday over the controversial firing of reporter Julie Blacklow. And their testimony may affect the nature of their jobs as much as Blacklow's future at the station.

At least five KING-TV reporters will be called on to testify at the hearing between KING Broad-

Shortly after, the parents of th kidnapped girl took legal action, charging that the news crew had jeopardized the safe return of their daughter. The matter was settled out of court.

KING fired Blacklow, who was covering the kidnapping, and the night assignment editor in April after the two gave depositions in the case. The station never public-

I GOT SUPPORT FROM WITHIN THE NEWSROOM...MY COLLEAGUES WERE BRAVE.

One after another, my co-workers took the stand, testifying under oath about their respect and admiration for me, statements made glaring at KING managers sitting just a few feet away. Hal Green offered as evidence several depositions given by my colleagues about the events during the kidnapping coverage. Every one contained minor inconsistencies similar to the ones I was accused of having. Several depositions contained far bigger disparities. Hal called one of the country's leading experts on memory who testified it would be impossible for statements taken months apart to be identical. Hal summed up that portion of our case and with a hint of a smile on his face, looking at KING lawyers, said, "Julie Blacklow's statements seem to have the fewest inconsistencies of all of them."

At one point a colleague, a lawyer himself known for his irascibility, had to be forcefully removed from the witness stand after launching into a tirade directed at KING management: "What the hell is wrong with you people? How dare you apologize for what we did? How could you possibly think that apologizing and firing Julie was the right thing to do?" Hal approached him with a smile and escorted him from the witness stand. He continued his verbal assault as he was shown the door.

Green then called several KING managers back to the witness stand who had testified earlier against me. Hal got each to admit that none had any personal knowledge of the events surrounding the kidnapping coverage. They did not respond to Hal's belief that KING "was looking for a scapegoat following Bellingham Police Chief Terry Mangan's public attacks on the station." I always believed that was true and prayed Joseph Kane would agree.

Hal Green said, "Either Mark Anderson [the photographer on assignment with Blacklow] and Julie Blacklow are telling the truth about what they understood when they left the station, or they have perpetuated a conspiracy of perjury. Aside from the fact that there is not a scintilla of such a conspiracy in the record, this notion simply belies common sense. The company has utterly failed to establish by proof beyond a reasonable doubt that Blacklow engaged in a pattern of calculated deceit in her sworn deposition. Blacklow has established by a preponderance of the credible evidence that she testified honestly. Just cause for her disciplinary discharge does not exist."

Hearing over on Blacklow firing

By Kit Boss
Times arts reporter

One side was contented, the other not talking as testimony concluded Friday in the arbitration hearing involving KING Broadcasting and Julie Blacklow, a KING-TV reporter who was fired last April after covering a local kidnapping.

Now both sides must wait about a month for a decision from the arbitrator who heard the matter.

Blacklow and assistant news editor Bill Baker were fired after KING's coverage of the October 1985 kidnapping of a Bellingham girl.

Testimony at the arbitration hearing dealt largely with who knew what on the night of Oct. 30, 1985, when Blacklow and a cameraman assigned to cover the story reportedly crossed paths with a police and FBI operation to capture the kidnapper. The pair were among several KING employees involved in the coverage.

Broadcasting and the American Federation of Television and Radio Artists (AFTRA), Blacklow's union.

According to sources close to the trial, KING attempted to prove that Blacklow knew she was being sent out to cover a life-threatening kidnapping situation that involved a young girl; further, that in testimony given to lawyers representing the Mauceris, Blacklow lied about her knowledge of the situation; finally, KING argued

FINALLY...THE END OF THE ARBITRATION...THE WAITING BEGINS.

Those harrowing four days in November were over. I was numb, sickened by the words the station's lawyers and their witnesses used to describe me, and paralyzed with fear that, despite the union's belief we would win, we would never prevail over the revered KING Broadcasting Company.

We would have to wait three more agonizing months before Joseph Kane announced his decision.

In the month following the arbitration, I wrote a letter to Hal Green, the union's lawyer.

> *Hal . . . your shoulders have carried me above all others through this frightening passage. You are a rare human being . . . possessing great professional intelligence and deep compassion. Your legal skills guided me through this maze and your belief in my innocence never wavered. Through all of it, you maintained dignity and grace, but for that one moment when you lost your temper with the KING News Director. Forgiveable. It was a privilege to go through this with you. In the case of this complicated saga, the truth has had to be patient. It waited for its rightful venue and last month it was heard. No matter the outcome for me personally, we have won. Of course I pray for complete vindication, both for myself and for the Union, but please know that whatever happens, I will be fine.*
>
> *Julie*

The arbitration took a terrible and frightening emotional toll on me but a financial toll on the union, which paid for the entire costly defense. My colleagues and I decided to have a party, a fundraiser to help offset the cost of seeking justice.

Hosted By:
Julie Blacklow
Aaron Brown
Ted D'Arms
Jean Enersen
Robin Groth
Jim Harriott

Hosted By:
Mike James
Lori Larsen
Don McGaffin
Bob Royer
Mayor Charles Royer
Pepper Schwartz
Art Skolnick

ON SATURDAY, JAN. 24TH...

The American Federation of
Television & Radio Artists
Invites You
And 2,000 Members and Friends of AFTRA
to Celebrate...

"THE BATTLE OF BELLINGHAM"

A Legal Fundraiser & Buffet
in Support of
Seattle TV Reporter Julie Blacklow
in her Arbitration Fight against KING-TV

A CAUSE FOR CELEBRATION...AND TO RAISE MONEY.

The Battle of Bellingham was held on January 24, 1987, with an impressive line-up of hosts who helped raise thousands of dollars.

TV newscasters band together to support Blacklow vs. KING

By Susan Paynter
P-I Television Critic

Win or lose — and a decision is imminent — Saturday night's fund-raising party to pay for TV reporter Julie Blacklow's union-backed legal arbitration against KING-TV will be more celebration than wake, say its high-profile hosts.

secondhand that management is upset over staff participation in the benefit, Enersen said she ha heard nothing against her involv ment.

James, who will be one several speakers Saturday n said the Blacklow case is answer to the question "W we need a union?" "So, coll ly, when something like th

to any one of them.
_ou run out the door
_ing story) and
_hat you'll
_ use

A welcome by Julie Blacklow.

9:15 to 11:00 .... Tonight's entertainment
provided by:

KIRO-TV Newsman Aaron Brown

TheatreSports Performers Josh Conescu
and Randy Dixon

Artist Ted D'Arms

Seattle Talk-Show Host Pat Finley

Actor John Gilbert

Veteran KOMO-TV newsman Jim Harriott

KING-TV Anchor Mike James

Former Seattle Seahawk Sam McCullom

Former Seattle Jo_   Don McGaffin
_en
_ckham
_ussell
_chwartz
_ow...

MARKETING
The Area's First Marketing Monthly   Feb '87
Vol. 1 No. 2

Blacklow – Benefit & More!

The "Battle of Bellingham" benefit for former KING-TV newswoman Julie Blacklow was much more than that! It was a fund-raiser, unio the theater, pot-luck reunion," and networ rolled into one.

Blacklow continued

wrote, "people working together to achieve something. Your support tonight means that AFTRA, our union, can go on to the next challenge with the special strength that only committed members can give."

Goateed Bill Russell, the towering basketball legend, TV commentator, AFTRA member, and notorious individualist, recalled how he once led the strike of an NBA All-Star game. He said the personal stance he was "most proud of" was when, in his second year in the NBA, he told the Commissioner to "sit _n a ruling against facial hair

lost. Julie was fired, but the viewers, THEY WERE PUNISHED."

Ted D'Arms in an off-stage aside before taking the mike from Don, who got sustained applause, lamented: "How do you follow that?" But the big, burly actor/artist did — in his typical booming style:

"We've just started," he declared, "this is just the first (bleeping) step! He also spoke of Julie's "integrity" and "toughness" during the nine-month ordeal from an up close and personal view as her companion.

Through the four-hour happening, the St. Michelle wine flowed far more freely

The martyrdom of
Julie Blacklow

What really happened that night? Did she break the rules? Or did KING sacrifice her in a panic?

Within a month, a federal arbitrator will issue a ruling in the still-simmering case of former KING-TV news reporter Julie Blacklow. On its face, that ruling will simply determine whether or not Blacklow should get her job back, and perhaps whether KING executives can put the case behind them.

later, when KING suddenly announced it was firing Blacklow and Bill Baker, who had been Blacklow's editor on the night of the incident. Baker and Blacklow claimed they were dumbfounded by the dismissal. KING manager Sturgis Dorrance explained only that a "discrepancy" emerged in sworn statements given by Blacklow and Baker. Whether Baker and Blacklow contradicted each other, themselves, or somebody

And a host no one ever expected, former NBA All-Star Bill Russell. After years playing professional basketball and being a strong believer in the player's unions, Bill made his post-basketball home in Seattle. He led a quiet and very private life and rarely ventured out into public. Though he did not know me personally, he saw press coverage about what happened to me, called the AFTRA offices, and offered to help in any way he could. Union executive director Mathis Dunn asked him to come to the Battle of Bellingham and bring along some basketballs he could sign and auction off at the party. Bill Russell was known to rarely give out autographs, but for this occasion, he did. For a price.

The Battle of Bellingham was a great success. More than three hundred colleagues and friends gathered to stand together as a family and to stand up for me. Among the statements said or written about the event:

> *That's all a union really is . . . people working together to achieve something. Your support tonight means that AFTRA, our union, can go on to the next challenge with the special strength that only committed members can give.*
> *—Mike James, KING 5 anchor*

> *Bill Russell, the goateed, towering basketball legend and AFTRA member talked about how he once led a strike of an NBA All-Star game. Russell said the personal stance he was most proud of was when, in his second year in the NBA, he told the Commissioner to "sit on it" when a ruling against facial hair came down. . . .*

> *The most moving moment was the appearance by former KING-TV commentator Don McGaffin, who suffered a stroke that left him partially paralyzed and previously speechless. He noted "he was still under a seven-year old libel suit, but was protected by KING. Julie never got that kind of protection. The other side—the young kidnap victim's family—filed a bizarre suit. And KING fired Julie and paid the family off. We don't know how many pennies that cost. They*

tried to prove Julie derelict. Not bloody likely. No, Julie didn't deserve this. But, more importantly, neither did the viewers. They were the ones who really lost."

—John Marshall, former
Seattle Post-Intelligencer *columnist*

Former Seahawks running back Sam McCullum, the player's union representative cut by management, spoke of the fear employees have of speaking up, or attending an event such as the Blacklow benefit.

While waiting for the arbitrator's decision, the story of the kidnapping debacle continued making news, appearing in dozens of articles with no shortage of opinions about KING Television and me. In *Monthly* magazine:

> For 30 years or more, KING was acknowledged in the profession to be the leaders in the local TV News market . . . refusing to go the way of blow-dried anchors and happy talk news shows. Instead, they hired the best people, spent the money and took the risks on aggressive, innovative TV Journalism. But in recent years, many on the news staff said the news operation has been less willing to take those risks. To some of them, at least, the Blacklow case seemed to epitomize that trend. By firing two veteran journalists [Assignment editor Bill Baker was fired with me, but never fought the decision. As management, he had no union to stand up for him and died several years after being fired for doing his job.] the station seemed to be issuing an ominous message to the rest of the staff: play it safe, don't take chances.

SUNDAY, FEBRUARY 22, 1987, was my fortieth birthday. Still awaiting the decision that would determine my fate, I did not feel much like celebrating. Some friends took me to a small Italian restaurant with red-checkered tablecloths, free-flowing wine, and a tiramisu cake with candles. I appreciated their gesture but could not feign happiness. As we were leaving, I spotted a Tarot card reader, and my friends paid her to do a session with me. I sat down across from her as she instructed me to lay out the cards. She did not know me or know what had happened to me. At the end of the reading, she asked me to turn over one final card, which I did. It was the card of Lady Justice, the card indicating a fair decision will be forthcoming.

I looked up at the Tarot lady, staring at her, tears welling up.

"This must have some meaning in your life," she said.

"Yes," I answered, "I hope so."

I went to bed that night falling into the deepest sleep I had in almost a year.

On Monday, February 23, I felt rested, calm, and hopeful.

ON TUESDAY MORNING, FEBRUARY 24, Hal Green called me: "We won! We won! We won!"

Skimming through the fifty-three-page decision, Hal turned quickly to the final page, the Findings of Fact and Conclusions, and read them to me over the phone:

1. I find that when management discharges an employee covered under the Agreement as a disciplinary matter, the issue of just cause arises and that issue must be resolved by Arbitration as provided in the current Agreement:

2. I find that there was insufficient and speculative evidence presented by the testimony of the witnesses and evidence presented at the hearing and thus cannot find that the grievant gave inconsistent statements of credible testimony on a deposition taken March 25, 1986. I find further that the discipline administered by KING TV in discharging the grievant was without just cause.

Award:

1. That the grievant will be reinstated to her former position at KING TV as a News Reporter.

2. That the grievant will be awarded back pay from the date of termination until reinstatement.

3. That the grievant's back pay will be reduced by the compensation she received at termination by any unemployment compensation . . . and by any other income she has received during her time of discharge.

Joseph S. Kane
Arbitrator

```
                    In the Arbitration

                            of

                    JULIE BLACKLOW

                    Subject: DISCHARGE


             Hearing held in Seattle, Washington
                 November 11, 12, 13, and 14, 1986

APPEARANCES:

For KING Broadcasting Company      For American Federation of
                                   Television and Radio
                                   Artists (AFTRA)

Russell L. Perisho, Esq.,          Harold H. Green, Esq.
Perkins Coie Law Firm              MacDonald, Hoague & Bayless
1900 Washington Bldg.              Hoge Building
Seattle, Washington                Seattle, Washington




                    Decision Rendered this

                 24th day of February, 1987

                            By:

                 Joseph S. Kane, Arbitrator

                            at

                    Seattle, Washington
```

FINALLY...A DECISION. TEN MONTHS OF WAITING ARE OVER.

In his decision, Mr. Kane summed up the whole sorry episode saying this: "The lack of a command post, where information could be issued to all media at one time, was the basic cause of this turmoil. It was not provided. Thus, I find insufficient proof that the grievant made untrue statements in her depositions or engaged in any planned deceit.

I called my parents. I went and got Jeremy out of school. I rushed to Hal Green's law offices to see and hold the document in my hands. The phone rang in Hal's office. It was my colleagues at the station who had just heard the news. They were elated. The *Seattle Times* sent a photographer to Hal's office as he captured me on the phone talking with the best reporters in the business. Within hours, I was on the front page of the *Seattle Times*:

April 21st, 1986 was the worst day of my life. February 24th, 1987 was one of the best. Arbitrator Joe Kane was quoted too, saying, "There was insufficient and speculative evidence presented to support KING's allegations."

The next day I received a hand-delivered letter from KING news director Don Varyu:

Dear Ms. Blacklow:

Yesterday we received the arbitrator's opinion and award. While KING disagrees with the decision both with respect to the arbitrability conclusions and the review of KING's discipline, KING has decided that it serves no one's interest to prolong the dispute. Accordingly, KING has elected not to appeal the decision.

You are hereby unconditionally offered the position you formerly held as a KING-TV news reporter and KING will make you whole for lost wages and benefits following your discharge of April 21, 1986.

KING wants to emphasize to you its public statement that you are welcome back at KING as a member of the KING-TV News Team. We sincerely hope that this dispute can be put behind us and we can all get back to the task at hand, namely broadcasting television news.

Sincerely,
Don Varyu, News Director

cc: Hal Green

The Seattle Times

25¢
48 pages

WASHINGTON'S LARGEST NEWSPAPER ■ COPYRIGHT© 1987, SEATTLE TIMES COMPANY

TUESDAY
February 24, 1987

Reporter gets her job back

KING
continued from Page 1

third party for settlement.

Blacklow's victory opens the way for a possible defamation suit by the reporter against KING Broadcasting. KING can also challenge the decision in civil court by claiming the arbitrator ruled improperly on whether Blacklow's firing was open to arbitration.

Blacklow said she didn't know "what the next step will be."

"The next stage is obviously

consideration of further legal action," said Kate Pflaumer, one of Blacklow's attorneys. "The arbitration proceeding only partially remedied the damages done to Julie."

The arbitration decision does not stipulate when Blacklow must be reinstated. The amount of back pay was undisclosed.

"We hope it will happen immediately," said Harry Chesnin, an attorney acting as spokesman for Blacklow's union, the American Federation of Radio & Television Artists. "Every day that goes on from now is another day of back pay to which she's entitled."

Blacklow expressed no qualms about returning to her former employer. "I would feel comfortable in that room, no doubt about that," Blacklow said. "That's my family."

Blacklow and assistant news director Bill Baker were fired last April after KING's coverage of the October 1985 kidnapping for ransom of a 14-year-old Bellingham girl.

Testimony at the arbitration hearing focused on who knew what on the night of Oct. 30, 1985, when Blacklow and a camerawoman crossed paths with a police and FBI operation set up to snare the kidnapper.

The week-long ordeal ended that night when the girl was released unharmed; her suspected abductor was killed in a police shootout early the next morning in a park near Steilacoom.

In a press release issued that day, Bellingham police criticized KING-TV for interfering in the ransom drop. KING reporters, tipped off by information broad-

cast on police scanners, were said to have followed the kidnapped girl's father and undercover law enforcement officials who were following an elaborate ruse laid out by the kidnapper.

Immediately after police leveled their criticism, KING news director Donald Varyu defended KING's handling of the story. A week later, after police had filed their report of what happened during the ransom drop, Durrance, KING general manager, publicly apologized for his station's behavior, conceding that KING-TV had "interfered with critical police activities."

Soon after, the parents of the kidnapped girl filed suit against KING-TV for jeopardizing their daughter and causing them emotional distress. That suit was settled out of court in July, 1986.

BANKING'S SUMMIT
...me one of the most profitable ...nony, E 1.
..n acquiring Rainier, adds a ...st chain. E 1.
...t Sound Bank are the next ... say analysts. E 4.

...bigger, but contingent on the latter's dwindling profits.

The move would put four out

...ion-dollar bid

five of Washington's largest commercial banks in the hands of institutions with headquarters outside of the state.

Seafirst, the largest commercial bank in the state, is now owned by California-based BankAmerica. First Interstate of Washington is owned by First Interstate Bancorp of Los Angeles. Old National Bank of Spokane is working on a merger deal with U.S. Bancorp. of Oregon, Peoples National

Please see RAINIER on A 8

KING-TV reporter gets her job back

Arbitrator rules for Julie Blacklow, fired in kidnap coverage

by Kit Boss
Times staff reporter

Julie Blacklow has won "the battle of Bellingham" and her job at KING-TV. The station must rehire the reporter — who was fired last April after her involvement in KING's controversial coverage of a Bellingham kidnapping case — and pay her back wages, according to a binding settlement handed down this morning by a local labor arbitrator.

"I've been waiting for this day for 10 months," said Blacklow, a reporter with 14 years of experience at the Seattle station. "I feel an incredible, wonderful sense of justice."

In testimony reproduced in arbitrator Joseph Kane's 53-page ruling, KING station manager Sturges Dorrance said Blacklow was fired because statements she made to lawyers about the kidnapping story which she was sent to cover "clearly indicates a pattern that she was trying to deceive us."

"We cannot afford," Dorrance later testified, "nor can any TV station afford to have a reporter on staff where predictability has basically been destroyed."

In Kane's ruling, he said, he found "insufficient proof" that Blacklow "made untrue statements in her statements, or depositions, or engaged in any planned deceit."

A flier promoting a Jan. 24 benefit to pay Blacklow's legal fees termed the dispute "the battle of Bellingham."

KING executives were in the process of formulating a response to the decision.

Arbitration is a quasi-judicial process where two parties agree to submit their disagreement to a

Please see KING on A 5

Reporter Julie Blacklow speaks with colleagues in the KING-TV newsroom by phone from the office of her union's lawyers after an arbitrator's ruling which reinstated her.

Eugene Tanner / Seattle Times

North suit challenges prosecutor

New twist in Iran arms scandal as Regan faces 'crunch' time

Times news services

WASHINGTON — Attorneys for fired White House aide Oliver North today filed a lawsuit challenging the constitutionality of the law empowering the special prosecutor to investigate North and the Iran arms scandal.

The suit, filed in U.S. District Court in Washington, charged that prosecutorial authority belonged exclusively to the executive branch and that the law violated the constitutional requirement on the separation of powers.

North, a Marine lieutenant colonel and former National Security Council aide, was the only publicly identified target when a special three-judge court two months ago appointed Lawrence Walsh, a former top Justice Department official, to investigate criminal wrongdoing in the shipment of arms to Iran and diversion of profits to the Nicaraguan rebels. President Reagan fired North and National Security Adviser John Poindexter resigned on Nov. 25 amid disclosures of the Iran arms sales.

A spokeswoman for Walsh, who has been issuing subpoenas and granting immunity as part of his fast-moving investigation, had no immediate comment on North's suit.

North's suit was filed on the day the White House reluctantly conceded for the first time that Reagan and his embattled chief of staff, Donald Regan, were going to discuss the latter's future.

After standing behind Regan for more than three months despite increasing pressure to oust

ILL-ADVISED ROMANCE
■ Oliver North's secretary was romantically involved with Arturo Cruz Jr., son of the Nicaraguan contra leader. U.S. officials feared he was a Sandinista agent. A 4.

him, the president finally decided that the only way to remain an effective leader during the final two years of his presidency is to replace Regan, according to sources.

In the most public statement to date hinting that Regan's job was in doubt, presidential spokesman Marlin Fitzwater said today that Reagan and Regan will "talk about his (Regan's) future after the Tower board report, but not before."

Fitzwater, asked about reports that Regan was searching for a new chief of staff, told reporters, "To my knowledge, it's not true. I'm not aware of any search for a successor."

However, several sources said that among candidates the president is considering is Charles Price, the ambassador to Britain and a longtime friend. They said Price is scheduled to arrive in Washington Saturday.

Former Sen. Paul Laxalt, a Reagan confidant who now practices law in Washington, also reportedly is being considered, as is former Secretary of Transportation Drew Lewis.

Regan has continued to insist

Please see NORTH on A 4

Searches can be legal despite police error

Associated Press

WASHINGTON — Honest mistakes by police officers may excuse what otherwise would be an unconstitutional search of someone's home, the U.S. Supreme Court said today.

By a 6-3 vote, the justices reversed a ruling that had thrown out a Baltimore man's heroin-distribution conviction and 15-year sentence.

They said heroin seized from Harold Garrison's apartment in a 1982 police search properly was used as evidence even though the officers had no authority to enter his apartment.

"The validity of the search ... depends on whether the officers' failure to realize the overbreadth of the warrant was objectively understandable and reasonable," Justice John Paul Stevens wrote

for the court. "Here it unquestionably was."

Baltimore police on May 21, 1982, obtained a court warrant to search the third-floor apartment of suspected drug dealer Lawrence McWebb, and spotted McWebb outside his apartment house.

Accompanying him to the third floor, the officers waited while McWebb unlocked a door at the head of the stairs and then entered a hallway.

The officers testified they did not realize the third floor contained two apartments divided by the interior hallway; one rented to McWebb and the other to Garrison.

From the hallway, one officer saw marijuana in Garrison's bedroom. A search of that room

Please see COURT on A 8

Shutdown of PUREX plant ends, but concerns over safety do not

by Eric Nalder
Times staff reporter

RICHLAND — The auditor whose findings contributed to the shutdown of two plutonium plants on the Hanford Nuclear Reservation declined to close the books on one of his audits on a plant that was reopened last Saturday.

Department of Energy officials said at a briefing yesterday that some safety rules were relaxed or simplified, and some new accident-prevention equipment was installed, at the Plutonium-Uranium Extraction Plant (PUREX) before it and associated laboratories and shipping facilities at the nearby Plutonium Finishing Plant were restarted.

Auditor Casey Ruud said he refused the request of his employer, Rockwell Hanford Operations, to close his audit on design changes at the huge PUREX plant because the DOE did not allow an independent review of the plant's safety. Ruud did close out audits regarding safeguards and security of plutonium.

Instead, Ruud transferred weeks ago to another division in the company. The audit was closed by his former supervisor, John Baker, said Rockwell spokesman Mark Musolf. That paved the way for the reopening of PUREX.

Ruud's unhappiness with the

DOE's handling of the audits became known in November when he refused to sign an investigative report on the two plutonium plants. Shortly thereafter he indicated that he would not close out his audits.

Though a government investigation confirmed many of Ruud's findings of unsafe work and design practices at PUREX, Ron Gerton, the DOE's chief safety officer at Hanford, said there was no reason for the independent review that Ruud had sought.

"Rockwell's disposition of each audit finding was judged to be adequate," said A.J. Rizzo,

Please see HANFORD on A 8

INDEX

"Get back to the task at hand, namely broadcasting television news." That was the sanest statement to come out of KING Television in more than a year. It was a task that should never have been interrupted. The station chose an ill-advised, short-sighted, and senseless path, assuming that placating a pompous police chief with a public apology and firing me would stop the criticism. It only made things worse, for KING and for me. After a year in exile, I was now invited back to my professional home, but after such an exhausting year, I was not physically or mentally prepared to go back to work.

Hal Green spoke with station managers who agreed to let me decide when the time was best for my return. They asked one favor. Would it be possible for Hal to escort me to the station the day after my victory? My colleagues wanted to see me, if only for a few minutes. I agreed. We walked into 333 Dexter Avenue North with its slanted-glass windows. I was trembling. I never thought this day would come, and I never imagined what was waiting for me inside. More than one hundred people were standing on the stairs and in the upstairs balcony, applauding me as I walked through the doors and into the lobby. They welcomed me home.

As I stood there, soaking up this unexpected reception, Hal stepped aside to chat with station manager Sturges Dorrance. After this emotional reception in the lobby, Hal, Sturges, and I went into a small conference room. Hal insisted that I get my back pay, ordered by the judge, immediately. Sturges balked, mumbling something about not being able to cut a big check so quickly, at which point Hal leaned into Sturges's face and said, "You should, you could, and you will . . . and we're not leaving until you do." Sturges went up to the accounting office. After deductions for unemployment benefits and income I earned from writing jobs, Sturges handed me a check for twenty-five thousand dollars. Before leaving, I told him I would be back at work in a couple of weeks but needed time to begin withdrawing from my Xanax addiction and to get unencumbered sleep. I went to the bank, deposited the check, and went home.

When I woke up the next morning, I called the Colonel and invited him over for a cup of coffee and to settle my debt with him. It was the first check I wrote after winning my case, written to G. M. Pembrook in the amount of $4,999. For a dollar down, he gave me a new roof for my home, protection from the rain, and a show of faith. No amount of money could ever repay him for that.

Within days of the Union's and my victory, the story was still big news, and hundreds of letters arrived from viewers and friends, among them:

Congratulations! From the Seattle Education Association!

Dear Julie . . . how wonderful to hear your distinctive voice again!

Welcome back! We've missed you!

It takes a good and strong woman such as yourself to best a KING!

One in particular came from the law firm that argued my case:

Dear Julie . . .

My joy over your reinstatement continues. Very, very pleased for you and all that it represents. You and AFTRA have pushed the rock up the hill. We share a little of that deserved high.

Love,
Ken MacDonald, Senior Partner
MacDonald, Hoague & Bayless

As I WROTE THIS, more than thirty years past the trauma, I spoke with some of the people who fired me and to those who carried me through the ordeal. One of KING's vice presidents, Eric Bremner, said, "No one can feel good about what happened . . . those were really bad times. Mistakes happen. Sometimes management has a responsibility to protect the institution even at the cost of the individual."

"I guess," I answered. "I guess I was one of those mistakes."

Fired KING-TV reporter is reinstated

By Susan Paynter
P-I Reporter

Last night's victory celebration for TV reporter Julie Blacklow started without the guest of honor, who joined the party after a late session with attorneys and union officials over one key question: Will she ever again be seen on KING 5 News?

KING must rehire Blacklow and pay her 10 months in back salary, a labor arbitrator ruled yesterday. But KING management and attorneys also wrestled the issue of Blacklow's on-air future into the evening, pausing to release a carefully worded statement saying the station will comply with the labor arbitrator's decision.

The statement said Channel 5 "will welcome Ms. Blacklow back to KING TV," and will pay her 10 months' worth of back salary.

Blacklow briefly interrupted last night's legal session to say there good chance" she will go back for KING, adding, "That's what negotiating now.

Such a comeback has ne pened in the annals of the A Federation of Radio and 'T Artists, said local AFTRA director Mathis Dunn. Other winning such suits have mo other stations, presuman tension.

But, Blacklow said, "" it."

apologize, saying it may have violated the bounds of good journalistic con duct.

The Mauceri family then filed a lawsuit against KING, which was settled out of court.

In yesterday's ruling, arbitrator Joseph S. Kane said he found no evidence that Blacklow gave inconsistent statements in separate accounts of the kidnap coverage. He also ruled that KING discharged Blacklow without just cause and called for the awarding of back pay from the date of her termination until she is reinstated. The money will be minus the unspecified amount Blacklow has already been paid in severance.

The Blacklow case, which went into arbitration in November, is the biggest and costliest legal fight ever waged by the Seattle unit of AFTRA.

KING anchorman and union spokesman Mike James said yesterday that this case proves the union has muscle and will stand behind its members. He called the decision "a great thing for AFTRA" because it proves the union contract counts for something.

The case became a cause among local reporters who staged a benefit to pay about $50,000 in legal fees. Attorney Hal Green, who handled the case for AFTRA, was out of town when the decision was announced yesterday ... fought back tears when

...ow gets a hug from Terry Tazioli, a section editor for The Seattle ...arty last night while Laddy Kite, left, KING-TV photographer.
BILL HUNTER P-I
...hotographer smile their approval.

...led in a shootout with police near
...e unfolded over sev-
...ile stretch of
Moun

Seattle AFTRA VOICE

You are the Union First Quarter Spring 1987

Arbitration win for Julie Blacklow and AFTRA

The Julie Blacklow arbitration is over, and Julie and AFTRA have won. The familiar KING TV newsreporter is back on the air and has been awarded full back pay for the ten months since her dismissal. Many believe this has been the most important legal fight in the history of our local. Clearly it's been the most expensive.

But what does it all mean? One o the best explanations so f from a recent article of the Sea neer

vestigate unusual police radio traffic. Bellingham police officials accused KING TV of interfering with their investigation and jeopardizing the life of 10-year-old Leah Mauceri, who was released by her abductor later in the day.

The station first rejected the police charges but later ...cly apologized. The Mau...

led a lawsuit ...gering their ... was settled ...6, but not ...n April.

...ned that ...for what ...encies ...parate ...ction ... has ... of ...or ...ce ...of

Photo by Ted D'Arms

Julie Blacklow

more complex legal issues, but the significant point for AFTRA members is made clear by the SPEEA newsletter article.

Rich Hawkins

(Cont. on page two)

KING'S JULIE BLACKLOW: 'EMPLOYERS MUST TREAD LIGHTLY'

MEDIA / J. Kingston Pierce

BLACKLOW'S VINDICATION

....

A fired reporter has the last laugh at KING

Joseph Kane that day had made known his decision in a ten-month-long arbitration case pitting Blacklow against her former employer, King Broadcasting Company; despite the odds, it seemed David had bested Goliath. Blacklow had been fired in April 1986, several months after her controversial coverage of a kidnapping case that involved Bellingham police and a missing 10-year-old girl. Kane maintained that her dismissal was "without just cause," and that as a result KING-TV should reinstate her as a reporter and award her back pay. Though KING had offered evidence in defense of its actions even after the time the case was initially supposed to have

"No doubt," he replied.

I thought to myself, *They completely failed to protect the institution with their incompetent decisions and, in fact, damaged the institution and the individual.*

Then AFTRA executive secretary Mathis Dunn now works for the national SAG-AFTRA Union. He told me, "We were a little ragtag group of union activists and a community that believed in doing the right thing."

This decision, won by this little ragtag union would have lasting and national repercussions. It strengthened and solidified the rule of just cause and insured that proper procedures and actions must be followed before an AFTRA member can be fired. The decision was sometimes referred to as the "Blacklow clause."

Ancil Payne, the former president of KING Broadcasting and the man I hold responsible for what happened to me, was replaced within a year of my return by Steven Clifford as head of the company. Payne passed away in 2004. Former station manager Sturges Dorrance refused to speak with me about what happened, saying only "he had nothing to add to the story." He was also let go some time after I returned but stopped me on the stairs in the newsroom one day to apologize. I accepted that gesture. Don Varyu, whom I believe did not want me fired, left the station as well. We remain friends.

I was encouraged by my private lawyers who helped me in my legal battle against KING to file a personal injury lawsuit against the station for pain and suffering. They believed it was a slam-dunk case, one that could net me millions of dollars. I did something I rarely did. I prayed about it. I sought the counsel of a rabbi. He said to do whatever I needed to do, but to remember "you already won." I agreed with him.

Steve Clifford, worried I was going to sue the company, called me up to his fifth-floor office one day, asking me what I wanted from the station.

For a moment, I thought about his question. "A dollar," I said, "and an apology." He gave me both.

I did not want to fight anymore. I had no fight left in me. Though subsequent books and articles claim that I sued KING, I never did.

What remains, though, and will likely never be erased is the powerful memory of what happened to me so long ago. I hope there will come a time when the date April 21 passes without notice, without my being engulfed again in darkness, without becoming sad, physically ill, and shaken to my core. I look forward to April 21 being just another day.

SOME VIEWERS WERE GLAD TO HAVE ME BACK.

In late March 1987, while on a slow, withdrawal regimen from Xanax and out from under the plague of anxiety I had suffered for a year, I went back to work. The last story I did before being fired was about Spider-Man visiting an elementary school, precisely the kind of assignment I needed to re-enter the erratic world of television news. The last thing I wanted was controversy and drama. It was the first thing I got.

Chapter 34

Pariah

H E WAS, TO USE A CLICHÉ, tall, dark, and handsome. Movie-star handsome. It was hard not to notice Steven George Farmer, but he wanted to be noticed. He was a beautiful, young gay man. He was also a sex predator who was HIV-positive and knew it. The teenagers he solicited for sex did not know that, but two of his friends did.

THE PHONE RANG at my desk.

"Is this Julie Blacklow?"

"Yes . . . who's this?"

"My name is Mavis Jones. You don't know me, but a friend of mine and I need to talk with you right away."

"About what?"

"We can't tell you over the phone . . . we need to see you. We're troubled about something, and we need to talk with you."

The urgent tone in her voice startled me. I had been back at work for only a few weeks, still withdrawing from Xanax, still shaken from my ordeal of the last year, still unsure and insecure about how the people who fired me would deal with me.

I should have handed the phone to another reporter. I did not.

ON FEBRUARY 17, 1987, Steven George Farmer picked up sixteen-year-old Eric in the Capitol Hill area of Seattle to have sex with him. Farmer told Eric to say he was fifteen and to call him "sir." According to police records, they went back to Farmer's apartment and engaged in multiple acts of oral sex. Farmer then took nude Polaroid pictures of Eric in a variety of sexual poses. When Eric tried to leave, Farmer would not let him go. Eric eventually fell asleep and woke up as Farmer was having anal sex with him. Eric later said he could not get away because Farmer was too big and overpowered him. The next morning, Farmer paid Eric twenty dollars and allowed him to leave. A few months later, Farmer picked up Jim, who was subjected to the same treatment. He was told to call Farmer "sir," pose for sexually explicit photographs, allow Farmer to penetrate him anally, and paid twenty dollars for his services.

Eric and Jim were not Farmer's only victims. Another teenager who did not get paid for going through the same ordeal went to Seattle police. On May 31, 1987, Steven Farmer was arrested, charged with sexual exploitation of seventeen-year-old Robert P., a minor, and booked into the King County Jail. While he was there, he called his friends Mavis and Patrick and told them to go to his apartment, remove a box of nude photos of young boys, destroy them, and throw out some illegal drugs. When his friends told Farmer what they'd done, he said they had destroyed the wrong pictures and sent them back to the apartment to get photos of Robert P. They also discovered something else when they went back, an official document confirming Farmer was HIV-positive.

Though Farmer's friends, Mavis and Patrick, destroyed the photos, the images of hundreds of young boys were indelible. And the knowledge that Farmer was HIV-positive was impossible to ignore. It haunted them.

We met at a coffee shop the day after they called. Mavis and Patrick found me in a dark corner of the room. Clearly torn about their decision to talk about Steven, the photos of the young boys angered and upset them, forcing them into an uncomfortable choice—to hold their disturbing secret or disclose the truth that their friend was a predator, having unprotected sex with minors. They showed me the document containing his HIV-AIDS status and gave it to me.

Mavis and Patrick were well aware of the explosive nature of these revelations. They brought it to me thinking, because I was brave enough to take on KING Television, I could handle something like this. It was precisely the kind of story, with its inevitable drama, that I did not feel ready to do, but now I had no choice.

In the early 1980s, years before hearing Steven Farmer's name, stories about HIV-AIDS were mostly medical and impersonal. Young gay men were dying of the human immunodeficiency virus, but the names and faces of these young victims were never made public. Stories focused on the medical and research aspects of the disease, on the doctors and scientists trying to understand what was happening. Seattle was a hub of these efforts, and I did dozens of stories about their work. Because so little was known about how AIDS was transmitted, those who were infected kept a very low profile. By the late 1980s, when I heard about Steven Farmer, some treatments were available to help manage the disease and prolong the lives of people who had it, but there was no cure. It was clear, though, how it was spread— through unprotected sex, through semen and blood.

In 1987, prosecutors in King County, Washington, also heard the name Steven George Farmer. They charged him with four counts of sexual exploitation of minors and would later charge him with destroying evidence. Though it was not illegal to be HIV-positive, prosecutors nonetheless saw him as a public health risk, aware he knew he had AIDS and was possibly spreading the disease to victims ignorant of the threat he posed. While the charges focused on the sex crimes, it was one of the first times the subject of HIV-AIDS found its way into the American justice system. Prosecutors knew this case would be explosive.

Farmer posted bail and was back out on the town. I knew where he lived. With a KING photographer, I went looking for him and found him in the Capitol Hill area of Seattle. We followed him, shot video of him walking, and tried to get him to talk. He refused.

His friends who had done his bidding by helping destroy evidence did want to talk and came to KING Television to sit down for a lengthy interview. Though they were nervous, Mavis and Patrick spoke openly about Steven, the photos they had found in his apartment, and conversations they had with him about his HIV status. I was nervous too. We all knew the risks of airing a story such as this. The facts of the case, that a sex predator was knowingly endangering lives, would be overshadowed by accusations that KING was homophobic and condemning those with AIDS. It was never about that to me, to prosecutors, or to Mavis and Patrick. It was about a sex predator who was a public health menace.

I put together the pieces of the story I had in place, Farmer's picture, interviews with Mavis and Patrick, documentation of the legal proceedings underway, but I never revealed the proof I had of his HIV diagnosis. Mavis and Patrick acknowledged it, as did the prosecutors, but it was not enough to calm the nerves of KING Television's managers. They demanded to know my source of the information, the medical documentation. How did I know this? The station's general manager and the news director called me into an office and insisted I give them proof. They had every right to ask. I felt I had every right to withhold the information. These were the same people who had fired me, and I did not trust them.

"If you're wrong," said KING's general manager, "Farmer will own the station."

"I'm right about this . . . and you'll have to trust me."

After showing the edited story to KING management, we did something we never did. We brought in some of the leaders in Seattle's gay community. It was unheard of to show any outsider a news story before it aired. We were trying to do damage control before showing this blistering, hot-button story. We attempted to garner support in anticipation of the furor we knew it would ignite. None of those who watched disputed the truth of the story or its importance. Before *State v. Steven George Farmer* went to trial, we went on the air.

The story opened with a close-up of Farmer's face, a still frame from the video. The opening lines went something like this: "This is Steven George Farmer. Take a good look at this face. Remember it. He is HIV-positive. He knows it and is having unprotected sex with minors."

My mentor, Don McGaffin, taught me at the beginning of my career that if you are tackling a giant or revealing some explosive truth, you must aim to kill. You cannot soft-pedal truth to try to avoid controversy or criticism. As a journalist, you must sometimes use words as weapons.

I unleashed a bomb and, despite support from leaders in the gay community, a shock wave came towards me. I got hate mail, angry phone calls, and accusations of being a rabid homophobe. I was vilified. My life was threatened in a couple of letters, which I turned over to KING management. They called Seattle police who could not do much with letters from anonymous accusers. The *Seattle Gay News* singled me out as an enemy of gay people, adding fuel to what was becoming an out-of-control situation. One day, walking with my eleven-year-old son along a Seattle street in a predominantly gay neighborhood, a man said, "I'd sure like to get in that kids' pants." In that moment, I was petrified, not only for my own life, but for the safety of my child. KING management, aware of death threats to me and threats to Jeremy's well-being, was concerned about our safety and paid to install a security system in our home.

Amidst the furious calls came a calm and welcomed one, from KING County prosecutor Rebecca Roe, who wanted a copy of my documentation proving Farmer was HIV-positive. I did not give it to KING management, and I did not give it to her. I felt I needed to protect the doctor who had administered Farmer's HIV test. Roe did not get heavy-handed about it or try to pressure me in any way. She told me years later she never really expected to get it. She said, "I would not have given it to me either."

Becky Roe was indefatigable, as smart and tough as they come. We were alike in many ways and respected each other's role in the drama that was unfolding.

As intense as the uproar was before the trial, things got far worse once it began. Becky Roe and her assistants, with my photographer and me trailing behind them, walked through a phalanx of Steven Farmer's friends and supporters towards the courtroom of Judge Charles Johnson. They yelled, cursed at us, and spit on us in the hallways every time we arrived and every time we left. Judge Johnson himself often had to be escorted in and out of the courthouse by armed sheriff's deputies. It was frightening and confusing. How could anyone support Farmer's flagrant behavior, having unprotected sex with minors and possibly older men as well? Becky Roe and I both had jobs to do. I was informing the public, and she was prosecuting a man endangering it. I drew strength from her resolve. And, once again, I had to fortify my interior shield to keep doing my job.

At the trial, Mavis and Patrick testified about Farmer's HIV status, that he knew he was positive and that he was having unprotected sex with minors. They, too, were subjected to shouts and recriminations from the gay community. I have little doubt they lost friends over this terrible trial. More than one hundred photos of some fifty naked boys were found by police in Farmer's apartment, but the evidence was ruled inadmissible due to an illegal search. Nonetheless, Steven George Farmer was convicted of three sex crimes and one count of tampering with evidence.

After the verdict, announced in a tension-filled courtroom, Judge Charles Johnson directed what is believed to be the first court-ordered HIV test in the United States. To no one's surprise, the test came back positive, and Judge Johnson sentenced Farmer to ninety months in prison. The AIDS test was challenged, and an appellate court later ruled the test violated Farmer's right to privacy. Nonetheless, based on witness testimony that Farmer exposed minors to the AIDS virus without regard to their welfare, the higher court found Farmer's actions "constituted a deliberate, cruel and malicious act that could result in their [the victims'] deaths". The court upheld Judge Johnson's seven-and-a half-year sentence.

In September 1991, with protestors gathered and shouting support, Steven Farmer walked into the King County Jail to begin serving his sentence. Four years had passed since his first arrest and since his case wound its way through the maze of the legal system. He once told friends he expected only to pay a small fine and get probation. His defenders were steadfast in believing he had been prosecuted for being gay and having AIDS. That was never the case. He was prosecuted for breaking laws making it illegal to have sex with minors. He committed crimes. He endangered lives.

Before he went to prison, Steven Farmer sent me a Christmas card with a poinsettia, a candle, and a Bible on the front.

A CHRISTMAS CARD FROM STEVEN FARMER.

Inside he wrote:

DEAR MS. BLACKLOW —
 I JUST WANTED YOU TO KNOW THAT I SPENT MOST OF THE YEAR HATING YOU,
 I CHOOSE TODAY NOT TO HATE YOU, AND REALIZE THAT WE ARE ALL HERE AS PART OF GODS WONDERFUL SCHEME OF THINGS. I RELEASE YOU TO YOUR HIGHEST GOOD —
 MAY GOD BLESS YOU AND KEEP YOU SAFE —

*This special prayer
is said for you
As Christmastime draws near—
God grant you
all the season's joy
And a happy and blessed year.*

SINCERLY IN SPIRIT,
STEVEN G. FARMER

LEFT: A MESSAGE INSIDE A CHRISTMAS CARD FROM STEVEN FARMER. RIGHT: THE MESSAGE FROM STEVEN FARMER'S CHRISTMAS CARD.

Dear Ms. Blacklow—

I just wanted you to know that I spent most of the year hating you.

I choose today not to hate you. And realize that we are all here as part of Gods {sic}wonderful scheme of things. I release you to your higher good—

May God bless you and keep you safe.

God grant you all the season's joy . . . and a happy and blessed year. [his underlining]

Sincerly [sic] In Spirit,
Steven G. Farmer

I was astounded and shaken by his letter. Though his own actions led to his undoing and ultimately to prison, I was the one who publicized it. I was the one who put his face on television and, in a very real sense, acted as judge and jury before his actual trial. I revealed it all to the city in which he lived and to many of his unsuspecting friends. Was he truly forgiving me and abandoning the hatred he harbored for years? All through a Christmas card with a Bible on the front?

Weeks after I received it, I started to believe Steven Farmer had found peace after the public turmoil. Perhaps he was resigned to his fate and taking responsibility for what he had done, instead of blaming others. As I have come to understand forgiveness, I know it is often done as much for the person expressing it as for those to whom it is directed. I took some comfort from the words on his Christmas card, which pierced a barrier I had constructed to keep away the pain some of my stories caused me.

Steven Farmer did not live long enough to serve out the exceptional sentence he received. After spending four years in prison, Washington State governor Mike Lowry granted him conditional clemency based on information that Farmer was near death. I was never able to learn the fates of the young men with whom he had unprotected sex. In September of 1995, Steven Farmer died at the age of thirty-nine of AIDS. His family did not disclose the location of the funeral or where he was buried.

Chapter 35

O

IN THE LATE SPRING OF 2003, the peerless, powerful, one and only Oprah Winfrey embarked on a four-city tour billed as "Live Your Best Life." On May 31 in Seattle, she descended from the plush, leather seats of her chauffeured, black Cadillac, resplendent in a gold pantsuit with silver cuffs and collar, indisputable proof that she was clearly living her own best life, practicing what she was preaching. On spiked heels, she effortlessly floated towards the doors of the Washington State Convention Center accompanied by shrieks of delight from her worshippers hoping a little of her magic would rub off on them. Hundreds of women who could not get tickets to the event just wanted to see her. The only men there were police officers standing next to ropes, holding back Oprah's devoted congregation, while a few thousand lucky fans with tickets waited for her inside the cavernous building.

Photographer Kevin Ely and I wanted to see her too and were hired by *Entertainment Tonight* to capture some of her presentation and conduct a quick interview with the most famous woman in the world. We were told in advance by her people that we would have just a couple of minutes to chat with her. For *Entertainment Tonight*, that was enough. Her image alone, with the ET logo on the microphone under her face, was all they really wanted.

After a few minutes of waving to her devotees, Oprah was guided over to Kevin and me. I felt an aura radiating from her, a powerful wave of energy. Twice before, I had felt this—a positive one from the Dalai Lama and an evil darkness oozing from maniacal killer David Lewis Rice. The warm and welcoming vibration emanating from Oprah embraced me before we ever made physical contact.

Smiling and beaming, she reached out her hands with their perfectly polished nails and introduced herself, as did I. She talked about the upcoming daylong event and its mission to help people become their best selves, which included receiving a gift bag, lunch, and several hours of Oprah being Oprah. I found it hard, though, to concentrate or think clearly, not only because I was in the presence of true greatness, but also because she was wearing the biggest diamond earrings I had ever seen. I thought to myself, *Why aren't her earlobes sagging more? Those things must weigh a lot!* I think they were heart-shaped or tear drops, but whatever shape they were, they were massive, startling, and distracting. It never occurred to me that they were fake. There was nothing fake about this woman.

"I've never seen earrings like that!" I said, slightly embarrassed by my unplanned comment.

"Oh . . . just a little something I bought for myself," she responded.

"Would you like to try one on?"

I was tempted. "I'd better not . . . you just keep wearing them for all of us women."

She liked that comment. It rang true to her.

Our few minutes with this truly wondrous woman passed, and she headed into a crowd of thousands who paid $185 for a day with Oprah. A bargain by any measure and worth its weight . . . in diamonds.

WITH OPRAH ON HER VISIT TO SEATTLE, WEARING THE BIGGEST DIAMOND EARRINGS I HAD EVER SEEN. *LAURA LIPPMAN*

Chapter 36

The Mutilator

O N MAY 20, 1989, around eight in the evening, Helen Harlow was beginning to worry. Her little boy, Ryan, had gone out for a bike ride earlier and had not yet come home to his Fern Hill neighborhood in Tacoma. She got in her car, went looking for him, thinking he had gone to see a friend and parked his bike outside a home somewhere. She called her mother, and they both drove around, searching for Ryan.

Meanwhile, as Helen frantically looked for her son, a disheveled ex-con went into a nearby Winchell's to buy doughnuts, temptations he would later use as a lure for any innocent victim who had the misfortune to cross his path. The man with the doughnuts went into the woods not far from Helen's home and waited as an animal would for its' prey.

Helen Harlow was not the only one who was worried. Newly elected Pierce County prosecutor John Ladenburg was sick with fear. Some months earlier, he had been notified by officials and doctors from Western State Hospital that a dangerous pedophile, having served his sentence for unimaginable crimes, was about to be released into the Fern Hill area.

While most murderers, rapists, and child abusers leave clues from their past explaining why they do the terrible things they do, Earl Kenneth Shriner was truly one of a kind. At the age of three, he was diagnosed as mentally deficient and tested showing he had an IQ of 67. As a young boy, he was caught setting off firecrackers in the rectums of dogs and once led his teachers to a tree where he had tied up a girl and strangled her to death.

Despite Prosecutor Ladenburg's efforts to keep this monster in prison, the officials at Western State Hospital said, "He had served every day of his sentence. He served all the time he was supposed to serve." They set him free to wreak havoc again and soon face charges of attempted murder, rape, and assault.

Without laws on the books to keep Earl Kenneth Shriner incarcerated, Ladenburg nonetheless filed papers and appealed to Western State to keep Shriner locked up. There were no precedents for holding sex offenders in prison after they had served their time, no matter how dangerous they were. Failing that, he notified local police of Shriner's pending release and sent photographs to some residents so they would know who he was. To the best of Ladenburg's knowledge, no public officials had ever taken such brazen steps to protect the public in an attempt to warn people that a predator was living among them. Helen Harlow and her son lived just outside the notification area. Ladenburg was told he could face lawsuits for doing what he did, but he did not care. All that mattered to him was that an extremely dangerous pedophile who drew pictures in prison of his sick fantasies and who threatened to attack, rape, and mutilate children was now free.

Ladenburg alerted police to watch out for Shriner and said that if they ever saw him near a child to arrest him. In late winter of 1989, Shriner grabbed a young boy at a local 7-Eleven. The child struggled to get away and escaped Shriner's grip when the store employee intervened. Shriner was immediately arrested, and while such a crime would normally be charged as a misdemeanor, John Ladenburg made sure Shriner was charged with a gross misdemeanor. That landed Shriner in jail for ninety days. After that, he was back on the streets.

Three months later, on May 20, the man with the Winchell's doughnuts and a twenty-four-year record of violent assaults and murder pulled little Ryan off his bike, dragged him into the woods, tied a noose around his neck, raped him multiple times, stabbed him, and in one final horrific act, cut off his penis. Earl Shriner left his human prey for dead, but Ryan did not die.

Helen Harlow's neighbors went down to the woods that night to bury a cat, to have a quiet, little family funeral for a beloved pet. In the midst of doing that, they saw a little boy stumbling out of some bushes, bloody, covered in mud, looking like a "little deer in the headlights." Without cell phones, they wrapped Ryan in a blanket and carried him home to call 911, tending to him as best they could until help arrived to take him to Mary Bridge Hospital in Tacoma. Helen and her mother were still out driving around, combing the neighborhood, now frantically searching for Ryan, unaware of what had happened to him, sick with worry because they had not found him. They came home and finally called police. They told her to wait. They were coming to her house, and she remembers sensing something odd in their voice.

Before that spring night in 1989, the Pacific Northwest had seen its share of horror. This was where Ted Bundy began his deadly crime spree, and as if not to be outdone, the Green River killer began and ended his deadly swath all over the Seattle area, killing as many as one hundred women. Both monsters brought unwanted infamy to the region, not the notoriety any region wants. I covered those appalling murders by Bundy and Green River killer, Gary Ridgway, and the violent acts of other child killers. All were terrible, sickening, and frightening events. As tragic and shocking as the carnage carried out by Bundy and Ridgway was, sometimes it is a singular, violent act that crushes the soul of a community. These horrific acts by Shriner, loosed on a little boy riding his bike, were going to be the crime that sent an icy chill through the Pacific Northwest and, soon, throughout the world.

Around eleven that night, police officers, accompanied by a chaplain, approached Helen Harlow's door. She knew what a visit from a chaplain could mean and thought to herself, *I'm not ready for an end to Ryan's life.* She silently made a deal with God: *No death for my child. And I will forgive anything that has happened.*

Police told her that Ryan had been involved in a serious accident, and she needed to gather her things and head to Mary Bridge Hospital. She felt in control in that moment and kept saying to God, "I need some help." By the time Helen and her mother got to the hospital, Ryan was in surgery to repair some of his injuries and stop the bleeding. When Helen heard what had happened to her son, she remembers asking God again for more help. She said, "I decided in that moment that I had to lay it all on God, that it wasn't my fault, and so even before I knew who had done this to my boy, I forgave him."

Police knew exactly who had done this to her boy. They knew where he lived. They knew what he looked like, and they knew he had now committed the act he once bragged about in prison, to capture, rape, and mutilate a young boy.

HELEN HARLOW INTERVIEW

From terrible ordeal come words of wisdom

AMONG all the cries of outrage resulting from that awful incident in Tacoma, where a little boy was raped and sexually mutilated, some of the calmest and wisest words have come from what might seem an unlikely source: the boy's mother.

Despite her ordeal, Helen Harlow touched all the right chords in a heart-wrenching interview with KING-TV reporter Julie Blacklow. No one who heard it or read excerpts could come away unmoved by her quiet voice of sense and reason.

Poignantly, Harlow said she had found inspiration in the attitude of her son, whose spirits remain high.

"The strength that I was hoping to instill in him is definitely there," she said. "He's not looking at this as a problem. He's just looking at it as how it is. And so now, let's get on with life."

Her son has become "every child," Harlow said insightfully. "And that's what we're having to deal with next, making sure that every child has a safe environment."

AN EDITORIAL IN THE SEATTLE TIMES ABOUT MY INTERVIEW WITH HELEN HARLOW.

Soon after Shriner was arrested, I was assigned to cover this story. My shock, disgust, and fury were no different from the thousands of others who lived in the region. As the story came out about what had happened to this child, local television, radio stations, and newspapers received thousands of calls from an outraged and shocked public. It was, in my memory, the biggest response ever to a criminal act.

The first and only time I saw Earl Kenneth Shriner was at his trial in Tacoma. I learned, after almost twenty years of covering stories of killers, rapists, and child molesters, they often act and appear as the guy next door and often are that person. Earl Shriner hardly fit that description. He looked like the savage he was. His face was bloated, his hair disheveled, and his features contorted and almost deformed. He did not look human, and of course, his actions indicated he was not. There he sat, at the defendant's table, undeserving of justice, I thought, but getting it anyway.

Helen Harlow could not bring herself to attend the trial. She stayed home with her son Ryan, still recovering from the physical and emotional scars of his ordeal. She did go one day, when Ryan had to testify and identify the demon who attacked him. As the prosecutor said in her closing arguments, Ryan identified Shriner "with certainty and confidence." Helen watched as her son faced his tormenter, and I watched her. She seemed calm and serene, noble and very brave. How, I wondered, could she not scream out her hatred for this monster? Ryan's father, Lowell, traveled from Oregon to see his son's attacker. I thought at any moment he might lose control and try to kill Shriner. I might have done that, but both parents stayed calm, at least on the outside.

Helen remembered the deal she had made with God: "No death for my child. And I will forgive anything that has happened."

I had a young son, just a few years older than Ryan. Watching this vile creature during the trial, I doubted I could ever forgive such a gruesome and unspeakable act had it happened to my child. I fought my own urges to scream at him. I steeled myself, quashed my emotions and did my job. But it was this crime, more than any I covered in my entire career, that managed to pierce my interior shield. Knowing of the horrific attacks on this little boy and imagining the suffering he endured made me physically ill. I could not shake the images and emotions I was feeling. My carefully constructed armor had cracked. Thirty years later, as I write this, I am crying again.

From the very beginning of this nightmare, Helen Harlow prayed for help. She said, "I hurt so much I could not handle the pain, so I needed to turn to God and to all of the champions who surrounded me."

On May 20, 1990, a year to the day after his blood-curdling crime, six men and six women on the jury took only four hours to find Earl Shriner guilty of two counts of first-degree rape, one count of attempted murder, and one count of assault. Soon after the verdict, Shriner was sentenced to more than one hundred thirty-one years in prison. The prosecutor said in her closing argument that there was "no doubt Shriner, a man with a lengthy, violent history, was the man who committed the crime." News of the verdict rippled throughout the region and the world.

Helen Harlow remarked at the end of the trial, "Praise God, it's over."

Soon after the trial ended, Helen Harlow invited me into her home to give the only interview she would allow. It was, as noted in a *Seattle Times* editorial, "heart-wrenching." Ryan's mother told me, and many residents of Washington State who wanted to hear from her, "The strength that I was hoping to instill in him is definitely there. He's not looking at this as a problem. He's just looking at it as how it is. And so now, let's get on with life."

She was, as the *Times* noted, "a quiet voice of sense and reason" who had found inspiration in the attitude of her son. Here was the mother of a child, a victim of one of the most horrifying crimes anyone could have imagined, comforting *us*.

The *Seattle Times* editorial said: "She was justifiably critical of loopholes that allow known sex criminals to roam free and strike again."

"We have preventive medicine," Helen said. "How come we don't have preventive corrections?"

I asked her what could be done, what did she want to see happen?

"I don't want to hear any more about 'we can't do it, we don't have the money. We can't do it, we don't have the space.' You have to tell us how we CAN. You have to give us an outlet."

Following her son's attack, Helen Harlow became a crusader for children's rights and helped start what was called the Tennis Shoe Brigade, along with parents of other child victims. The *Seattle Times* editorial board urged Washington State public officials to listen. And they did. Soon after Shriner was convicted and sentenced, John Ladenburg worked to adopt a notification law in Pierce County to let residents know if sex predators were living in their neighborhoods. The Washington State Legislature soon passed similar legislation, the Community Protection Act of 1990, making it a state law that all jurisdictions must notify communities where sex offenders were living. A three-tier ranking system was created to assess the danger levels of sex offenders. The law passed by the Washington State Legislature became the first in the country to lengthen terms for sex offenders and allow indefinite confinement for high-risk offenders after they served their full sentences. The statute also allowed police to notify communities where sex offenders were living. Similar legislation was subsequently adopted in all fifty states.

ONCE THE SCENE OF A HORRIFYING CRIME…NOW A PARK…DEDICATED TO RYAN.

Ryan, meanwhile, known at the time of the crime only as "the little Tacoma boy" in order to protect his privacy, underwent a series of surgeries to repair the physical damage to his body and went into therapy to help with the psychological trauma. His bravery astonished his mother. As he got older, he decided he did not want or need further counseling; he felt ready to move on with his life. And he did. The park where he was attacked was cleaned up, bushes cut back, and trash removed. Mother and son frequently walked there, and one day Ryan said to his mother, "I just see a park here."

Helen said that on more than one occasion she could not figure out who was healing whom. They were each other's strength and ballast. Not surprisingly, Helen said Ryan would lash out from time to time, punching his fists through walls in their home. She never asked him to repress his anger, just told him to please confine his rage and fists to one wall in their home.

Hundreds of thousands of dollars poured in from all corners of the world, and a trust fund was set up to help Ryan go on with his life. He lived off a monthly stipend, which put him through college where he studied upholstery. He bought a house, sold it, bought another, and had big plans to open a skate park someday. He had girlfriends but never married.

According to *Tacoma News Tribune* writer Paul Sand, Ryan "lived every day like there wouldn't be another."

On June 9, 2005, twenty-three-year-old Ryan Alan Hade ran out of days. A little before 10:00 p.m., about five miles from his home, Ryan's motorcycle collided with a pickup truck, and he died at the scene, sixteen years after Earl Shriner grabbed him from his first bike. News of the accident listed the victim as Ryan Hade, and at first, there was little publicity about his death. He had been known only as "the little Tacoma boy," so at first people did not make the connection. Soon, Helen said, the floodgates opened again, as the community realized who died in that accident. Ryan was cremated, his ashes scattered in places that he loved. A recreation center and a park near their home was, in time, named after him.

Today, Helen says she is "in a good place," living in Tacoma where she can see the sun rise and set every day, where she washes her dishes, does her laundry, and remembers, through occasional tears, that the too-short life of her son had great purpose. "We'll never know," she said, "whose lives were spared because of changes made after Ryan's ordeal."

Pierce County prosecutor John Ladenburg, who tried desperately to keep Shriner in prison, has no doubt many children are alive and safe today because of the laws passed after Ryan's attack.

"What happened to Ryan was," he said years later, "extremely predictable and yet we could not stop it. This crime was the worst of the worst . . . the most terrible thing I ever had to deal with. There were no laws on the books, so we had to create them. All of us—the parents of victims and lawmakers and the public—we all tried to do some good after so much evil . . . and I am certain we did."

Hundreds, perhaps thousands of violent predators, Ladenburg said, "will never be set free to harm anyone again. In his death we found purpose. That is Ryan's great and lasting legacy."

Chapter 37

Enough Was Enough

BETWEEN COVERING ASSORTED NORTHWEST CATASTROPHES for ABC and NBC, I had the great, good fortune to work for *Entertainment Tonight* (*ET*), conducting interviews with various celebrities shooting movies in the Puget Sound area or just making a stop to promote themselves or a product they were hyping. I recall lines of salivating women outside a Seattle department store waiting to stare at Jim Palmer, the former star baseball pitcher and Hall of Famer. He was there to sell his line of men's underwear, but there was hardly a man to be seen. The women claimed to be there to buy briefs for their boyfriends and husbands, but they were transfixed by the stunning good looks of Mr. Palmer. So was I. Sadly, he wore a suit that day. When Vanna White came to town to sign her book, a line of excited men stretched for blocks with hardly a woman in sight.

ET gave me the opportunity to meet Sylvester Stallone (a very nice guy), Arnold Schwarzenegger (also charming), and among others, Sean Penn, reputed to hate the press and be among the most difficult people to interview. It did not help that when Sean Penn was here to promote his film at the Seattle International Film Festival, some of the *ET* executives flew up from LA and sat behind me as I talked with him. Before the interview, I made sure to see all of his movies, and the subject of his new film, about an abused wife, was an issue I often covered in my news stories. I found common ground between us, and he was ready, willing, and easy to interview.

Enough, starring Jennifer Lopez, was another movie about an abused wife, shot partly in the Seattle area. *ET* hired me to go to the set, shoot a little video of people shooting film, and do an on-camera, sit-down interview with the star. I was prompted to try to interview co-stars Billy Campbell and Noah Wyle, if they were standing around waiting to be called for a scene. I never saw Billy, but Noah was a very nice and casual guy. I remember his comment to me, referring to Ms. Lopez: "So are you enjoying dealing with the corporation?" He was sarcastically referring to the coterie of handlers always surrounding her, lest anybody get just a bit too close.

The *ET* crew, which included the cameraman, audio engineer, and me, walked over to an out-of-the-way spot, set up our lights, camera, and audio equipment, and waited for the arrival of the very busy and much-in-demand Jennifer Lopez. An hour passed. Another. Then another. We were bored and well aware we were not going to make it back to Seattle to feed the video to Los Angeles in time for that night's show. I called *ET*. They said no problem. "Just feed it by satellite when you can, and we'll run it tomorrow night."

Then, finally, she appeared, cranky, a bit disheveled, with very little make-up, looking plain and plainly annoyed. Clearly, she had had a long and tiring day. While the end result of movie-making is a movie, the process of making a film is anything but glamourous. Hours are spent waiting around as technicians and set designers do the necessary drudgework. In terms of stimulation, it is akin to watching paint dry or grass grow, but less dramatic. Ms. Lopez apparently had had about all she could take as she approached us.

It was abundantly clear she did not want to be there. Neither did we. Working for *Entertainment Tonight*, we were there, as always, to publicize a film and let celebrities say anything they wanted. We were not there to investigate, probe, or make trouble. *ET* today is basically the same as it ever was, a program promoting pop culture. Easy and free publicity.

As she sat down in front of our camera, she was sullen and pouty to the point of rudeness as if to say "let's get this over with."

I agreed. Instinctively, without thinking too much, I turned to my crew and told them to pack up our equipment. We were leaving without conducting the interview. This confused and infuriated her handlers, those young people with clipboards and walkie-talkies pinned to their shirts, often the scourges of most movie sets. Nobody walks out on Jennifer Lopez. Almost nobody. She seemed shocked at what was happening. I was too. I could not believe what I had just done.

I did not immediately call Los Angeles to tell them we would have no video to send. I just left. After producing dozens of successful stories for *ET* over the years, I knew they would support my decision, which, despite protestations from the Lopez "corporation," they did. As the movie poster for *Enough* says above the title: "Everyone has a limit."

A MOVIE POSTER FROM THE FILM 'ENOUGH'...
SHOT IN SEATTLE...STARRING JENNIFER LOPEZ.

That day, I reached mine.

Chapter 38

The Most Handsome Man in the World

BY LATE 1995, after more than twenty years at the NBC affiliate, KING Television, after being fired, reinstated, covering a conglomeration of murderers, child molesters, and political scandals, I had enough and resigned, this time of my own volition.

The phone rang with an unexpected caller on the other end, from Ken Hatch, the president of the local CBS station, KIRO Television. At the time, KIRO was owned by the Mormon Church, so I was more than a little shocked that Ken wanted to hire me, the Jewish, well-known troublemaker, to work in his newsroom.

"We need you to stir things up a little bit," Ken said, "and you're the perfect person to do it. We've become a little boring and predictable, and we need some new blood here."

I accepted his offer, and because I was already doing freelance work for *Entertainment Tonight,* which aired on CBS in Seattle, I would be able to work for both KIRO and *ET.* John Fitzgerald Kennedy Jr. was coming to town, and both wanted me to cover his visit promoting his new magazine, *George,* a blend of celebrity and politics. After appearances in other cities, other freelance producers hired by *ET* were unable to get an interview with him. I was their last hope. Seattle was his final stop.

"We really need you to come through for us," an *ET* producer said. "He isn't talking to anyone."

How weird, I thought. *He's trying to advertise his product, a magazine, but he does not want to talk to the media about it.*

My video crew and I began searching for him in the cavernous Washington State Convention Center. The setting for JFK Jr.'s event was in one of the largest rooms in the building, half the size of a football field. An assortment of public relations people was vying for seats towards the front to ogle the man and the enlarged sample of his magazine propped on an easel. Supermodel Cindy Crawford dressed as George Washington was featured on the magazine's first cover. I scoured the place looking for my colleagues to see where everyone was setting up their equipment but could not spot them. Then, I saw dozens of television, radio, and newspaper reporters relegated to the very back, far away from the star of the show. My *ET*/KIRO crew and I were directed to join them.

We stayed where we were, much closer to the main stage but still too far away to capture the event, even with a powerful zoom lens. I had to quickly devise some plan to get us all closer to the man the world knew as John-John, son of the assassinated president. I walked over to my media cronies and told them we had to do something to get closer. I asked if I had their support and would they be willing to walk out of the room if my strategy did not work. I was planning on playing hardball with JFK Jr.'s handlers. My cohorts agreed being confined to the back of the room was not going to work, that there was no way to get decent pictures or hear what he might say. Excluding the press from a media event ostensibly seeking publicity about it was ridiculous. There was no way we could do our jobs stuck in the back. They wished me luck.

I walked toward the stage, aware I had to get to his handlers if I was ever going to get to him. I began waving my arms around, hoping someone would see me and come over to talk. I caught the attention of a very short, dark-haired woman standing close to John and mouthed the words: "Please come here . . . I need to talk with you."

She casually walked over, and it crossed my mind I recognized her, even though we had never met. She was, like me—a pushy, cocky Jewish girl who loved being in charge and telling people what they could and could not do. I was, however, older, taller, blond, bitchier, more experienced, and more determined. She introduced herself as Nancy:

"What do you want?" she asked with unmasked hostility.

"Well," I said, "I want you to listen to me very carefully."

"What is it?"

"You see all those people at the back of the room? They're all reporters and photographers from the local newspaper, TV and radio stations, and there are national reporters here from the Associated Press. I'm here working for *Entertainment Tonight*. We all work for different people, but we're all unhappy about the same thing . . . being sent to the back of the room where we really can't do our jobs."

"Well, I'm sorry," she said, "That's the best we can do."

"Well, I'm sorry too because if we can't get closer, we're all going to leave, and your boss will not get the publicity he wants. Nobody is going to win here."

"They won't leave," she insisted.

"Yes, we will."

As she started to turn away, still doubting my threat was real, I called her back. "Hey, Nancy, let me tell you something. It's your job to go over to your boss and tell him exactly what I said to you. I want to watch you pass on my request, and if he says he doesn't want us up there, we'll leave and we can all get on with our day. And one more thing. I would appreciate it if he would give me a one-on-one interview after he's done with his presentation. It's for *Entertainment Tonight*. They would be very grateful . . . and they want it for tonight's show."

With a slight smirk and a "yeah, sure, that's not going to happen" look on her face, she walked back to the stage and passed on my request. Instantly, JFK Jr. gestured to me and told his little minion to bring the entire press corps closer to the front of the room. Everyone packed up his or her equipment and relocated closer to the stage. We all shot video and still photos as he talked about his hopes for his new magazine, that he wanted to get younger generations interested in politics and provide substance with a little glitter thrown in.

The toddler in the blue jacket who had saluted his father's casket decades earlier grew up and became breathtakingly handsome. It was hard even to look at him. He was chiseled, masculine perfection, more beautiful in person than in his photographs, which were pretty remarkable. During his presentation, he captivated his audience, whom I think were as interested in seeing him as hearing about *George* magazine. When he was done, almost everyone stayed, huddled in small groups just to stare at him for a few more minutes.

JFK, JR...THE MOST HANDSOME MAN IN THE WORLD.

Nancy, the grumpy assistant, had agreed earlier to my request for an interview with JFK Jr. after allowing all the media closer to him to record his remarks. My crew and I went down to the front of the stage and positioned our tripod and camera in front of the easel with a sample cover of the magazine with Barbra Streisand dressed as a peasant. Then JFK Jr. walked over to me and said, "Okay . . . I'm all yours."

If only.

He belonged to someone else, to his future bride, Carolyn Bessette. Rumors abounded he was engaged and about to be married, but I thought I should just stick to questions about his magazine. All *Entertainment Tonight* really wanted was some video of the iconic *ET* microphone flag underneath his handsome face. What he said really did not matter all that much.

He answered a few questions about where the idea for the magazine came from. Politics was in his blood, he said, and he had been raised in the spotlight with photographers using him to sell magazines. He thought he should use other celebrities to help sell his. After a couple of minutes, knowing the public was hungry to know more about his personal life, he said, "It's okay . . . I'll give you three questions about my private life."

Though personal questions were often *ET*'s stock in trade, I said, "Mr. Kennedy, I really don't want to pry into your personal life. You get hounded enough. I'm just grateful you agreed to this interview and allowed the press to get a little closer to you." He seemed surprised but relieved I declined his offer to nose into his private life. "Thank you," he replied.

A WEIRD PHOTO OF ME TO THE LEFT OF JFK, JR. WHO I WAS ABOUT TO INTERVIEW.

JFK Jr. was as polite and patient as he was powerful and patrician. Four years later, in 1999, he was gone, along with his wife Carolyn and her sister Lauren. He was flying a small plane that crashed off Martha's Vineyard in Massachusetts in the fog. Without its star founder and editor, *George* magazine did not survive either. The final issue was published in 2001 with the most handsome man in the world on its cover.

Chapter 39

With a Little Help from My Friends

I HAD AGONIZED OVER WHAT TO WEAR for a month before the first Beatles concert in America in Washington, DC, in 1964. Then I only got within one hundred feet of Paul McCartney, and he missed his chance to meet me, fall in love with me, and sweep me off my feet.

Twenty-six years later, he was going to have another opportunity to fall in love with me. Again, I fretted over what to wear because this time I was going to get closer, at a press conference before his 1990 concert at Seattle's Kingdome. I was now a successful television journalist, a reporter of good standing, and having regaled everyone ad nauseum with my story of seeing the first Beatles concert, I was determined to cover Paul McCartney's performance.

Heading into the bowels of the Kingdome, setting up our cameras and microphones, I was as nervous as the seventeen-year-old girl who saw him onstage at the Washington Coliseum. Dozens of metal, folding chairs awaited the arrival of a throng of television, newspaper, and radio reporters. When I arrived, I noticed a couple of empty seats at the front of the room, just across from the table where my idol would soon arrive. My media friends, tired of hearing me brag about the first Beatle concert, had generously left a front row seat just for me.

Paul walked out alone and sat down at the table, no more than ten feet away from me. It would be seven years before he was knighted by the Queen of England, but he was already royalty to me. In an instant, I was transported back to my seventeen-year-old self, the girl in the herringbone jumper hoping to catch his eye and eventually marry him. My adoration was not dulled at all with the passage of time. The Beatles brought joy to millions of us in the wake of the assassination of President Kennedy. I worshipped all of them, but Paul was my great teenage crush.

I started to cry.

Before any questions were asked, before Paul had a chance to say anything, he looked straight at me and asked, "Are you all right?"

"I'll be okay," I responded. "I just need a minute here."

He smiled. My colleagues seemed amused, seeing their take-no-prisoners, tough reporter friend actually reveal a softer side. As I composed myself, others asked questions. I was too embarrassed to say anything, transfixed on his handsome face and seductive British accent. By then, of course, he had found the love of his life, his wife Linda. My childhood fantasy that he would fall in love with me was to remain just that, a fantasy, a delusion no doubt possessed by millions of women who, like me, were once hysterical teenagers screaming at the Beatles.

One of his road managers heard I had been at that first concert on February 11, 1964, and invited me back to the private sanctum for a few minutes alone with Paul McCartney. I had stopped crying but was no less star-struck and mesmerized, now standing inches away from him. He said the first American concert was one of the few the Beatles vividly remembered. It was, he said something of a blur after that. He was charming, as handsome as ever, and understanding of my weepy display. I guess he was accustomed to similar reactions since the Beatles had stepped onto the world stage almost thirty years earlier.

I still wonder, though . . . if only we had met in 1964.

Chapter 40

Elvis Has Entered the Building

JUST BEFORE 9 A.M. in late December 1970, Egil "Bud" Krogh (rhymes with "rogue") received a phone call from Dwight Chapin. Both were aides to President Richard Nixon. Within two years' time, Nixon, Chapin, and Krogh would all be embroiled in the scandal known as Watergate, but at that moment in time, Watergate was just the name of a hotel and shopping complex in Washington, DC.

EGIL 'BUD' KROGH STANDING BEHIND RICHARD NIXON. *FAMILY OF EGIL KROGH.*

Chapin alerted Krogh that the "King," Elvis Presley, was in town, and he wanted to meet with President Nixon. Elvis had a present for Nixon and wanted to be made a federal agent to help in the war on drugs. Chapin asked Bud Krogh to make it happen. At noon on December 21, 1970, Elvis arrived at the White House wearing a dark-purple velvet cape, tight-fitting velvet pants, a white shirt, gold chains dangling from his neck, and a large, gold belt buckle. The gift he brought Nixon was an ornate gun with silver bullets in a display case, a collector's item Elvis thought the president would appreciate. It was not appreciated by the Secret Service, which confiscated it. Firearms are not permitted in the Oval Office.[1*]

RICHARD NIXON WELCOMING ELVIS INTO THE OVAL OFFICE. *FAMILY OF EGIL KROGH.*

Bud Krogh met Elvis, one of his teenage idols, before taking him to meet Nixon. The King showed Bud pictures of his wife and baby, and Krogh showed Elvis into the Oval Office. Elvis and President Nixon shook hands, smiled a lot at each other, and posed for pictures.

Before he left, Elvis Presley, at Nixon's request, received a badge designating him a special assistant in the Bureau of Narcotics and Dangerous Drugs.

---

1   * The gun, a Colt .45, is on display as Exhibit 119 in the Nixon Library in Yorba Linda, California.

INSIDE THE OVAL OFFICE AS ELVIS GLANCES AT EGIL KROGH. *FAMILY OF EGIL KROGH.*

ELVIS' BADGE FROM THE U.S. DEPARTMENT OF JUSTICE. *FAMILY OF EGIL KROGH.*

Seven years later, Elvis died of a drug overdose, and within two years, Bud Krogh stood before a federal judge who sentenced him to prison. Neither could have imagined his fate the day Elvis entered the White House due to the efforts of Bud Krogh.

EGIL KROGH was raised in Seattle, graduated with highest honors from Principia College in Illinois, and after serving in the US Navy for three years, came home and graduated from the University of Washington School of Law in 1968. He joined the law firm of family friend John Ehrlichman. Both soon left to become aides to Richard Nixon, Ehrlichman as counsel to the President for Domestic Affairs, Krogh as liaison to the Federal Bureau of Investigation and the Bureau of Narcotics and Dangerous Drugs. Krogh was barely in his thirties, and the heady atmosphere of working in the White House could be, as Krogh said himself, "intimidating." Overpowering enough, perhaps, to deflect the heading of one's moral compass.

In June of 1971, the so-called Pentagon Papers were secretly leaked to the press, government documents about the failing war in Vietnam. The official government story was far more optimistic than what was being discussed behind closed doors by military commanders. Military analyst Daniel Ellsberg immediately admitted he was the man who had leaked the papers.

The Nixon White House, facing increasing public pressure about Vietnam, became obsessed about discrediting Daniel Ellsberg. About a month after the release of the Pentagon Papers, a covert Special Investigations Unit, nicknamed 'The Plumbers', was formed to stop further leaks and attempt damage control. White House counsel John Ehrlichman appointed Bud Krogh to head the group and carry out its first mission, an illegal break-in to the office of Daniel Ellsberg's psychiatrist. Ehrlichman told Krogh this order was "of the highest national security importance," as stated by the president. It was an attempt to find disparaging information about Ellsberg's mental health and to smear him. G. Gordon Liddy and E. Howard Hunt ransacked the office, found nothing incriminating and left.

One year later, another illegal mission was undertaken, the break-in at the Democratic National Headquarters at the Watergate complex in Washington, DC. Some of the burglars were former members of the covert plumbers group, which had been disbanded earlier. This time, the prowl-ers were caught wiretapping phones and stealing documents and later were connected to Richard Nixon's reelection campaign. While Krogh was not part of the Watergate burglary, his role in the Ellsberg crime came out in the later investigation. The scandal, branded as Watergate, turned into flood-gates that ended Nixon's presidency and the careers of many people who broke the law trying to salvage it.

In 1973, under federal indictment, Egil Krogh pleaded guilty to crimi-nal conspiracy for violating the civil rights of Daniel Ellsberg's psychiatrist. Krogh was one of the few men in the wreckage of Watergate to enter a guilty plea saying, "I came to accept that I could no longer defend my conduct." At his sentencing, Judge Gerherd Gesell read a quote from the renowned Justice Louis Brandeis which read in part: "Crime is contagious. If the gov-ernment becomes a lawbreaker, it breeds contempt for law; it invites every man to become a law unto himself; it invites anarchy."

Those words bore deep into Bud Krogh.

Dozens of others were tried, convicted, and sent to prison. Krogh served only four and a half months of a longer sentence, due in part to his admission of guilt.

When he was released from prison, he went to see Dr. Lewis Fielding, Daniel Ellsberg's psychiatrist, to apologize for his part in the break-in. He also spent a couple of hours with his former boss, Richard Nixon, at his San Clemente, California home. He asked the former president whether he felt any guilt about Watergate. Nixon told him he did not.

Bud Krogh returned home to Seattle and was soon disbarred from practicing law by the Washington State Supreme Court.

On June 7, 1994, I walked into the law offices of Krogh & Leonard in down-town Seattle, twenty-five years since the creation of the plumbers unit. For some time, I tried and failed repeatedly to reach Bud Krogh, to talk about Watergate, and find out what life was like for him after the scandal. Then my luck changed. My former husband, Richard Blacklow, was a friend of Krogh's, part of a group of lawyers who regularly jogged downtown during their lunch breaks. I asked Richard to call Bud for me and help get me in the door. It worked.

Bud Krogh greeted me with a handshake, a big smile, and a bigger hug. It surprised me, but I think his friendship with my ex-husband helped him feel comfortable with me, and he seemed to know me from my years on television as a reporter. As cameras and lights were positioned, I entertained him with stories of my trespassing on John Ehrlichman's Seattle property to get an interview and shoving aside Secret Service agents to get to Richard Nixon. He smiled at my antics and said he was surprised I was not arrested or shot on either occasion. I told him I was also surprised. As the subject turned to his past and to Watergate, he became solemn and deeply reflective talking about the mistakes he had made, his skewed sense of right and wrong, what he called "ethical fading." He struggled and lost his internal battle about what he had been asked to do, believing his actions were justified in the name of national security, decisions sanctioned by the president. Over time, he was haunted by what he had done and realized the seriousness of his breach of duty as a lawyer and as an American citizen. Though I mentioned how young he was when he lost his way, he would not allow his age to be used as an excuse for what he did.

His remorse was heartfelt, deeply moving, and honest. It was not an easy path back from the darkness, as he explained it to me. As he talked, he paused more than once and closed his eyes, remembering the arduous, long road he traveled to be readmitted to the bar. His first attempt was rejected. But in 1980, the court was impressed with work he had done in public administration and classes he had taught in a number of colleges, focusing on ethics. A majority of the Washington State Supreme court approved Bud Krogh's bid for a second chance to practice law.

As our cameras, lights, and audio equipment were being packed up, Bud stood up with a big smile on his face and said he wanted to show me something. He walked over to a large, cardboard box saying, "This just arrived today . . . about one of my happiest days in the White House."

He pulled out a copy of his just-released book, *The Day Elvis Met Nixon*, his detailed account of the King's visit to the White House. It is hilarious, weird, and quite wonderful. In one of the pictures, Bud and Elvis are smiling at each other. Bud talked about how down to earth Elvis was and thrilled to get his badge from the Department of Justice.

Bud inscribed a copy for me:

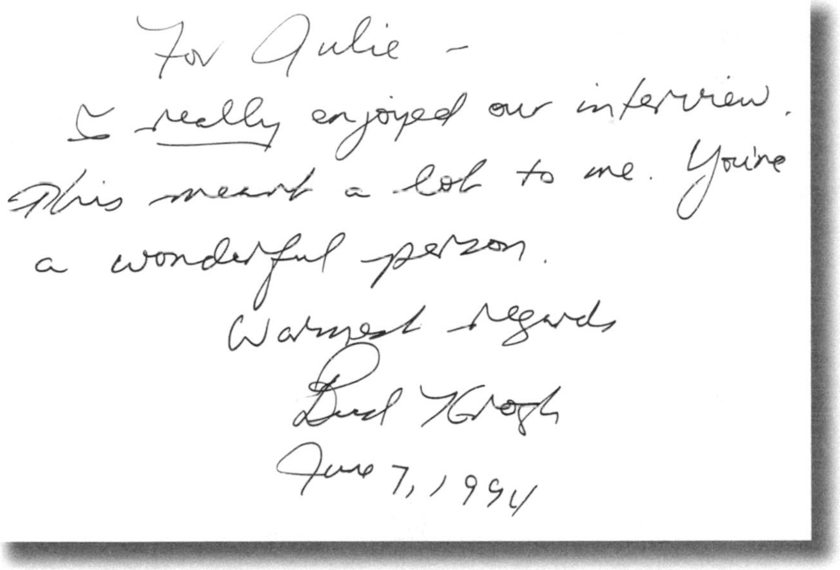

> *For Julie—*
>
> *I <u>really</u> enjoyed our interview. This meant a lot to me. You're a wonderful person.*
>
> *Warmest regards,*
> *Bud Krogh*
> *June 7, 1994*

For Julie –
I really enjoyed our interview.
This meant a lot to me. You're
a wonderful person.
Warmest regards
Bud Krogh
June 7, 1994

INSCRIPTION FROM BUD KROGH IN THE BOOK HE GAVE TO ME. JUNE, 1994.

I felt the same way about Bud Krogh, a wonderful man who found his way back after veering far off course, and resetting his moral compass with dignity, deep remorse, and a renewed sense of purpose. He and his son Matthew Krogh wrote a book, *Integrity: Good People, Bad Choices and Life Lessons from the White House*. Bud is currently living in Washington, DC, recovering from a stroke, ever mindful of the message he hopes we all will remember:

Never fail to ask . . . is this right?

I HAD THREE ENCOUNTERS in my career with men of the Watergate scandal: John Ehrlichman, Richard Nixon, and Bud Krogh. There is another connection . . . a sweeter one . . . a recipe my mother copied from the Watergate Bakery in that infamous hotel where the break-in occurred, not far from my childhood home. She called it the Watergate Cake. The confection is green, the color of Christmas, and I've been baking it for decades every December. It is foolproof, cheap, and as unhealthy as it is delicious.

THE WATERGATE CAKE

Mix together:
> 1 Duncan Hines Yellow Cake Mix
> 1 package Jell-O Pistachio Pudding
> 3 eggs, beaten
> 1 cup vegetable oil
> 1 cup club soda
> Poppy seeds/pistachios/walnuts (optional)

Pour into a Bundt pan. Bake for 45 minutes at 350°.

Remove from Bundt pan, and for additional calories, sprinkle powdered sugar over the cake.

Chapter 41

Love Is Real

L OVE IS A NOUN, a verb, an emotion, and the name of a man. Love Israel. A visionary who founded one of the biggest and longest surviving communes in United States history. It began in the late Sixties, grew to more than 350 members, fractured in the 1980s, regrouped in the Nineties, and survives to this day in smaller numbers and in disparate places.

Love Israel began life as Paul Erdmann. He spent part of his childhood in Seattle, part in California and came back to the Pacific Northwest in 1968. He opened a drop-in center for disillusioned young people, but he was, in fact, an older version of the kids he was trying to help. He wanted a more spiritual life, divined a new name for himself, and began buying houses in a quiet, Seattle neighborhood. Paul Erdmann became Love Israel, a name when divided and slightly rearranged—Love Is Real—expressed the core tenet of his and his followers' beliefs.

"We are one."

"Love is the answer."

"Now is the time."

These were familiar phrases to anyone who lived in the 1960s and enticed hundreds of people to join the Love Israel family. What began in a little bungalow grew to more than a dozen homes on an upscale hilltop in Seattle's quiet Queen Anne neighborhood.

A HOME ON SEATTLE'S QUEEN ANNE HILL,
BUILT BY THE LOVE ISRAEL FAMILY. *LOVE ISRAEL FAMILY.*

In the early 1970s as a freshly minted television reporter, I began getting calls from neighbors, fearful the Charles Manson family had moved north. Charles Manson led a notorious cult known for slaughtering innocent people in California, including pregnant actress Sharon Tate. A disciple later told authorities the family wanted to commit a crime that would shock the world, which indeed it did. Now some Seattle residents feared the same fate awaited them.

Aware that they looked and lived differently than others, members of the Love Israel family went out of their way to embrace nearby residents and not kill them. They introduced themselves, cleaned up an overgrown park, shared food, and started a nighttime neighborhood watch. Two robed men at a time walked the streets at night to protect homes and people, trying to keep the peace, not disrupt it. Whatever their good intentions and good deeds, the generous reach of the new Love Israel family did not extend far enough to calm everyone. Some neighbors were still nervous. I decided I needed to go meet the family myself.

I knocked on the door of the ornate, wood-framed house and was welcomed inside to meet the Love Israel family. If I had any concerns about entering a demonic cult of devil worshippers, my fears instantly disappeared. Perhaps the only traits this family shared with the Mansons were beards and long hair.

Like their leader, these followers adopted the Israel surname and took on new first names symbolizing positive virtues such as Honesty, Devotion, Confidence, Endearment, Healing, and Serious Israel, to name just a few. Some were married, others were not, and many were single followers, but all considered themselves part of one large family, bound by the same last name and shared core beliefs.

MEMBERS OF THE LOVE ISRAEL FAMILY
ATOP ONE OF THEIR HOMES IN SEATTLE. *LOVE ISRAEL FAMILY.*

Serious Israel was well named. Tall, handsome, and reserved, he exuded calm and confidence without having to say a word. It was soothing just to stand near him. From the genesis of the Love Israel family, he was considered the number 2 man behind its leader. Quiet, compelling . . . Serious. Like so many young people in the Sixties, the former Robert Brewer wanted off a traditional life track and headed west in search of something different. He found what he was looking for in his new life with the Love family.

Love Israel, the head of the growing clan was also well named. He was devastatingly handsome, charming, and seductive. With outstretched arms and a big smile, he hugged me as if he had known me forever. With his robes, long hair, and generosity of spirit, he seemed Christ-like . . . beatific, wise, and rapturous. His demeanor conveyed the impression that he knew things most of us did not, and that aura drew people to him. He was utterly captivating.

We interviewed several Love family members, filmed the interiors of the impressive, immaculate house, and returned to KING Television with a convincing story about the quirky family setting down roots in Seattle. We assured viewers the family was focused on setting up businesses, expanding their tribe of followers, and not killing anyone. Within a few years, the compound grew to eighteen homes filled with more than two hundred people. As the family expanded, it outgrew its Seattle neighborhood and moved sixty miles north to a large ranch in Arlington, Washington.

Love Israel preached love and kindness as a way of life and sought a peaceful, collaborative way of living together for his family, aspirations held by millions in the Sixties but put into practice in the Love compound. Describing themselves as "very, very clean hippies," they helped raise each other's children, shared communal meals, occasionally shared beds, and tried to dismantle societal boundaries they believed separated people instead of connecting them. They practiced what Love Israel preached. For a while it worked.

Despite its credo of love being the answer, the family suffered some of the same troubles as other households, with fights over money and struggles over power.

They lost hundreds of members but regrouped at their farm, growing organic food, which supported their local restaurant, and hosting an annual festival open to the public. It was known as the Garlic Festival, a three-day event featuring dozens of bands, including Country Joe and the Fish, and devoted to all things garlic. Country Joe McDonald was a close friend of Love's. I went to the festival once as a regular person, not a reporter. With the tie-dyed clothes, smell of pot wafting through the air, and an abundance of children with flowers in their hair, I was transported back to the 1960s.

Two decades passed before I visited the Love family again.

By the late Nineties, I was working at the CBS affiliate in Seattle, producing a series of reports about whatever happened to people I had covered decades earlier. In 1997, the Love Israel family was on my broadcast bucket list. I was invited up to the ranch in Arlington, acres of meadows and trees, dotted with small homes, yurts, a beautiful lake, and a large barn converted into a magnificent home and gathering place for the family. Love Israel, still the eponymous head of his smaller but thriving family, lived in the big house. We were free to roam around, interview people, shoot video, and just hang out, observe, and get a sense of life in their bucolic commune. Unlike their Seattle neighbors in the early days, most of the family's neighbors had no problem with the family. Members of the Love Israel clan were master carpenters, experts on land use and hydrology, and happy to share their skills with anyone who needed help, which included working as consultants with Snohomish County officials.

Before I sat down to interview Love in the sanctuary above his home, I wanted to talk first with the still handsome, calm, and perfectly named number 2 man, Serious Israel.

He escorted my crew and me to his beautiful yurt, and we began setting up our camera, tripod, and lights. Serious had some quick business to attend to and stepped out for a moment. Since the photographers forbade me from helping with or even touching their equipment, I passed time snooping around the yurt, staring at objects and pictures on his desk and on his walls. One picture caught my attention and stopped me cold. I stared at it, fixated on one face in what seemed to be an old family photo. Shocked by what I saw and in total disbelief, I asked Serious a question the moment he walked back through his door:

THE PHOTO I SPOTTED INSIDE THE HOME OF SERIOUS ISRAEL WITH MY BEST FRIEND FROM HIGH SCHOOL, MARTHA, AT THE CENTER IN THE BACK. *LOVE ISRAEL FAMILY.*

"Why is there a picture on your wall of my best friend from high school? Why is Martha Brewer's picture here?"

Serious answered in his quiet way, "She's my sister."

Oh my God, I thought.

She was also my best friend from Washington-Lee High School in Arlington, Virginia, and I had been trying for years to find her.

"Martha Brewer is your sister? Seriously, Serious?"

Before he was Serious Israel, he was Robert Brewer, Martha's older brother whom I had never met. He left the middle-class comfort of home in the suburbs of Washington, DC, headed for college, and then searched for a more meaningful life, which he eventually found thousands of miles from his hometown. His little sister, Martha, was my ballast in high school, the rare person who always has your back and is more than happy to let you be out front. She was that friend who understands how wacky you are but loves you anyway and who gives you a certain kind of look that tells you whether to keep going or pull back from a line you should not cross. We were in the same clubs, ran with the same group, attended the first Beatles concert together, and even double-dated on the night of our senior prom, the night I lost my virginity. After high school, we lost track of each other.

For decades, I tried to find her. I saw her once looking forlorn at a high school reunion, but we were living on different coasts, busy working, raising children, and trying to sustain failing marriages. Now here she was in a picture frame, standing at the center of her beautiful family, to the left of brother Robert Brewer, now Serious Israel, the man I was about to interview. Serious and I were both amazed at the coincidence of this discovery, and after our interview, we called his little sister, now living in Pennsylvania.

She was as shocked and delighted as we were. "It blew my mind," Martha told me years later. "It was just so, so powerful. It felt mystical to me. Serious was always the most important man in my life, and imagining you . . . so important to me . . . standing next to him astonished me and made me so happy! It was hard to take in . . . and I guess it was just serendipity at work. It was magic!"

Two weeks later, Martha came and stayed with me in my Seattle home. We looked at our high school yearbook and caught up with more than thirty years of life gone by. Her brother brought us together, and we discovered another link. Standing in my kitchen during another visit to Seattle, she told me her daughter was gay, as was my son. Despite our liberal politics and open minds about pretty much everything, we both struggled with the sexual identity of our children and helped each other with that challenge. It was never about disapproval, only about having to change what I call the "film in our heads" about what life was going to look like. We imagined our children would get married to partners of the opposite sex, have kids, and give us grandchildren. Martha and I helped each other re-edit our scripts. In 2004, Martha moved west, closer to her brother, her daughter, and me.

That same year the Love Israel family was forced by bankruptcy to sell the property in Arlington but regrouped once again to a smaller enclave in Bothell, south of the big ranch, closer to where it all began in Seattle almost fifty years earlier.

Love Israel himself, the powerful patriarch who founded his family, died in 2016 at the age of seventy-five of prostate cancer. His steadfast friend, Serious, became the elder statesman and spokesman for what remained of the Love family. Now in his late seventies, Serious remained the same, quiet-spoken man I had met decades earlier as I prepared to talk with him again.

LOVE ISRAEL, IN PRAYER AT HIS HOME IN ARLINGTON, WASHINGTON... WITH SERIOUS ISRAEL ON THE LEFT. *LOVE ISRAEL FAMILY.*

"I'm enjoying the ride," he said, "watching it all unfold again. No one is quite sure what to make of it all now. We seem to be focused on just enjoying one another in whatever ways are comfortable and convenient for each of us. Regardless of why or when we stopped living together, we all share a common experience in the family . . . unparalleled love and support."

THE LOVE ISRAEL FAMILY, ARLINGTON, WASHINGTON. *LOVE ISRAEL FAMILY.*

Serious's long hair is a little thinner, a little whiter now, his face as handsome as ever, his aura of calm still soothing everyone around him. On this day of our meeting, his little sister Martha is sitting next to me on a comfy sofa, no longer a photo on a wall.

In thinking back on my time with the Love Israel family, I am heartened that half a century from its beginnings, the family, though smaller, remains intact. Some live in homes near Seattle, others in the northeast part of Washington state. Though not physically connected as they once were, they are still bound by the deeply felt belief that love is the answer for all of us. A laudable aspiration for any family.

Chapter 42

Then There Was Ramtha

*"Condemnation without investigation
is the height of ignorance."*
—ALBERT EINSTEIN

RAMTHA IS A SEVEN-FOOT TALL, thirty-five-thousand-year-old Lemurian warrior. He claims to have led an army of two million soldiers, battled the Atlanteans, and conquered three-fourths of the known world. Before taking an extended hiatus, he promised to return someday.

Ramtha was true to his word.

ON A SUNDAY AFTERNOON IN 1977, JZ Knight was standing in her kitchen in Tacoma, Washington. (The *Z* in her name stands for "Zebra," a sobriquet she was given because of her ability to see things in black and white.) Until that moment, life seemed normal. The mother of two young boys was married to a dentist, going about her business when Ramtha appeared without warning. JZ recalled the moment.

He said, "Beloved woman, I am Ramtha the Enlightened One, and I have come to help you over the ditch. It is called the ditch of limitation. I am here, and we are going to do a grand work together."

For the former Judith Darlene Hampton, life was never the same again. She was still a wife and mother but became Ramtha's channel, his medium, a human through whom he was able to speak. Ramtha was a discarnate, a spiritual soul who still had much to say and chose JZ Knight to help him say it.

After two years with Ramtha, JZ bought eighty acres in Yelm, Washington, mostly undeveloped farmland about an hour south of Seattle. Residents of this rural town were disquieted and suspicious by talk of a thirty-five-thousand-year-old neighbor speaking through the body of a beautiful blonde. JZ built a huge house and established Ramtha's School of Enlightenment, bringing in students from around the world to study his teachings. For the sake of privacy, an imposing wall was constructed to keep out a curious public and press.

I was in that latter group, having tried and failed for many years to get behind the intriguing and imposing barrier. Then, in 1997, almost twenty years after moving to Yelm, JZ Knight invited local journalists to come for a visit, allowed onto the grounds and behind the wall for the first time.

The tall, black gates slowly swung open to a beautiful, cascading waterfall in front of a magnificent French-styled chateau. The house that JZ and Ramtha built was dazzling. Ramtha's School of Enlightenment was clearly thriving, both popular and profitable.

Television, newspaper, and radio reporters with their cameras and audio and video equipment were guided into an opulent room filled with large trees, surrounding a stunning, blue-tiled swimming pool.

A group of scientists and theologians sat behind a long, cloth-draped table at the front of the room. Their credentials were impressive, from Colgate and Temple Universities and from the Chicago Theological Seminary. They had observed Ramtha and the school for a couple of years, studied JZ as she channeled Ramtha, and watched as he taught his students in an attempt to understand or debunk what was happening. They measured her heart rate, brain waves, and muscle tension as she invoked Ramtha.

JZ had purpose behind our visit, to gain validation from respected professionals revealing their findings to a suspicious press corps, "to scientifically eliminate," Dr. Robert Moore from Chicago said, "the possibility of fraud. When you look into the eyes of this body when JZ is channeling, it's very striking."

"We cannot say what this is," said another researcher, "but we were able to show what it is not. It is not role playing, it is not mental disease, it is not delusional, it is not panic attacks."

Dr. Stanley Krippner, in a masterful understatement summed it up quite well: "It is puzzling."

There was little time for questions. JZ thanked everyone for coming and shook hands, but we were all on a deadline and needed to get back to put together a story of our brief encounter with Yelm's most famous resident. Ramtha, the real star of the show and the reason for this event, did not attend this particular gathering. For me that quick visit was a mere appetizer. I wanted the full meal and asked if we could come back the next day. JZ agreed, and I wanted to meet Ramtha for myself.

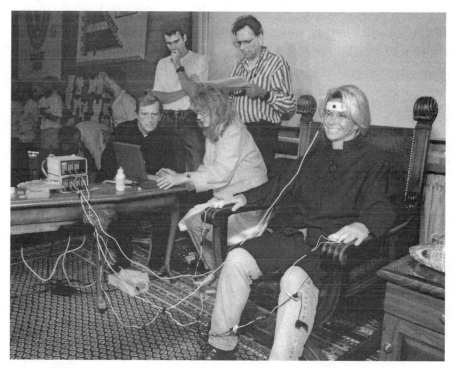

JZ Knight wired and ready for testing by scientists. *JZ Knight*

Photographer Glenn Aust and I had, in his impeccable phrase, "seen a lot of weird stuff in our time as journalists," the entire gamut of human experience from the ridiculous to the horrific and everything in between. We had never observed a thirty-five-thousand-year-old warrior speaking through another human being. The next day we returned to Yelm, pressed a button on the intercom to announce our arrival, and drove towards the big house once again.

"What the hell have we gotten ourselves into?" Glenn said. "I feel as if I'm going to a memorial service . . .but I don't know who died, and I don't know anyone here."

"I have no idea," I answered, "but we're in it now . . . we're here to see something we've never seen, so it'll be an adventure."

JZ Knight's chunky bulldogs ambled up to our news car as we unloaded our gear. She walked up behind them, greeted us, and to our complete surprise, said we could have the "run of the place" for the day. We were free to talk to students, interview the researchers and scientists we met the previous day, and watch Ramtha teach later that evening. Our cameras were not allowed to record him, but we could watch, the first journalists ever permitted inside the Great Hall. The school would provide us some videotape of the lecture, but we would be able to see it for ourselves. Good enough.

Before the evening lecture, I spoke with and interviewed several students who had been coming to Ramtha's school for years. All shared a common experience. Their lives had improved dramatically, they never felt coerced or controlled, and they understood the doubts people had about Ramtha. Longtime student Linda McCollom said, "The doubters have a right to doubt. I doubted. Everyone's skeptical at a certain point because you have to stretch what you're comfortable with."

Actress Linda Evans, of *Dynasty* and *The Big Valley*, moved to the Northwest to be closer to Ramtha's school. She, too, had had her doubts: "What was that? How do I know she's not acting? So I watched her to see how she would do it if she were acting. After a while, I determined not only would she be a brilliant actress if she were acting but who's writing her material? How did she know all that? And if she knew it, why didn't she just do it herself? I know my friend very well . . . JZ . . . I know her. She's not there. When he comes in, my friend leaves."

JZ Knight walked into the Great Hall and stood before hundreds of enthralled students. She wore a pink blouse and black pants, thanked the audience for coming, clasped her hands, and spoke briefly from the elevated stage. "Thank you . . . very kind . . . I've thought a lot about [these] twenty years and the journey it's been, and it's been a son of a gun . . . I love everything that I've learned and who I've become, and I'm certainly not there, but I'm on my way. I have to leave now and take all this garb off and transform myself."

RAMTHA...IN THE BODY OF JZ KNIGHT. *JZ KNIGHT*

She later told me, "It takes me about three minutes to get out of my body, and at great velocity, I move through this tunnel, and Ramtha's energy comes in as a ball of light that is shaped like a teardrop. That teardrop encases my physical body."

Thirty minutes later, to the sound of drumbeats, Ramtha arrives. JZ's long, blond hair is pulled back into a tight braid. The person on stage, resplendent in a dark, blue tunic and not a hint of femininity in sight, raises a glass of wine and in a commanding voice says, "God bless my life! So be it! To life!"

For two hours, in a deep, guttural voice, Ramtha talks about the core concepts of his beliefs: "You are God. The mind creates reality. The challenge is to conquer yourself."

Glenn and I watched Ramtha and the faces of the students hanging on every word. The gestures, the sound of the voice, the way Ramtha stared intensely at the captivated students and strutted confidently on the stage were unquestionably masculine behavior. JZ Knight was gone.

"I don't think we're in Kansas anymore," Glenn whispered to me.

Ramtha ended his talk as he began it, raising a glass of wine and exclaiming: "To life!"

An hour later, we sat down with Ramtha's channel in her comfortable den. Ramtha is gone. JZ is back: "During the time that I'm absent . . . moving into this wall of light . . . [in] which I have no memory of what happens to me after I re-emerge from this place . . . what is five minutes to me, Ramtha may have had my body for twelve hours. So I have a twelve-hour gap of time . . . or four hours or three hours."

Since Ramtha selected JZ as his spokesman, it has not been an easy partnership. She has been the target of withering criticism from some disgruntled students and even from famed astrophysicist Carl Sagan who said he believed JZ was inventing Ramtha and that she had no contact with disembodied spirits. How he would know that raises its own questions. There is no proof on either side of the controversy. Others have claimed to channel Ramtha and were successfully sued by JZ to stop. She has never denied the challenges of life with a thirty-five-thousand-year-old man: "All of my difficulties and my confrontations that I've had to deal with in the last decades . . . mainly because of Ramtha . . . have made me a much greater person in my eyes . . . and I think I understand people much better now than I did before, so I find that I couldn't have grown without him . . . and I appreciate it, and I don't regret any of it."

After two days immersed in all aspects of Ramtha's school, after interviews with JZ, the scientists, and some of her students, and after witnessing Ramtha teaching, we produced a twenty-minute segment for the CBS affiliate in Seattle, *Reconsidering Ramtha*. It can still be seen on YouTube and ends with my conclusion: "Only one of two things is true . . . the entity called Ramtha is either a twenty-year-old deception involving thousands of people worldwide, or something else quite impossible to explain is happening . . . and either one of those two things is remarkable."

The expressions on the faces of the two news anchors at the end of the story was amusing to see. They were incredulous, befuddled, and clearly out of their comfort zones. They did not know what to say. They smiled and simply said, "The weather is coming up next."

Cut to commercial.

THE NEXT YEAR, my local television news career was over. A new news director was brought in, and I was soon let go, more of an "I quit"/"you're fired" moment. Station managers and I clashed professionally and personally. Television news was becoming a daily repository of what I called "road kill," easy assignments covering car crashes, fires, and inconsequential junk, lacking journalistic nutrition and offering little of substance to viewers. I worried about how I would support myself and my son, but Ramtha came to my rescue.

JZ's assistant called and said she was thrilled with the story I did, that it was the fairest and most balanced report she ever received since Ramtha first arrived on the scene. Would I be interested in producing a couple of documentaries for the school? Yes . . . I would.

I, along with two cameramen, audio engineers, and a stockpile of equipment waited in a comfortable living room in JZ's mansion. In my decades as a reporter, I interviewed thousands of people, but never a thirty-five-thousand-year-old warrior. Since there was no way to prepare for such a moment, I drank some tea, ate a cookie, and waited.

JZ never came out to greet us. Soon, bedecked in a red velvet tunic, Ramtha, in the body of JZ Knight, walked boldly into the room. He sat down, put his hands on his knees, looked around, and called for wine-filled glasses to be handed to everyone. He toasted the occasion of our gathering: "To life!"

It was the first time a reporter, a mere mortal who was not a student at the school, faced this disembodied spirit. He, and I say "he" because there was nothing feminine in evidence, seemed forceful, a little brash, not angry . . . just cocky. He looked straight at me sitting just a few feet away as if to say, "Bring it on! I'm ready!"

I, however, was not. I could not think of anything to say that might be intelligent. So I started with obvious questions, but he answered back with his own questions.

"Tell me more about where you came from."

"Where do you think I came from?"

"Why did you choose JZ Knight?"

"Why do you think I chose this beloved woman?"

"Why come back now?"

"Why do you think I returned now?"

I found that annoying and told him I needed him to answer questions, not ask them.

He told me who he was and that he chose JZ because he thought a woman would be a better messenger: "I am a teacher and a god. I am a god because I experienced all of these things, and I am a teacher not of truth but of philosophy. I have already lived my truth. It's my truth. It's not yours!"

But Ramtha knew something of my truth and shocked me to my core. He leaned close, pointed his finger at me, and looking straight into my eyes, said, "You died! You died, and you could no longer have children!"

I was stunned and told the photographers to turn off the cameras. How could he know that? How could he know that twenty years earlier I had died for a moment during surgery, bleeding profusely from a hysterectomy. No one in the room knew that. Neither Ramtha nor JZ knew my family or the few friends who knew that. He leaned back in his chair with a look of compassion and a gentle smile on his face. It occurred to me that his astonishing revelation was a way of proving himself, trying to convince me he was real. The rest of our time together was less startling as he spoke about his teachings, but I was shaken by what he had said and what he seemed to know.

Over the next several days, we watched hundreds of students endure challenging tests of their physical and mental abilities—blindfolded archery, walking through mazes, and hours of Ramtha teaching.

Huston Cummings Smith, a renowned religious scholar visiting the school, sat down with me for an interview. "You know," he said, "what is far more surprising than the idea of Ramtha is that there is so much doubt about entities like him in the United States. Many, if not most of the world's religions, put great faith in the existence of souls of humans who are no longer living, but borrow the living to speak." To him, Ramtha was real.

JZ Knight herself has a sense of humor about Ramtha: "I assure you that had I had any inclination or desire to concoct such a story, I don't think I would have made him quite so old."

Forty years have passed since Ramtha appeared in JZ Knight's kitchen, and as I write this, twenty years have elapsed since I was invited behind the walls. In the fall of 2018, I went back for a visit. JZ Knight walked into her plush, comfy den and gave me a big, lingering hug. She looked beautiful, ageless, and we held onto each other as old friends do who have not seen each other for a very long time. She and Ramtha are basically retired, but the school continues to thrive with thousands of students around the world, taught by instructors trained by Ramtha. In addition to events in Yelm and in thirty-six countries, JZ and the Ramtha school community are active on Twitter and Facebook. Despite his age, Ramtha is clearly active in the modern world of social media.

The entity she once described as looking a lot like Yul Brynner, but darker and taller, rarely visits anymore. JZ says she "loves being in her seventies now and experiencing, for the first time, the beauty of all four seasons" on the grounds of her home in Yelm. Ramtha took up so much of her life and time she literally had no time to stop and smell, let alone see, the roses. She is still busy creating new businesses.

In 2015, JZ invented the Blu Room for which she received a patent in 2018. There are thirty-five Blu Room services in the United States and eleven other countries with additional locations under construction. She describes these rooms as "providing an environment of deep tranquility that our modern lives no longer offer. It provides the user a mind/body/spirit/consciousness lifting environment that creates a sense of well-being." She offers free time at her Blu Room in Yelm to war veterans suffering from post-traumatic stress. It has, she says, "always been my purpose in life to help people in any way I could."

The question about Ramtha's existence is one of those great mysteries of life, a phenomenon that can neither be proved nor disproved. If you believe in him, you do so on faith, and if you do not, it is also an act of faith. There is no incontrovertible evidence to support either side. Many, if not most, of the students who have studied with Ramtha believe their lives are much improved, which is enough validation for the believers. Skeptics dismiss the possibility of JZ's claims because they are preposterous and incredible. For them, that is sufficient enough to reject Ramtha's existence. On one side lies truth and on the other fabrication. The lingering question is which side is correct?

When I ended my television story in 1997, twenty years after Ramtha arrived in the Northwest, I said only one of two opposing things was true about Ramtha. He was either a fraud and figment of JZ Knight's creation, or he was real. As I write this, forty years have now passed since Ramtha first appeared in JZ Knight's Tacoma kitchen, and I still believe only one of those conclusions is probable. I think often about my time in Yelm behind the wall and yield to the mystery of Ramtha and to that which I cannot explain. If I were forced to choose, I would, with some hesitation, select the second option. I mostly believe in the messenger, but I absolutely believe in the message.

Chapter 43

Away in a Manger . . . the Last Straw

MY CAREER IN LOCAL TELEVISION NEWS began in a bizarre way, grabbed in the ass by a city official, and ended in a similarly ignominious fashion, forced to do a story about a piece of stolen plastic.

A North Seattle resident called the CBS affiliate, KIRO, on behalf of her distraught friend, a next-door neighbor who was bereft and heartbroken, too devastated to speak for herself. In the middle of the night, a thief trespassed on the lady's property, peered into an outdoor nativity scene, and snatched the plastic baby Jesus from the comfort of his makeshift manger.

I was assigned to investigate this local tragedy and ranted about the absurdity of the assignment before I left the station. "This is ridiculous! Are you fucking kidding me? This is not a story!"

On what must have been a very slow news day, the assignment editors, many of whom never ventured outside a newsroom to actually cover a story, sent me north to Seattle's Ballard neighborhood to investigate the mystery of the stolen, plastic Son of God. To justify their reasoning for this ridiculous undertaking, the managers said it was December and getting close to Christmas. It was a seasonal story.

It was mid-afternoon as I walked up the steps of the scene of the crime. Before knocking on the woman's door, I peered into the wood-framed nativity set. The little lambs and sheep were there. The shepherds were holding their crooks, and the Virgin Mary with arms folded looked mournful, which seemed peculiar, as she had just given birth to the Son of God. Sadly, she was holding an empty blanket. Her newborn child, baby Jesus, was gone. I walked up the stairs to meet another woman in mourning who was robbed overnight.

As the door opened, I instantly understood why this woman relied on someone else to call the station and report the theft. She could barely form a single word, paralyzed on one side of her face from a recent stroke. She sounded the way most of us do following dental surgery, unable to speak clearly with tongues and faces numbed by novocain.

I introduced myself and listened as she tried to convey her sense of loss. The nativity set belonged to her grandmother, then her mother and was passed on to her. I felt compassion for her but realized as I took in the sad story that there was no way we could televise this. I asked the woman to wait a moment, went out to the news car, and called the assignment desk at the station. "Brian . . . we cannot do this story! I feel bad that her baby Jesus was stolen, but the woman's had a stroke, she's drooling, and we can't put her on television! Please don't make us do this!"

Brian took my plea to the news director, who typically chose not to listen to what reporters in the field were saying, that there was no story here, certainly not one we could broadcast. This time was no exception. "Sorry, Julie . . . he says we have to go with it. You're now the lead AND we're going to go live with the story at the top of the five o'clock show."

"Jesus Christ! You're kidding me!"

"I wish I was, but the live truck is on its way now."

The cameraman was as disgusted as I was. I considered putting our gear back in the car, thanking the lady for her time, and returning to the station in defiance of the news managers. My colleague said he could not afford to lose his job. I said he could blame it on me. We stayed.

The photographer shot video of the manger with the missing baby and set up his camera and lights in the woman's living room. We felt it was best to focus on the unparalyzed side of her face and to keep the interview very, very short. The enormous satellite truck, almost as wide as the street, pulled up in front of the house, raised its thirty-foot-high microwave mast enabling us to go live from the scene of the crime. I would bookend the story—open it live with a few words, toss to the video insert, and wrap it up standing in front of the sad, little manger, its main character still missing.

As we edited the video insert, I begged again to stop this insanity. I called our main anchorman, Steve Raible, and pleaded with him to intervene and kill the story.

"I'm sorry, Julie. I tried. They wouldn't listen to me either."

I went "Live at 5," but something inside me died on that late afternoon, in much the same way that standards of excellence and integrity in broadcast news had been dying for years. Television stations throughout the country focused more on technology and less on the quality and content of the stories being reported.

Since the arrival of new technology costing millions of dollars, going live often became more important than reporting serious journalism. A triumph of form over substance. The arrival of the ENG (electronic news gathering) trucks allowed television stations to broadcast from just about anywhere. No matter if it was an empty street corner where a murder occurred earlier in the day or a nighttime shot where nothing but the reporter was visible, going live was what mattered most. In their infinite stupidity, station managers throughout the country listened to consultants who convinced them the words "live from the scene" would captivate viewers. They often spent more money on things than on people. They bought the pricey equipment and had to use it. At every afternoon editorial meeting, the first words often uttered from the show producers were "Where are my live shots? How many trucks do I have?"

It often had less to do with substance and more about just being live from the scene. That is the only explanation as to why the saga of the stolen baby Jesus led the newscast on that chilly December day.

I went back to the station, stormed into the news director's office and tore into him. I said we should be ashamed of what we did. There was already little love lost between news managers and me. My contract was soon to expire, and I was at home days later when I received a call that my contract was not being renewed. I was fired but had already decided to resign. They did not want me or the kinds of stories I wanted to produce.

I was privileged to have worked in what I believed was the golden age of local television news, but the luster was fading both locally and nationally. I wanted and needed to leave. I had no idea what lay ahead, but I knew what I was leaving behind, an almost thirty-year-span of encounters with the entire spectrum of humanity. I met and interviewed movie stars, musicians, and murderers, annoyed news managers, confronted infamous politicians, survived personal medical crises and my own attempted suicide, and raised a son along the way. I now faced the challenge of forging a new path. I desperately hoped I would find a new career . . . or that it might find me.

PART THREE

In the Shadow of the Mountain
—A Quieter Life

Chapter 44

Scattering Daddy

MY GUILELESS, GENTLE, and much-loved eighty-five-year-old father, Leonard Honick, fell and hit his head in his Seattle apartment in the early summer of 1999. I arrived within minutes of my mother's frantic phone call. He was bleeding, disoriented, and as was typical of him, said he was fine and did not need to go to the hospital. He did. My father never put himself or his needs before anyone else's, and it was always surprising to me that half of who I was came from him. He was quiet and unassuming. I was loud and presumptuous. He was gentle. I was pushy. He hated confrontation. I welcomed it. He was short. I towered over him.

No matter our differences, he adored me, loved that I was a local celebrity, and even loved my notoriety. Daddy had my back both literally and figuratively, from the time his hand held me as a baby in diapers on the back of a black pony to supporting me throughout my controversial career. It was now my turn to be there for him.

Though CT scans showed no evidence of permanent damage, Daddy's behavior changed. His short-term memory, still impressive at eighty-five, now failed him. He did not remember where he lived, who was president, or what year it was. Sometimes he did not immediately recognize me. But propped up in his hospital bed one day, he recounted his many trips across the Atlantic during World War II on his Liberty ship and recited the names of most of the men who served under him.

As I listened, I deeply regretted not paying more attention to him when he had wanted to talk about the Great War. I had had no interest in his stories when he wanted to tell them to me as a child. Now, I was fascinated, but it was too late for him to appreciate that. Daddy left the hospital after a week or so, but he never went home again to the apartment he shared with his beloved Esther, my mother.

LEONARD WITH HIS NAVY BUDDIES AT THE END OF THE WAR. 1944.

In a dramatically short time, Daddy could no longer walk, dress himself, or do any of the things he had done for most of his life. Since my mother could not take care of him, we made the painful decision to move him to a Jewish care facility in South Seattle. It was immaculate and well staffed but nonetheless devastating. After sixty-one years of marriage and living together almost every single day of their adult lives, Esther and Leonard were now separated.

We went to see Daddy almost daily. On most days, he was sitting in a wheelchair, chatting with other residents, seeming to recognize his family, though he smiled at everyone. He saved his biggest grins for my shaggy wheaten terrier, Bob, who lit up every aging face in the nursing home. Bob was one of those dogs who never sought attention and always gave the impression that you were lucky to pet him. He never played with toys, never chased after anything. If you threw a ball for him, you had to retrieve it. He could not be bothered. In the nursing home, though, he was an entirely different dog. He snuggled up to anyone who called to him, chased a toy and brought it back if someone was strong enough to throw it, and sat patiently by my father's side. His soft fur comforted people, and Bob sensed that.

MY INSCRUTABLE WHEATEN TERRIER, BOB.

After a few months, Daddy's health steadily declined, and we knew he would soon die. Bedridden now and in his last days, he was still able to understand what I was saying, though he had difficulty speaking. I spent a couple of hours with him and thanked him for all he had done for me and for his beloved grandson, Jeremy. My father, often absent from my childhood because he was frequently working six days a week to provide for us, became Jeremy's daycare grandpa. From the time Jeremy was three years old until he graduated from high school, Pop Pop picked him up from school, took him to his activities, or was waiting at home for him when Jeremy came home from school. By the time he was driving and very much on his own, Jeremy said to me one day, "Mom, you know Pop Pop doesn't really need to wait here at home for me anymore."

"You may not need him at the house," I said, "but he needs to be there."

I thanked Daddy for his patience with me, for waiting in line all night to get tickets to the first Beatles concert, for never raising his voice, for teaching me to drive in the Pentagon parking lot, for not punishing me for wrecking his new Oldsmobile convertible, and for never once showing me a disapproving face. He embraced every one of my friends, from our early days in Arlington, Virginia, to our lives in Seattle. Everyone loved him, and he loved them.

In that last conversation, he called me by his childhood name for me: "JuJu," he said, "you really should go back to horses. It's what you loved most as a little girl."

Leonard hoped he would survive to see his eighty-sixth birthday on 9/9/99, and he almost made it. He died on August 27, just a little shy of his goal. He stated in his will that he wanted to be cremated, a practice not explicitly prohibited by his Jewish faith but often frowned upon. Historic, cultural, and spiritual beliefs argued against it. In Jewish mystical tradition, it is believed the soul does not immediately depart the body so putting a body into the earth allows for a more gradual separation. The Torah stipulates the body is considered the property of God, and so humans are forbidden to defile it. Willful burning of a human being is also discouraged. More modern thought cites the burning of millions of Jews in the Holocaust as an argument against cremation. But, as with most religions, there are conflicting opinions. Modern Reform Judaism, which my parents had migrated to from their Orthodox upbringing, also says children are not forbidden from honoring a parent's request for cremation and it is not considered a sin to follow a dying person's wishes. Cremation is what Leonard wanted, and that is what he got.

My mother, brother, and I, along with a good friend of mine, went to the funeral home seeking advice from the professionals about what we needed to do to cremate Leonard. We were led into a room and encouraged to select a casket in which my father's body would be placed into a 1,400°-1,800° crematory and subsequently reduced to ashes. The caskets were wooden, shiny, and beautiful and carried an average price tag of around five thousand dollars.

My mother asked, "Do you have anything a little bit cheaper?"

It made no sense to us to purchase an expensive item that was going to be immediately destroyed.

"What price range were you thinking about?" was the somewhat startled response of the funeral director.

"Well . . . just something less expensive," my mother replied.

"We have something for a couple thousand dollars," he said.

"Even cheaper," I replied.

He said, "You wouldn't want to put your father in something tacky, would you?"

"Actually," I said, "my father is dead and gone, and he was always careful with money, so I don't think he'd want us to spend it on this." I asked about the cardboard boxes that contained the caskets, which utterly shocked the man in the dark suit. "What do those cost?" I asked.

"About one hundred dollars," he answered with a look of obvious disgust and disapproval on his face.

My mother and I looked at each other. Perfect. The simplest of coffins. Not a pine box but a cardboard one. Daddy would have approved.

His remains, now a fine, gray dust inside a velvet pouch, were handed over to us about a week later and placed inside a tasteful blue urn.

THE URN THAT HELD MY FATHER'S AND MOTHER'S ASHES...
AND WILL SOMEDAY HOLD MINE.

The challenge now, where to scatter Daddy. Being a navy man, he told us he wanted to be in the water. Esther, Jeremy, and I, along with Bob the dog and some family friends, headed east from Seattle, searching for a river in which to put him. We had no particular destination in mind on that clear, sunny day but pulled alongside a road nestled near the Snoqualmie River, thirty miles from our home. We found a trail leading down to the rocky riverbank, paused, and said some words about Leonard. Then we took turns emptying small portions of what was left of Daddy into the chilly water. Jeremy and I reached into the bag to feel the consistency of the ashes, scooped Pop-Pop's remains into our hands, and gently let them fall into the water. We watched as the ashes turned a milky gray color as the current swept the dust away. We embraced each other, smiled, cried, and headed home.

LEFT: ESTHER, ME AND BOB...JUST AFTER SCATTERING DADDY'S ASHES INTO THE SNOQUALMIE RIVER. RIGHT: WITH DADDY IN THE BACKYARD OF MY SEATTLE HOME...LOVE THE POLYESTER PANTS AND WHITE SHOES. 1980

Unaware at the time, I was just a mile away from the next chapter of my life, near a horse ranch where, within two years, I would heed Daddy's suggestion and "go back to horses."

DADDY...DAPPER AS ALWAYS.

Chapter 45

The Ranch

A great horse will change your life.
The truly special ones define it.
—AUTHOR UNKNOWN

THE FIRST TIME I INHALED the scent of a horse, took the reins, and clutched a saddle horn, I was only eighteen months old, and if a baby can convey such a thing, I looked calm and confident, as if I belonged there. The patient pony likely had to endure dozens of toddlers on its back as a roving photographer captured a keepsake of the parents' child on horseback. As I look at that picture now, more than seventy years later, it seems to capture a moment impossible to put into words. I was feeling and learning something before I could talk or even comprehend language. I am certain a powerful connection was made, one that would stay with me forever and grow stronger over the years. The day that picture was taken was the day I fell in love with horses.

BY THE TIME I COULD READ, almost every book I owned was about horses. My favorite was *Misty of Chincoteague*, published in 1947, the year I was born. It tells the story about the wreck of a Spanish galleon along the shores of Assateague Island off the coast of Virginia, not far from where I grew up. Some of the ponies swam to a nearby island, and a foal born from the wild herd was raised by a family who lived there. They named the foal Misty.

CHUNKY BABY JULIE IN A DIAPER ASTRIDE A PATIENT, LITTLE PONY...
THE DAY I FELL IN LOVE WITH HORSES.

Throughout the 1950s, every one of my favorite television shows had horses in them: *My Friend Flicka, The Lone Ranger* with beautiful Silver and Tonto's Scout, *Spin and Marty* from *The Mickey Mouse Club* with the beautiful palomino, Roy Rogers and Dale Evans with Trigger and Buttermilk, Gene Autry with Champion the Wonder Horse, and *Fury* the powerful black stallion. I could smell their scent through our black-and-white TV set, and the sound of their hooves as they galloped was mesmerizing.

Bernie's Pony Ring was a ten-minute ride from our house in Arlington, Virginia. We drove by it a dozen times a week, on the way to the grocery store, to have a meal at the Hot Shoppes Restaurant right across the street, or to crack crab at Steve's Diner right behind Bernie's. The little ponies were tied to a long, wooden post under a striped canopy, saddled up and waiting for their next young rider, another chance to walk in a daze around a large circle. At age seven, I felt sad for them, but I was grateful every time I got to be near them. The only way my parents could entice me to go to Sunday school, which I loathed, was to bribe me with a trip to Bernie's as a reward for behaving myself at the Arlington-Fairfax Jewish Center. Bernie's tent was my preferred house of worship. Even as a young child, when I was on a horse, I felt I was in heaven, near God, in the presence, figuratively and literally, of something much greater than myself.

After I got too big for ponies, I took riding lessons in the suburbs of Northern Virginia and begged my parents for years, without success, to buy me a horse. It was all I ever wanted. Almost every vacation I took as I grew older had to include horseback riding as part of the action. By the time I was a teenager and heading off to college, my obsession with horses faded as I began to focus on other things—boys, marriage, babies, and a career. But the smell of horses and the calm that came over me when I was near them was deeply etched in my soul and memory, a passion dormant for the next three decades but never gone.

On my fiftieth birthday, my son, Jeremy, gave me a copy of my favorite childhood book, *Misty of Chincoteague*. We affectionately referred to each other as 'Devil Child' and 'Devil Mom'. Inside he wrote: "Mom . . . one day you'll get your Misty . . . it's a promise."

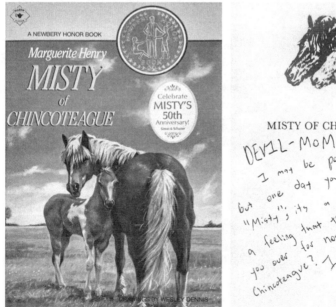

MISTY OF CHINCOTEAGUE

LEFT: THE COVER OF "MISTY OF CHINCOTEAGUE"...MY FAVORITE CHILDHOOD BOOK... GIVEN AS A PRESENT FROM MY SON ON MY FIFTIETH BIRTHDAY. RIGHT: AN INSCRIPTION FROM JEREMY INSIDE THE BOOK.

A few years later, his promise came true.

MORE THAN TWO DOZEN, gnarly, old sycamore trees line the sides of the road leading to Rosebud River Ranch, where my dear friend Pepper Schwartz lived and bred horses. A month after September 11, 2001, knowing how much I loved horses, she invited me to come spend an afternoon with her. It was one of those perfect fall days . . . bright blue skies with not a cloud in sight . . . a good place to forget for a moment the horror of the previous month. The air was crisp, the colorful trees were just starting to drop their leaves. As I slowly drove under the canopy of sycamores, I felt as if I was being transported back in time, driving to Bernie's to ride ponies. It was a road that paralleled the Snoqualmie River where, just two years earlier and only a mile away, we had scattered my father's ashes. Now as I turned into the driveway, I remembered my father's last words to me: "You should go back to horses . . . it's what you loved most as a little girl."

ROSEBUD RIVER RANCH...NESTLED AGAINST MT. SI.

Rosebud River Ranch is nestled under the imposing rock of Mt. Si, a four-thousand foot peak, part of the Cascade Mountain Range. The mountain was named after local homesteader Josiah 'Uncle Si' Merritt, but made famous in the quirky television show, 'Twin Peaks', filmed partly in the

Snoqualmie/North Bend area. The 'twin peaks' are the two humps at the top of Mount Si, which, on a clear day, can be seen as you drive east from Seattle. Thousands of people hike to the top every year. For them, Si is a recreational peak. To the Snoqualmie Tribe, the mountain is hallowed ground. The tribe's legend tells the story of Snoqualm, the moon, who ordered that a rope of cedar bark be stretched between the earth and the sky. It is said that a face resembling Snoqualm can be seen among the rocks near the summit.

On that sparkling October day when I made my first trip to the ranch, every rock formation, every crag and crevice on the mountain was visible from the ranch. Thousands of trees growing on the mountain and surrounding the ranch were beginning their transition to winter, splashes of yellow, gold, and orange among the fading green leaves. It was overwhelmingly beautiful—the mountain, the trees, the river nearby, the azure blue sky . . . and the horses. Pepper met me outside the big green barn and took me inside. In an instant, I inhaled an intoxicating and familiar scent. If you love these animals, you will understand the calming and exhilarating impact of the redolence of horses. I stopped for a moment, closed my eyes, took a deep breath, and felt I was home.

We walked through the barn, which leads out to acres of pastures filled with these enchanting animals, doing what they do best . . . eating, every head down munching on the early, fall grass. As we walked down the lane separating the fields, Pepper pointed out every horse and knew every name, some thirty in all. It was impressive. As we stopped by each gate, the horses trotted up to us, stretching out their long, furry necks, reaching for a carrot. As I fed them, I leaned into their warm coat and was instantly transported back to my childhood, inhaling the scent of Bernie's ponies. I was fifty-four years old but felt like a little girl again. I kept gazing up at formidable Mount Si looming over the ranch and imagining it keeping guard over everything, a protective, ancient fortress. This was heaven on earth.

On the way back to the barn, I said to Pepper, "I always wanted my own horse. I begged my parents to buy me one, but my mother never went along with it. She said it was too expensive, that I might get hurt. There was nothing I could say to change their minds."

"What kind of a horse?" she asked.

I knew exactly what I always wanted. "A chestnut filly with a big white blaze," I answered instantly.

Pepper looked at me for a moment and told me to wait at the front of the barn and close my eyes.

A few minutes later, she walked out and stopped inches from me.

"Open your eyes," she said.

At the end of the lead rope in her hand was a chestnut filly with a big, white blaze. "This is Hollywood! She was so flashy with her white face and socks we thought it was the perfect name. We just weaned all the foals from their mothers. She's six months old. Is this what you had in mind?"

BABY HOLLYWOOD...THE FOAL THAT CHANGED MY LIFE.

Standing in front of me on long, spindly legs with a head that seemed too big for her gangly body was the horse of my childhood dreams. I took the rope from Pepper and just stood there. Awestruck, stunned, with tears welling up in my eyes. I had no idea what to do, how to put on a halter, or even how to take her for a walk. I knew only that I loved her and that my life was about to change forever.

I heard echoes from my father and my son. On October 14, 2001, more than five decades after sitting on a pony in diapers, I got back to horses and finally found my Misty. Two months later, after taking a little time to think about it, I bought her for five thousand dollars. It was the biggest impulse buy of my life and the best money I ever spent . . . a life-changing decision that took me in a direction I could never have imagined, as far removed from the world of television as one could be.

JULIE L. BLACKLOW

113

DATE 12/17/01

1–7029/2260
67

PAY TO THE
ORDER OF Rosebud River Ranch $ 5000.00

Five-thousand and no/100........................DOLLARS

DIME.

THE DIME SAVINGS BANK OF NEW YORK, FSB
New York, NY 10017

FOR Hollywood

THE BEST MONEY I EVER SPENT.

I kept working as a freelance television producer for all of the major networks, covering the occasional Pacific Northwest disaster or conducting interviews with local experts who were part of a national news story. My freelance television life kept me busy several days a week, which left me precious time to go to the ranch and stare at Hollywood. I spent hundreds of hours watching her gamboling in the pastures, bossing around the other eight foals born the previous spring and spent many Sunday afternoons sitting on a chair in her stall, reading the NY Times, and listening to her chew her hay.

Hollywood knew exactly how to be a horse. She was living, breathing proof of more than fifty million years of evolution. Despite the fact that horses are prey and not predators, they are survivors. They are smart and intuitive, aware of everything around them. They can hear, see, and smell things we humans cannot, and they come out of the womb with those skills deeply embedded. Hollywood had all the intelligence of her ancestors, a free, wild, animal child, unfettered, unrestrained, untrained yet by humans. Sassy, bossy, and pushy. A perfect mirror of me. She knew precisely who she was and what to do. I, on the other hand, was clueless about being a horse owner and overwhelmed by the burden of being responsible for teaching her what she needed to know to be successful in a human world.

Any savvy horse person will tell you a green horse with a green owner is a terribly bad combination. I was scared I would make a mistake and ruin this innocent creature. In my favorite Joseph Campbell book, *An Open Life*, a transcription of a conversation with Michael Toms, he asks: "Can anything happen to you for which you're not ready?"

In my case, I chose to believe the answer was no. But I knew I needed a lot of help.

Hollywood's and my first instructor was a woman named Debbie, a tough-as-nails trainer who had little patience for people but unlimited tolerance for horses. The first thing she did was put duct tape over my mouth, admonishing me for talking too much around the horse. For my entire life, the most insulting thing anyone could do to me was try to shut me up. I reluctantly surrendered to Debbie.

"It confuses them when people babble so much. Less is more with horses. Don't ever forget that. So just be quiet. And remember every gesture you make, every turn of your head, means something to them."

The first year with Hollywood was humbling and harrowing. I came from a world where I made my living by talking and was now in a place where words meant very little, where words only complicated things. I went from a world where I was always in charge and knew what to do to a place where I was completely ignorant. I spent hours learning how to put on a halter, brush Hollywood, and clean her hooves. I rarely was afraid facing murderers or child molesters, but I was terrified picking up the back legs of a horse who, with one swift kick, could cause serious pain or even kill you. I remember one day a child, no more than five years old, came over to me as I was cleaning Hollywood's feet and with a sharp rebuke said, "Julie, you're not doing that right! Get your face away from her back leg! You're gonna get hurt!"

Hollywood's stall became a safe and sacred place... quiet, peaceful, tranquil.... just her and me. It occurred to me that buying Hollywood was the only thing I had ever done in my life that was just for me. When you get married, have a baby, start a job, whatever you do in life is almost always done in concert with other people . . . part of a human chain. But Hollywood was mine alone . . . a decision made by me and for me. She would occasionally stop eating, walk over to me and put her big head on my shoulder, and in those moments, I felt a sense of contentment and gratitude unlike anything I had ever experienced.

Our routine for the next two and half years, the standard time needed for her bones to develop, mostly focused on teaching her ground manners and spending time in the pastures. She was growing bigger and stronger, sassier and pushier. The foal I met weighed only two hundred pounds. She now weighed more than a thousand pounds and stood sixty inches at the withers, a big, bossy, domineering, and intimidating creature. I had met my match and was cowed by her. I remember thinking by bringing this particular horse into my life, the universe was teaching me to be humble. I suppose it was a much-needed lesson.

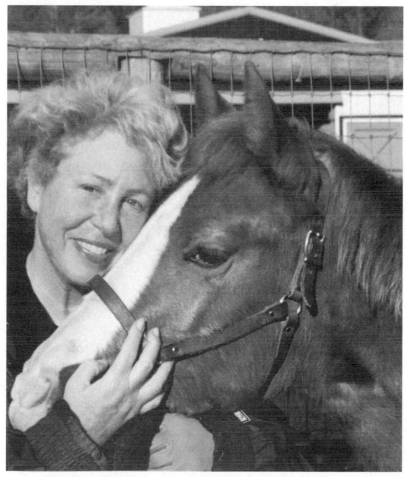

ME AND HOLLYWOOD...A POWERFUL LOVE CONNECTION. 2002.

I learned to ride again on some of the other ranch horses as Hollywood got older. That, too, was terrifying. As a child, I had not yet learned to be afraid. Now in my mid-fifties, I learned I could get hurt. And I did. I fell off more than once. I got back up. I suffered three broken ribs, a broken toe, and a broken leg and ankle. All worth the suffering.

"How do you learn to ride?" my friends asked.

"You ride," I answered.

I watched with incredible jealousy as other owners cleaned their horses, saddled them up, and effortlessly put on bridles, getting ready to head out to the trails accessible from the ranch property. I wondered, with great envy, if I would ever be able to do that.

I had good and patient teachers along the way as Hollywood grew up. I learned the importance of silence, calm, and patience. It is never a good idea to be in a hurry with horses. With the ability to feel a fly land on their backs, they absorb every human emotion and react accordingly. If you are tense, they are tense. If you are sad, they reflect that, and if you are calm and relaxed, they mirror that as well. They do not like to be rushed . . . ever. I still struggle to remember that.

As Hollywood grew, I gently put a saddle on her back, eased a bit into her mouth, and taught her to stand to get her hooves trimmed by the farrier. I walked her around the trails on the ranch property, exposed her to the rustling of tarps, the sounds of the tractors, and the racket of weed eaters, getting her accustomed to scary things. Slowly, we both gained confidence and began to trust one another. She frequently messed with me, pinning her ears back and threatening to bite, which she never did. Hollywood reminded me she had limits and would tolerate only so much. A one-thousand-pound alpha mare with ears flat back is a scary force to encounter. I taught her, or tried to teach her, to respect boundaries between herself and humans. I intentionally broke the rules I was trying to establish and let her move into my body and rub her big head up against me. To make things worse I rewarded her for doing that and gave her treats as she nuzzled me. I stood on mounting blocks next to her so she could adapt to seeing me above her and waited with uncommon patience for her third birthday when I could finally ride my horse.

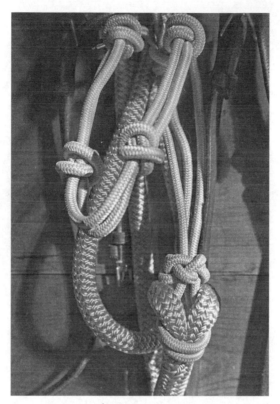

A rope halter.

In the spring of 2004, I brushed her, put on her saddle pad, saddle, and bridle, and walked into the arena. I brought her to the mounting block, slowly climbed the three steps to the top, put my left foot into the stirrup, and swung the rest of me over her back and sat down in the saddle. It was two and a half years since the day I met her, and that moment was, other than the birth of my son, the happiest day of my life. She stood there, turned her head towards me, and calmly waited for me to do something. She seemed to be talking to me as if to say, "I'm ready. Are you? Let's go."

I sat there for a couple of minutes, overcome with emotion. I leaned forward, touched the top of her neck, and kissed her mane. With little effort, just a gentle nudge from my legs, Hollywood moved forward, and we walked around the arena. In our first years together, we were two separate beings, side by side, both on the ground. Now, for the first time, we were one. It was the first of thousands of rides we would take together in the years to come.

PEPPER SCHWARTZ AND ME. THE WOMAN WHO MADE MY DREAMS COME TRUE.

Shortly after I bought Hollywood, Pepper Schwartz, my friend and owner of the ranch, divorced her husband. He had built and managed the ranch, but in the wake of the divorce, Pepper asked me to take over the financial part of the operation. I soon learned that was the easy part of running a ranch.

Paying the bills, signing paychecks, depositing monthly payments from people who boarded their horses at the ranch was effortless. I was skilled at managing money. What I was not proficient at was watching a revolving door of misfits move into the house on the property and pretend to care about the welfare of the horses or the well-being of their owners. In exchange for free rent, utilities, and a hefty salary, ranch managers were expected to supervise the staff, help clean stalls, manage thirty acres of pastures, and exercise Pepper's horses. If they were good with horses, they were often terrible with people. And if they had decent people skills, they seemed clueless about horses. What they all seemed to have in common was a penchant for alcohol, drugs, or both.

The final indignity unfolded early on a Sunday morning in spring of 2006. The phone rang in my Seattle home with a ranch employee yelling on the other end, "Senora . . . senora . . . baby is here! Baby is on the ground, and Mama is dragging part of it around!"

"What?!"

"You come now to the ranch!"

"Where's the manager? He should be in the house! Wake him up!"

"I try . . . I try . . . he no answer."

"Okay . . . I'll get there as fast as I can."

I got dressed and sped to the ranch about thirty minutes away. I ran to the paddock where we kept mares about to give birth. Beautiful Galaxy was standing over her foal, the placenta still attached to her, both mother and baby looking dazed and helpless. I ran to the door of the house and banged on it, screaming for the manager to come outside. Nothing. I screamed again and kept knocking, but no one answered. I opened the door, went inside, and saw the foreman and his girlfriend passed out in the living room. Even if I could have awakened them, they would have been useless to help me, the mare, or her baby.

I called our vet and pleaded with her to come immediately to the ranch. She told me what to do in the meantime. Get some peroxide, clean the umbilicus of the baby, gather the placenta, and place it in a plastic container. And try to get the foal to stand and nurse since the colostrum in the mother's milk is vital for the baby's health. I was overwhelmed and furious with the drunk lying inside the house. I had no time to indulge in my own emotions and fears. Galaxy and her baby needed me. With the help of two equally frightened stall cleaners, we did what we had to do. We cleaned the foal, packed up the placenta, and hoisted the baby onto his four skinny legs so he could nurse. The vet arrived, assuring us we did everything right. I kept thinking what is a nice, Jewish girl with a decades-long career in television news doing here, scooping placenta, and helping a foal to its mother's teats?

Later that afternoon, Pepper and I went into the house and roused the two drunks from their stupor. She fired them and told them to pack up and get out. We both had had enough and knew with a nod to one another that we were done hiring men with seemingly good resumes and recommendations who rarely lived up to their promises. They all looked the part, as if they'd come from central casting, with their western boots, faded jeans, and cowboy hats, but every one of them eventually succumbed to their demons. Pepper decided I had sufficient on-the-job training and turned over the entire ranch operation to me. I would not have to live there. We would allow one of the ranch hands to occupy the little house on the property, but I was now in charge of the whole operation.

I thought of Joseph Campbell again: "Can anything happen to you for which you're not ready?"

If television newsrooms are bastions of lunacy and craziness, which indeed they are, the world of horses and their owners is similarly wacky and unpredictable. Horses are people's treasured pets, which, for the most part, they are unable to bring home at the end of the day. Equine parents are forced to entrust the care of their four-legged babies to other people, a trust not easily won and never entirely bestowed. Even if horse owners have confidence in you and your staff, they never completely believe their horse is okay. They always worry . . . if only just a little.

I developed what I refer to as my "horse owner deviancy scale." At the extreme end are the owners who trust no one to care for their horses and who become apoplectic if their horse comes back to the barn at the end of the day with even a small amount of coat missing, the tiniest speck of blood from a bite or nick, or the slightest limp. They call the vet for everything. Fortunately, over the years, I have encountered only a few of those I place into the bat-shit-crazy category. But those few are memorable:

- One Saturday afternoon, I got a call from one of my staff telling me there was an astronaut in our arena, chasing a terrified horse. In fact, one of the boarders had donned a beekeeper's suit, a pure white outfit with a veil covering her entire head which, I guess if you didn't know better, looked a bit like a space suit. She was attempting to desensitize the horse, trying to get it used to scary things, but was, instead, frightening the poor animal into a frenzy.
- One owner had a psychotic breakdown on a Sunday afternoon, lost control of both her horses, who came running frantically back to the barn with no owner in

sight. She had overdosed on her anti-psychotic drugs, barely knew where she was, and would not allow us to call her husband. She left the barn, and I later found her parked on the road a mile from the ranch, slumped over the wheel in her truck . . . passed out.

- Another woman intentionally injured her horse's legs, scratched and picked at them until the vet had to be called. If Munchausen by proxy disease applies to a relationship between humans and animals, she had that condition with her poor horse.

- We had to issue a cease and desist order from our lawyers to one client who insisted on sleeping at night in her horse's stall. We pleaded with her to stop and warned her of the dangers of lying down next to a horse in a confined, small place, but she would not stop. Her sister had recently died, and she bought the horse to fill the pain inside her. I get that, but this was just too much neurosis for us to handle. We asked her to leave.

- There was the woman who saw a snail in one of the tack rooms and wanted the entire tack room exterminated immediately.

Also in the bat-shit crazy category are the constant complainers—the people who will always find something to grouse about, and you can always find something to complain about in a barn. "The floor mats are not perfectly aligned in the stalls." "The grain bucket has some leftover muck in it." "The water has some hay in it." "I don't want my horse outside in the rain." "There is too much mud at the gates in the pastures." The complaints never stop. It is a ranch, an organic entity where you are coping with people, weather, and animals. It is always imperfect.

At the other end of my personal spectrum are those who never worry at all, understand that horses are big animals that play rough sometimes, and call the vet only if there is a lot of blood, too much snot coming out of the nose, or the horse cannot walk. Even then, these owners often give the horses a couple of days to work through their problems on their own without medical intervention. Though they love their horses, they view the animal as just a horse, capable of surviving in nasty weather and able to recover from most wounds and mishaps. They figure horses have survived for fifty million years and trust their animals can survive most injuries for a couple of days.

Most owners, almost all women in my little horse world, hover somewhere in the middle. They comprise the largest group of owners at Rosebud, the ones who fret a little but not too much, coddle their animals, lather them with overpriced horse unguents and sprays, buy expensive blankets, pay for bodywork experts to massage the animal's muscles, and rely on their horses for a level of emotional support they cannot find anywhere else. I put myself in the middle group. After observing people at both ends, the middle is a good and fairly sane place to be. Not too crazy, not too indifferent, somewhat obsessed, a little nuts.

Hundreds of books and thousands of articles have been written about the relationship between women and horses. Some are complicated analyses about horses giving women a sense of power or fulfilling childhood fantasies about riding into the sunset, that horseback riding is romantic, or that taming a horse is like taming a man. I do not buy that last assertion. Most horses are much easier to train than men. From my experience and having watched so many women with their horses, I think there is a simpler explanation, though I am certain it varies slightly for each woman. In essence and at its simplest core, horses make us happy. Unlike husbands, children, aging parents, and needy friends, the horse asks nothing of us, except for the occasional carrot or sweet apple. It needs clean food and water, a pasture in which to play, and I believe, the company of other horses, and little else. Whatever we give the horse, it gives us back a thousand fold.

I have seen the faces of distraught mothers, daughters, and wives gently fall into the necks of their patient horses and lean into their large bodies, and watched the stress of any given day melt away. Horses are, to those who love them, a balm for everything that hurts. They have a remarkable ability to fix what is broken in us. Whether touching them, standing near them, or riding them, we are healed by them. To be with a horse, one must be present and focused, which forces us, in the best possible and most rewarding way, to leave other worldly problems outside the barn. I have seen posters and bumper stickers saying words to that effect: "My therapist has four legs and eats hay." True.

Horses are beautiful, captivating, kind, and prescient. They know things. I have seen the naughtiest pony and the most dominant mare become gentle and quiet in the presence of small children. And I have watched the best-trained horse pin its ears back and bite a person raising a hand towards the animal. They are sensitive in mind and body. As I wrote earlier, a horse can feel an insect on its substantial rear end and sense the plight of someone who is suffering.

When Hollywood was still a baby, only a year old, my mother wanted to meet my frisky mare, despite Esther being in a wheelchair, in her final days. My horse was still very much a wild child, unpredictable, and untrained. I got the wheelchair out of my car, placed my mother in the chair, and rolled her into the barn. I put a halter on Hollywood and brought her up slowly towards my mother. Esther had a small bag of carrots in her lap, and I had little faith this encounter was going to work out well. I was certain Hollywood would dive into my mother's lap, devour the carrots, and possibly cause my mother's death in an instant. But horses know things . . . even this young filly. In as slow a gesture as I ever saw her make, Hollywood gently approached my mother, bowed her head into my mother's lap, and let Esther feed her one little carrot at a time. Those moments with Hollywood brought a smile to my mother's face that I had not seen for a long time. For a few minutes, my mother forgot her pain.

Esther died shortly after that, and we scattered her ashes into the same river where we had put Daddy's ashes a few years earlier. In the months following my mother's death, Hollywood was gentle, quiet, and tolerant. She let me cry into her neck, hold her, and lean on her, literally and figuratively. As horses are wont to do . . . she healed me. Horses know things.

Rosebud River Ranch has been the birthplace of dozens of foals over the years. Few things are quite as amazing as watching a foal come out of its mother, fall on the ground, and within minutes stand up, wobble a bit, begin nursing, and then frolic around the paddock in a happy frenzy. Of course, where there is life, there is also death, and I have witnessed the passing of many horses. It is a sobering thing to watch the last breath of a big, beautiful animal as it falls to the ground lifeless. Some die of old age, some from the devastation of colic, which can take a horse in minutes, and some are gone just moments after they are born.

On a cold, early spring night, our big beautiful mare, Godiva, gave birth to a baby girl. The foal was stillborn. We watched as the mare kept licking the baby, trying desperately to bring her to life, but she could not give it breath. It was one of the saddest rituals I ever saw. She would not let us into the stall to get the baby as she hovered over the body protecting it. The vet had to come and sedate her so we could remove the lifeless foal. I remember how Godiva kept looking for the baby weeks after it was gone. Two years later, she gave birth to the last foal born at Rosebud, named Q, who now stands almost seventeen hands high. A big, healthy, happy boy.

In late summer of 2018, we lost Snoopy, a forty-three-year-old former racehorse who spent more than ten years with us at the ranch. It was a great privilege and honor to care for him, feed him endless treats, and let him graze all day in his pasture. He was noble, kind, and gentle and, despite his age, remained healthy until cancer suddenly ravaged his body. We watched as he tried with great difficulty to drink water and quench his withering body before we took him for his final walk out to the big maple tree so our vet could stop his pain and end his life. It was around dinner time, but the other horses in the barn, usually ravenous and whinnying for their hay, were quiet as if they knew the "old man" was about to depart. Perhaps in their silence they were paying respect. Horses know things. I am certain they knew Snoopy was about to leave them. Before our vet administered the first of three shots that stopped his heart and felled him, she stood behind him, braided part of his tail, cut it off, and gave it to his owner. As she did that, eagles circled overhead, poised, as the vet said, to guide him home. His two closest friends that preceded him in death were, I am certain, waiting for him. After the big horse went down, the barn family gathered around the owner and embraced her. A cherished and indelible moment. Snoopy never won a race at the track but won the hearts of everyone who knew him.

Hollywood and I are, as I write this, in our eighteenth year together. We have ridden hundreds of miles on the trails, encountered elk, bear, deer, and even a couple of heavily loaded logging trucks barreling at us with frightening speed. She never reared, bucked, or bolted on me and always brought me back from our trail rides safe and sound. Whatever I have taught her pales next to what she has taught me and given me. Patience and perseverance are two of her gifts. She always makes me smile. Sometimes when I go to her paddock or stall to put a halter on her, she turns away and pins her ears back as if to remind me she is bigger and does not feel like getting groomed or going for a ride. When she does that, I often send in a young child to get her. Hollywood lowers her head and practically puts on the halter herself. She saves the naughty treatment just for me. But she also gives me love. When she sees my car, she nickers at me, and if she hears my voice, even fifty feet away she whinnies. I tell myself she is calling to me, wanting to see me. I think that is part of what she is saying. The other part, "Give me a treat, now!"

HOLLYWOOD STRETCHING FOR A CARROT.

As I was nearing the end of my three-year journey writing this book, I went out to the ranch on an early Sunday morning, a reliably calm and quiet time. I cleaned Hollywood, hoisted the heavy saddle on her back, and mounted. As always, she turned her big head to the right for a treat and then stretched to her left for another piece of carrot. One is never supposed to give horses treats from the saddle. I always do. With a verbal click from me, we ambled over to a lush trail on the ranch property, walking slowly towards "our" mountain. Though she is a horse that is always moving forward unless asked to stop, she halted, turned her beautiful face around, and stared at me with her big, brown right eye. She held that position, and we shared a moment in another space and time:

"I know you," she said in a soft voice in a language without words. "I know you as no one knows you. All those hours in my stall when you were watching me, I was watching you. I know you. Every human who has ever met you . . . everyone who lays claim to knowing you, even those who love you . . . know you in their own distinct way. You are different to every person you have ever known. They see you from their own perspectives and all the judgments and experiences of their own lives. They see only whom they choose to see. But I know you with none of that past. I know you as you truly are because I am you. I am big and brave, as are you. I am sometimes frightened, as are you. I have carried you a thousand times and brought you home safely from the mountains. You have carried me through sickness and brought me back from near death. When you stand next to me, when you inhale the sweet scent of the hair on my neck, when you lean into me and I rest my head on your shoulder, we are one. I am fifty million years of evolution and wisdom . . . and you are my child. When you come to my world and I nicker at the sight of you, I am saying, 'Come be with me. I will heal you.'

ME AND MY GIRL. 2019. BEST FRIENDS. *CARRIE CRAWFORD*

Chapter 46

My Left Kidney

Cancer may have started the fight, but I will finish it.
—GOTCANCER.ORG

NOT COUNTING THE CATASTROPHIC, three-pound fibroid tumor that destroyed my uterus and cervix and ruined my ability to have more children, I never got sick. I never got the flu, rarely had a cold, and never ran a temperature. Until late in June in 2014 when I went into mild convulsions from a 102 fever. I staggered into the living room towards Laddy, now my partner and former KING photographer who worked with me for more than two decades: "I don't feel well . . . something's really wrong with me."

He helped me to the sofa and called my doctor who, luckily for me, was also a good friend. She said I needed to come to her office immediately. I stumbled into her medical suite, barely able to stand on my own. She took my temperature and vital signs and sent me to Swedish Hospital's emergency room. One advantage of being in your late sixties, in the older-age category, is that you sometimes get attention more quickly. By then, I was sweating, shivering, and desperately ill. The nurses quickly hooked me up to blood-pressure and heart-rate monitors and started me on a saline drip. With no reliable diagnosis, a young doctor speculated I had a bacterial or viral infection, but they would have to run more tests. They inserted a catheter to test my urine, ordered a CT abdominal scan, and admitted me to the hospital.

Laddy had long-standing plans to travel to Oakland to sell part of his collection of vintage photography. I urged him not to cancel the trip and assured him I would be well taken care of in the hospital. My fever would break, they would find the source of the infection, and I would have friends come retrieve me from the hospital and take me home. That is what I told Laddy and what I tried to believe. But as John Lennon famously said, "Life is what happens to you while you're busy making other plans." Deep inside my aching body, I had a sense once again of the undertoad rearing its head in front of me the way it did before the discovery of my tumor and before I was fired from my job decades earlier. The menacing undertoad was coming for me.

Throughout that Friday night and much of the next day, I was subjected to blood draws, more CT scans, and an MRI test. My fever broke, my vital signs looked good, but in the absence of a diagnosis and little attention from doctors, I panicked. On June 29, 2014, life happened, a life I never envisioned.

A young doctor—most of the weekend doctors are young—walked into my room and, in an ominous tone, abruptly asked the woman in the other bed to leave. Fortunately for my sick hospital acquaintance, she was ambulatory, got out of her bed, and went for a walk. With few introductory remarks and no attempt to soften the blow she said, "You have renal cell carcinoma. You have kidney cancer."

It takes a lot to shut me up or make me cry. Those nine words accomplished both.

She made no attempt to comfort me as she blathered on about not needing a biopsy to confirm the diagnosis. The mass was on the left kidney, not small, not particularly large. It was, she said, too close to the border of the kidney to resect it, to cut it out and leave the rest of the organ. It was most certainly cancer, she kept insisting. I kept not hearing her ramblings. I continued crying. She said my doctor would be in touch. And she left.

I called Laddy in California.

"I have cancer . . . a tumor in my left kidney."

By that night, Laddy was back in Seattle in my hospital room, both of us terrified about what we now faced. The unknown. The possibility of death. No one gets out alive to be sure, but most of us believe it will be later than sooner. This was life . . . unplanned.

A few days after leaving the hospital, we met with a much-respected kidney surgeon, known for her unusually small and skilled hands, able to retrieve kidneys with arthroscopy, without carving up your body. There was no option, she said, but to remove the kidney and try to prevent the cancer from spreading. She could do it by making three slits in my abdomen, sever it from whatever it was attached to, take some lymph nodes and surrounding tissue, and yank it all out from a small incision in my belly.

Until I was on the verge of losing a kidney, I never bothered to learn what exactly kidneys did. I knew what my heart, stomach, intestines, and my long-gone reproductive organs did, but I was remarkably ignorant about the rest of my abdominal body parts. Kidneys are very busy things. They extract waste from the blood, balance body fluids, form urine, and have a strategic relationship with the pancreas and bladder. I was about to lose one but fortunately had a spare.

We arrived at Northwest Hospital, about ten miles north of Seattle, on a warm, early July morning. I was calm and optimistic, about as ready as one can ever be to face major surgery and lose a body part. I relinquished insurance cards, a driver's license to prove I was whom I said I was, and signed a stack of documents acknowledging I could die during the procedure and, unless there was proof of malpractice, I would not sue the hospital or the doctor. You have no choice but to surrender in these moments and trust that the people you are relying on to save you will do just that.

I walked back into the prep area, took off my clothes, and donned one of those ugly, cotton hospital gowns that never quite cover your posterior. In going through the pre-operative ritual, you become less of an individual, just a body in a human assembly line, forced to abandon any sense of control and dignity you had in the world outside the hospital walls. To fight, complain, or resist would have been futile. So I complied, held out my arms for the intravenous needle that would first give me valium to calm me down and, eventually, deliver drugs to anesthetize me and erase any memory of what was about to happen.

Laddy was proud of me. He had rarely seen me so agreeable and relaxed and was surprised at my behavior. So was I. Until the anesthesiologist entered my curtained zone of privacy and disrupted the peace. He had a cold, calculating aura, as icy as the doctor who blurted out I had kidney cancer. He introduced himself without looking at me and announced he needed to insert an arterial line into my forearm to monitor my blood pressure during surgery. The surgeon herself interrupted him to say she did not think that was necessary, that I was not a high-risk patient, but it seemed in that moment the anesthesiologist was the alpha dog, determined to do things his way. I was just a body on a table and was in no position to argue with him.

His first attempt at getting a needle into the veins of my forearm failed, as did the second, third, and fourth tries to get the long, thin metal needle into me. He called for more needles, switched arms and failed again, repeatedly. Whatever calm I possessed was shattered. The tension in the room was palpable and disquieting. I was crying and terrified, precisely the opposite demeanor I had when I entered the hospital and a level of anxiety one should never have before surgery. If the anesthesiologist was at all embarrassed by his incompetence, he did not show it. Laddy was watching, trying to control the urge to scream at him and make him stop, but we both knew it would be futile and stupid to challenge the man responsible for keeping me alive and sedated while cancer was being removed from my body. Finally, he found the vein, and I went into a much-welcomed daze.

Five hours later, I was in a recovery room. I was woozy, but alive, and heard that the surgery went well. Two days later, I went home, still disoriented and without my left kidney. It would be at least a week, maybe more, before I would get a pathology report and learn if the cancer had spread beyond the kidney. Ever the journalist, wanting to see things for myself, I asked the surgeon to take a picture of my extracted kidney before sending it off to the pathologist so I could see it. I doubted it would resemble the bean-shaped organ it once was, and I was right. It was a messy blob of red, looking more like roadkill than a human body part. The cancerous mass, some lymph nodes, and surrounding tissue had been removed and sent off to a lab for analysis. I threw away the photo of my former kidney and waited for the test results.

Ten days later, I received a letter, the facts and findings of the pathologist. The margins and lymph nodes were clean.

I did not need chemotherapy or radiation. I was one of the really lucky ones. My primary care doctor told me if the cancer had not been spotted so early, I probably would not have survived. The five-centimeter tumor had been about to penetrate my kidney wall and spread throughout my body. In a word, the kidney that took care of me for sixty-seven years had turned on me and would have killed me. I believe the high fever and convulsions that rendered me helpless weeks earlier were my body's way of alerting me something was very wrong, though most of my doctors disagreed, but not all of them. My kidney specialist, the quirky Dr. Bruce O'Neill, agreed with me. He said, "We doctors don't really like to acknowledge something if we can't explain it. I don't know if the fever was your body's response to the cancer. But I can't say it wasn't. How could I know that? How could anyone?"

Not everything needs an explanation.

Whether it was the sudden, unexplained fever or just good fortune, once cancer invades your body, it never really leaves even if it is physically removed. Nothing can ever completely extract the nagging worry that, without warning, cancer could come back at any time. It happened once. It could happen again. My mangled left kidney, along with its potentially deadly two-inch tumor, was gone, but its specter remains. In the wake of the surgery, hardly a day passes without my overactive brain imagining a few malignant cells had managed to escape the shredded kidney as it was being removed from my body.

The first year in the wake of any crisis is, I suppose, often the worst. That was true for me. I dreaded each follow-up doctor visit, CT scan, and blood test. Was my right kidney managing to pick up the slack of its now-absent twin? Was my blood work normal? What did the urine test show? Every time I went through the obligatory, medical rituals, I tortured myself with worry.

As the years pass, I agonize a little less with each visit to my kidney doctor, the handsome, rail-thin specialist whom I will see every few months for the rest of my life. We have settled into an easy, almost welcome routine. I get a blood draw and leave a urine sample a few days before visiting him. He reads the results and forces me to look at the numbers in his computer. The charts and data mean nothing to me. I ask him, "Am I okay?" He says, "Yes . . . everything's fine." That is all I want or need to hear. We spend five minutes talking about my right kidney and thirty minutes railing about politics and the sorry state of the world.

Before cancer, I exercised, maintained healthy eating habits, and never smoked or drank. I always hated the taste of alcohol, which was a good thing. Kidneys have enough to do without having to deal with alcohol. After cancer, my routine remains much the same. I have to monitor my blood pressure and try to limit how much salt and sugar I eat. I try to confine my sugar binges to the weekends. My doctor did express some concern about riding my horse. He said, "You've got only one kidney . . . don't fall off," but he never advised me to stop riding. He knew the benefits of being in the saddle far outweighed the risks.

It gets easier. I am less anxious. Still, the ghost of cancer hovers over me. Sometimes it appears in a nightmare or for a fleeting, unexpected moment in the middle of the day. Most of the time, I vanquish the undertoad, but it never completely disappears.

Chapter 47

Legacy

Bloated, fat, and tired of carrying around the living creature inside me, I was, as most expectant mothers are, beyond ready to get the baby out. It was hard to breathe, impossible to sleep, and difficult to eat. I could not find any comfortable position standing, sitting, or lying down. I was off balance in every way possible, physically unsteady because of my seventy-pound weight gain, and emotionally rocky. I had no idea how to raise a baby or how this epic, life-changing event would affect me. June 5, 1976, the expected due date, came and went. I was assured by the obstetrician the baby would come when it was ready.

Baby Jeremy, 1976.

Jeremy Isaac Blacklow was born at 3:26 in the afternoon of June 10, 1976, after more than twenty hours of hard labor. I hoped to have a natural delivery, without drugs, but after fifteen hours of pain, I struggled to one side and received a much-welcomed epidural block, an injection into the spinal cord that numbs all feeling below the waist. Five hours later, my almost-ten-pound baby came into the world. As most newborns do, he looked squished and wrinkly, but to me he looked perfect. In exchange for having to give away tickets to a Paul McCartney concert that night at Seattle's Kingdome, I got a beautiful baby boy. More than a fair trade.

MY MOTHER, GAGA, WITH JEREMY, 1976.

Prior to his arrival, no television reporter in Seattle was ever visibly pregnant. KING management worried about this. They had only recently and begrudgingly accepted women in the newsroom at all. I do not think they were ready for a pregnant woman to be seen reporting on camera. Beyond being pregnant on the air, I think they worried I would not be emotionally or physically capable of handling the job. They would have to find a temporary replacement when I had the baby and wondered if I would even come back. I was a problem they did not know how to fix and they preferred not to have to deal with this issue at all.

A few months before my due date, I had the audacity to ask for maternity leave, a request they had never had to consider. At the time, there was no language in the AFTRA contract addressing the issue of maternity or parental leave. The American Federal of Television and Radio Artists, at least in Seattle, had never dealt with pregnant members, so the union saw no reason to ask for it. Then I, with my pregnant belly, arrived. In 1975, I asked for a seat at the bargaining table and sat across from a bevy of white, male, pin-striped lawyers seated next to KING managers.

I was told in no uncertain terms that I could use my sick leave but that was all they would allow.

"That's not enough," I said.

"That's all you're going to get."

It was not all I got. I demanded at least three months off and got it. It was an unpaid leave of absence, of course, but it was broken ground, and in the ensuing decades, maternity leave became parental leave, granting time off for mothers and fathers and for parents adopting babies. Change takes time.

I was grateful for those priceless three months with Jeremy in the summer of 1976. It was the most unfettered time I would ever spend with him. His lawyer father, Richard, went to work every day to support us, so it was just the two of us. I had all the right things a baby needs—the crib, the diapers, the tiny clothes, and the baby wipes but little confidence or experience about what to do with all of it and no faith I would be a good mother. As all parents do, you try your best and hope not to kill them. Love them, feed them, change their diapers, bathe them, and soothe them when they cry.

While doing all of that, you slowly come to realize that you have never loved anything as much as this baby, that you are no longer the most important person in your own life and never will be again. Babies own you from the moment they take their first breath until you take your last. Hopefully in that order. It is an indescribable bond.

As babies go, Jeremy was easy. He slept through the night after only a couple of months, and as much as I enjoyed nursing him, I stopped breastfeeding him when he was three months old and gave him a bottle with little resistance from him. It bothered me more to stop nursing, but I had to start thinking about going back to work. The term "child care" was not even in the vernacular in the mid-1970s. There were no professional daycare centers to speak of, and full-time nannies were too expensive. I found an unlicensed daycare and dropped him off daily where he spent the day with half a dozen other toddlers and babies. I took it as a very good sign that he cried when I came to pick him up and was happy when he arrived every morning.

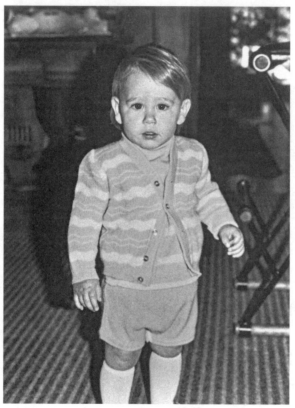

JEREMY ON HIS SECOND BIRTHDAY. JUNE, 1978.

By the time Jeremy was two, I used him as a lure to entice my parents to sell their Virginia home and my father's men's clothing stores and move to Seattle. As their only daughter, I alone was not enough to inspire them to move west, so I relied on their only grandchild as the irresistible bait. My mother, Esther, went to work at a downtown law firm, and Leonard became Jeremy's irreplaceable Pop-Pop, who picked him up every day from school, brought him home, and got a second chance at being a father. With my workload of at least fifty hours a week, my father would get to experience things I was now going to miss. I reasoned if I could not be present for much of Jeremy's childhood, knowing my father was there was comfort enough.

As I think back to his childhood, I remember two startling things Jeremy said, the words indelibly etched in my mind. When he was barely three years old, he was playing in a family room adjacent to our kitchen. I was cooking dinner and I heard him say: "My body's just a casket for my soul" as he continued playing with his toys. I stopped what I was doing, walked over to him, knelt down on the floor and said, "What did you say?" "Mommy, my body's a casket for my soul!" I asked him where he heard that. He did not answer me, went back to playing and I never heard him say anything like that ever again. Some years later, when he was five or six, he walked in the door from school with a very sad, droopy face. I asked him what was wrong. He thought for a moment and replied: "My happy tubes are clogged." To this day, I consider those words as the best explanation I have ever heard to describe sadness. I have used that phrase many, many times.

Jeremy went from being an easy baby and toddler to a bright, capable, and mostly responsible teenager. Mostly. As a screaming two-year-old, he once threw a bottle of pulpy orange juice at me while I was driving. It splattered over me and the dashboard. I stopped the car, leaned into the back seat and said "if you don't stop crying, Mommy's going to kill you." He instantly stopped and swears he remembers the incident. In elementary school, he was coerced by some reckless teenagers to spray-paint a brick wall at his school. Taking no responsibility for his actions, I called some cop friends and arranged for them to come to our house in full uniform and make Jeremy show them what he had done. I emptied his bank account, all one thousand dollars of his savings, and made him pay the school to repair the damage. The worst thing he ever did as a teenager, at least to my knowledge, was lie to me about going to a party where, he said, parents would be supervising. I ran into the parents at a movie theater, drove to their home, rang the doorbell, and asked if Jeremy Blacklow was there. I said, "Tell Jeremy his mother has come to pick him up." Humiliating, but effective.

In the fall of 1994, Jeremy left home for Columbia University, the school where I wanted to go, but as a woman could not even apply in 1965. My son would fulfill that dream for me. Many mothers and fathers are bereft at the prospect of children leaving the nest, but I couldn't wait for him to go. Neither could he. We were arguing a lot about inconsequential things, both of us fouling the nest, perhaps to make his upcoming departure easier to handle. Separations, even painful ones, sometimes free both children and parents. We needed a break from each other. He left for New York City with new clothes, a few personal items, and a colossal secret he was not quite ready to share.

Three months later, Jeremy came home for Christmas break. He arrived on a Saturday in the middle of my annual party where his stepfather, Ted D'Arms, was gathering everyone for the traditional holiday reading of Dickens's *A Christmas Carol*. At the end of the story when Tiny Tim exults, "God bless us, every one!" my guests were crying happy tears, ready to eat, drink, and celebrate. Jeremy, usually chatty and sociable, seemed unusually low-key. *Probably tired from the cross-country trip home*, I told myself, but I thought there was something more going on. I was right.

Sunday night, we met friends for a Chinese dinner, came home, plopped on my bed, and turned on the television.

Jeremy got up, turned it off, looked at me, and said, "Mom, I have something to tell you. I'm gay."

I said nothing but started to cry.

I was shocked. Stunned by his words. I staggered into the bathroom to get some Kleenex and crawled back into my bed. I muttered the first thought that came into my head, "Well, no woman would've been good enough for you anyway." A glib, insensitive, and wholly untrue thing to say, but it was all I could think of.

"Mom," he said, "I'm still the same person I was five minutes ago."

In his mind, that was true, but not in mine.

The movie in my brain of how his life would unfold—college, graduation, a career, marriage, and babies—was going to need extensive editing, and I did not know if I could do that. I would need time to revise that movie. Jeremy was obviously disappointed and frustrated by my reaction, and I reminded him he had carried his secret for a while, but it was a new revelation for me. He would have to give me time to adjust.

The next day, he called my parents, his beloved Gaga and Pop-Pop, and invited them over that afternoon. I worried how Leonard and Esther, now in their eighties, might react to Jeremy's news. We had a homosexual uncle in the family (we never used the word "gay") and a lesbian couple living across the street from our Arlington home. My parents never exhibited a hint of prejudice or judgment about anyone's race, color, or sexual orientation. But this was close to home, and I was nervous.

When they arrived, Jeremy sent me upstairs. He wanted to talk with them alone. I eavesdropped from a hidden spot on the balcony and secretly peered down on the three of them."Grandma, Pop Pop, I have something to tell you. I'm gay."

I did not know what I was expecting them to say in response to those words. Would they cry as I did? Would they express shock? Would they get up and leave? I heard nothing. If I had anticipated something disturbing or offensive, my concern evaporated instantly with my father's reply."Well that's fine son, but did you make the dean's list?"

My parents went over and hugged him and told him they were fine with whoever he was and whatever he wanted to do. They only wanted him to be happy. Since the day their only grandchild was born, he could do no wrong in their eyes. Eighteen years later, their vision of him was unchanged. We went out to lunch.

Jeremy returned to New York City for winter quarter, and I went back to work, rattled and wrestling with the realization that my son was not who I thought he was. I was upset not so much that he was gay but that I had not seen any clues in all our years together. How could I not have known that? I was a professional observer. *What did I miss? How do I process this?* I called every gay friend I had, read books they recommended, and began, slowly and with some trepidation, to create a new story in my mind of what his life, and mine, might look like.

As cliché as it may sound, life does in fact go on. The following summer, Jeremy brought his new boyfriend home. I remember watching my father at a picnic in our back yard, chatting away with both young men. It all seemed effortless and normal, and we adjusted because we had to and wanted to. I was grateful that my son felt safe coming out to his family, that he did not have to keep his secret for too long, and that he was never afraid of being rejected, condemned, or judged by those he loved the most and those who loved him.

He graduated from Columbia and followed his mother's path somewhat, mostly in the entertainment side of the news business, working for CNN, NBC, *Access Hollywood,* and for Yahoo Entertainment. When he could no longer, in his words, "tolerate covering the Kardashians," he turned to music, became a DJ to help pay his bills, but kept looking for a way to use his skills as a writer to make a difference in the world.

JEREMY AND ME...GETTING READY FOR COLLEGE...TRYING TO HANG ON. 1994.

In the fall of 2017, he was hired as director of entertainment media for GLAAD, the Gay & Lesbian Alliance Against Defamation, the nation's largest LGBTQ advocacy organization. As I write this, it is where he works today, helping to amplify the voices of people in marginalized communities. He still works too hard and pushes himself too much. He wants to help people. There is no higher purpose than that.

Some months into his job at GLAAD, before I began to write this chapter, I knew I could not and did not want to write it without his help and participation. The truth of who he is and my reaction to it were not just my story. It was our story. I told him I had questions that had been on my mind in the decades since he first told me he was gay, but if he did not want to answer them and allow me to share his thoughts, I would be fine with that. Soon after we talked on the phone, he booked a flight to come home, ready to give me the time I needed and answer anything I wanted to ask. On a Saturday morning in the early spring of 2018, Jeremy stretched out on the living room sofa and turned off his phone, a remarkable gesture of respect. Still somewhat haunted that I never saw even a small clue he was gay, I wanted to know when he knew. He was, he said, something of a late bloomer, that it wasn't until early adolescence that he felt different and only certain he was attracted to boys when he was sixteen. It was 1992. He mentioned within months of finally knowing who he was, the movie *Philadelphia* was released about a man dying of AIDS who hides his secret to protect his status at a law firm. Jeremy remembers it vividly. Talk of AIDS was everywhere, not just on movie screens.

"All I could see was gay men dying of AIDS. When I was sixteen, being gay meant AIDS, and AIDS meant death. My friends were starting to have sex, but for me it was not a primal force. I had girlfriends in high school, but I didn't want to have sex with them. I was different. And back then, being gay, to me, meant you were going to die. So I overcompensated. I became an overachiever . . . whether it was because I wanted to get into a good school or because I wanted to avoid dealing with being gay, I don't know. I wanted to make sure I didn't have time to think about it."

I told him how worried his father and I were about how hard he was working back in high school and how we wanted him to cut back on his activities. Now, finally, I knew why he kept up his frenetic pace. He could not risk slowing down and taking time to think about who he really was. Thoughts of suffering and death might creep into his consciousness . . . too much a burden for him to bear.

Though I was grateful he finally told us his truth on that first trip home from college, it broke my heart to hear his memories from high school. Learning that he suffered at all and was afraid of dying at such a young age was crushing.

He kept his secret because he was scared. Jeremy told me, "Once you tell your parents, or tell your friends that you are gay, you have a sense of losing control . . . losing control over your own narrative. It is scary for everyone who wants to come out.

"Being gay should never be the defining characteristic of someone's life. It is not who they are . . . any more than being straight defines your character. But when you're a minority of any kind, discrimination is a fact of one's life. Given the times we're now living in, if you're not a straight, white, Christian male or female, if you're black or an immigrant, transgender or Muslim, you are in the margins of American life. And it's not always a safe place to be."

JEREMY...ALL GROWN UP.

He went on, "I look forward to a day when no one is asked to declare their sexual orientation . . . to some day when people are truly free to love who they love and marry who they want to marry without fear of judgment, recrimination, or violence. That will be real equality."

As the day went on, I asked Jeremy what he remembered about his childhood with me growing up in Seattle. He remembers me as a "fighter . . . an advocate . . . an outspoken critic who would never take shit from anybody . . . including him." He remembers the battle I fought with KING to get my job back. He was ten at the time and proud I fought that fight. He remembers me as "a nurturer and a good mother who cooked dinner most nights" for him and that when I walked in the door at the end of my day, I mostly left my work outside.

"You never let those terrible stories into our home. You never let them intrude into our lives together."

His words comforted me.

Solid, steady, and loved by many, many people, Jeremy is now in his early forties. Though we named him Jeremy, I have called him Max since he was a little boy, named after the child in his favorite book by Maurice Sendak, *Where the Wild Things Are*. My Max is beautiful inside and out. I am so proud of who he is and how he lives his life and happy beyond measure he no longer feels different as he did at sixteen.

If I never do anything else worthwhile in my life, I know I did one thing right: I gave birth to and raised a remarkable man, my living legacy. The world is a better place because he is in it. That said, I will let him hold onto his memories of my cooking for him most nights after work. Without the take-out teriyaki restaurant and the nearby Red Apple market with its ready-made meals, he might have gone hungry.

Jeremy and me...Spring, 2019.

Epilogue

Either write something worth reading
or do something worth writing.
—BENJAMIN FRANKLIN

I HOPE BOTH OF FRANKLIN'S DIRECTIVES have been accomplished in this book. If you read these pages, thank you for your time and attention. I greatly appreciate that. I am now seventy-two years old, and it occurs to me that the bookends of my life are me with horses. In the first photo, I am just over a year old in diapers, and in more recent pictures I am, thankfully, fully clothed, still connected with horses. The decades between those bookends have been, to say the least, intense and very busy. As it is with most of us while we are living our lives, we rarely have time to stop and see the wake we have created. Four years ago, I stopped to turn around and take a look back. I am amazed at the life I lived and survived.

I always thought I would find some way to wrap up the end of this book with words of wisdom, pithy commentary about the lamentable state of broadcast news, or an inspirational message of some kind, but I realize I have nothing much to add. While not entirely true, television news is now sadly something of an oxymoron. There is too much opining and too little listening. Being first often seems more important than being right, and too many journalists seem more interested in serving their egos, instead of the communities in which they work. Enough said about that, except I hope the hallowed profession of true journalism gets back to the mission of informing people, rather than lecturing them. To quote the late, estimable U.S. Supreme Court Justice William O. Douglas:

"The function of the press is to explore and investigate events, inform the people what is going on, and to expose the harmful as well as the good influences at work. There is no higher function performed under our constitutional regime."

Although I've titled the book *Fearless*, that description is somewhat misleading. I was afraid of some of the murderers I met, terrified to fight KING Television to get my job back, frightened when I almost died from a gargantuan tumor in my body, and terror-stricken when I had kidney cancer, certain it would kill me. I am still occasionally cowed by my horse who I am convinced can smell my fear, fully aware she could take me out at any moment.

For most of my life, I took umbrage when others described me as pushy, loud, aggressive, pugnacious, occasionally intolerant, and impatient. Older now, I agree with those descriptions and am mostly at peace with the more complicated parts of who I am. I am also funny, sweet, kind to animals, a loyal friend, and a good mother. I pride myself at being able to complete the Sunday New York Times Crossword Puzzle in ink and most of the time without cheating.

Having encountered almost every type of human being in my career as a journalist, managing a horse ranch and going about the normal day-to-day things we need to do to survive, I believe we are all very much the same. We want to love and be loved and do our best in whatever we are doing. There is an abundance of good in most of us but also a touch of evil, which we manage to suppress most of the time. I want to scream at drivers in passing lanes going twenty miles below the speed limit and always feel like ramming my shopping cart into someone leaving theirs in the middle of a grocery aisle. I control those urges. I loathe people who hurt animals and children, and my dark fantasies about what I want to do to some politicians must never be put to paper.

The only absolutes for me are that none of us gets out of this alive, change is the only constant, and love, while not necessarily *all* you need, is what matters most. I also know this. We are all insecure, no matter our status or station in life. Supermodel Cindy Crawford once told me she worried about her looks. I heard Paul McCartney say he sometimes worries whether he is good enough and still feels he has something to prove. If *they* believe that, we are all uncertain about something.

I abide by a few rules I consider extremely important. If you make a mess, clean it up, whether it involves picking up clothes or apologizing for being thoughtless or unkind. Try never to be late for an appointment because it is disrespectful. It is one thing to waste our own time but inconsiderate to squander someone else's.

Speaking of wasting time, I have come to believe in the vital importance of slowing down and being still in the world. We are all too busy, overcommitted, and spend too many hours of our lives doing things we do not want to do with people we really do not want to be with. The word 'no' is powerful and should be used more often, especially by women, to allow time for rest and restoration. Time given to doing nothing in particular, whether sitting by a river, walking in the woods, or staring into the night sky, is time well spent.

The most important thing—always tell the people you love how much you love them, and tell them often. Those words can never be said too much.

We never know our expiration date.

Laddy Kite

About the Author

JULIE BLACKLOW is an Emmy-award winning journalist with more than forty years in the television news business, among the first generation of women in television news in the United States. As a journalist, she encountered the entire spectrum of humanity from movie stars to murderers and regular people overcoming everyday obstacles. Born and raised in Washington, DC, she migrated to the other Washington in her early twenties and settled in Seattle. Hers is a life writ large, a roller-coaster ride with a remarkable number of highs and terrifying lows. At the age of sixty, she switched careers, leaving the world of television news to manage a horse ranch, a dramatic career change where she learned animals are often far more sane than many humans. She has owned five dogs, four cats, one horse and has one son, Jeremy, whom she claims is the best "thing" she ever produced. Her friends describe her as complicated, tenacious, decisive, bossy, opinionated, loving, loyal, and most of all, brave.

An eBook and audiobook version of *Fearless*
will be available in 2020.

julieblacklow.com
Facebook.com/JulieBlacklowFearless

To contact Julie Blacklow for an interview or
speaking engagement email info@julieblacklow.com